DATE DUE

E e

Ethics and Experience

Moral Theory from
Just War to Abortion

Lloyd Steffen

ROWMAN & LITTLEFIELD PUBLISHERS, INC.
Lanham • Boulder • New York • Toronto • Plymouth, UK

Published by Rowman & Littlefield Publishers, Inc.
A wholly owned subsidiary of The Rowman & Littlefield Publishing Group, Inc.
4501 Forbes Boulevard, Suite 200, Lanham, Maryland 20706
www.rowman.com

10 Thornbury Road, Plymouth PL6 7PP, United Kingdom

British Library Cataloguing in Publication Information Available

Library of Congress Cataloging-in-Publication Data
Steffen, Lloyd H., 1951–
    Ethics and experience : moral theory from just war to abortion / Lloyd Steffen.
        p.   cm.
    Includes bibliographical references and index.
    ISBN 978-1-4422-1653-2 (cloth : alk. paper) — ISBN 978-1-4422-1654-9 (pbk. : alk. paper) — ISBN 978-1-4422-1655-6 (electronic) 1. Ethics. I. Title.
    BJ1012.S665 2012
    170—dc23

                                                                    2012020494

♾™ The paper used in this publication meets the minimum requirements of American National Standard for Information Sciences—Permanence of Paper for Printed Library Materials, ANSI/NISO Z39.48-1992.

Printed in the United States of America

To Nathan, Sam, and Will
gaudium patris

Contents

Preface

The question that has inspired this book is one that should be of interest to students and scholars of ethics: how might we best *think* about the moral life as people actually *live* it? While ethical inquiry can sometimes proceed confined to theory or, conversely, focused exclusively on practical applications, this question turns our attention to the connection between ethical thinking and moral experience, even suggesting that if experience informs our ethical thinking, so too does ethical thinking inform our lived experience. How the moral life ought to be lived is a question central to ethical reflection; it cannot be avoided, and no one should want to avoid it. Here, in these pages, that "ought" question will be raised in the context of lived moral experience. How do the experiences we have and the decisions we make to act one way rather than another affect our broader ethical thinking; how do the various ways we go about ethical thinking shape our practical decision making; and are our ethical theories adequate to address the complexity of the moral life as it is actually lived?

These questions require attention to both ethical theory and moral practice, and on the theoretical front there are many different resources that can be of help. Readers will not have to delve very far into these pages to see that in this project, a connection between ethics thinking and experience appears to depend significantly on ideas related to "just war." The idea of a "just war" is admittedly controversial, and for all the attention I give to just war ideas in the pages ahead, I join those who are critical of just war thinking as it typically arises in public discussions or is employed as a tool of international policy making. This is a book about ethics and how to think about ethics, however, and we cannot deny that just war ideas are important in our ethics traditions and are routinely discussed in the ethics literature. I believe that attention to just war thinking can advance our thinking about moral experience and ethics in general, and the argument I offer here is that behind just war—and beyond it—lies an actual ethic that can help us understand the connection between ethical thought and moral experience even as it may transform the idea of "just war" into something other than what policy makers want to make of it, even to the extent of making it unfamiliar if not quite unrecognizable. That ethic, conformed to the moral point of view and described here as a "hybrid" ethic, includes duties and obligations, principles, attention to consequences, and virtues. This hybrid ethic seeks to reconcile our ethical thinking with our experience of living the moral life, and as such it also seeks to overcome long-standing conceptual antagonisms between deontology and consequentialism, action ethics and virtue ethics. This hybrid ethic, called a "common agreement" ethic in the pages that follow, is grounded in the human capacity for reason and reasonableness, which is the heart of what is referred to in these pages as "natural law." Terms such as "reason," "duty," "consequences," and even "natural law" are used throughout these pages in the lowercase—use of these terms as uppercase realities are beyond the scope of this inquiry.

A few things may be said about this book by way of "preface" comments.

1. This book is meant to be a contribution to moral theory.

2. This book is offered as a supplement, even a corrective, to the division of moral theories into opposing camps—Kantian deontology, utilitarian consequentialism, virtue ethics. No one writing in ethics can ignore these theories, and I make use of them throughout the volume and acknowledge my dependence on them. My purpose is not to provide an exhaustive account of these theories or even attend to them more than is necessary for the case I am going to make. Numerous works, both scholarly monographs and textbooks, not to mention websites, can provide a more extensive grounding in any particular theory. Of significance to this study is that fact—and it is a fact—that no moral theory is free from problems, and all have been subjected to harsh, even hostile criticism, as any proponent of a particular theory would readily acknowledge. To be properly schooled in ethics is to know something about the criticisms that attend any given ethical theory.

In the pages ahead I offer neither an in-depth analysis of the major moral theories nor a comprehensive rehashing of the criticisms that attend them, but those criticisms, which do point to real problems and sometimes serious inadequacies, open up the possibility for a different approach to ethics, which my purpose here is to propose. I make reference to just war thinking more for what it exemplifies as a mode of ethical approach rather than as a self-enclosed theory with no relationship to the long-standing theories recognized in our moral traditions. This proposed "hybrid" ethic respects the best that is in, say, deontological and utilitarian ethics without directing attention once more to the inadequacies of the theories so often the focus of attention in standard accounts of moral theory.

3. The idea of just war is an oxymoron to many people, and I understand that—as already indicated, I even agree with that. Just war has a bad reputation, and I take criticisms of just war thinking with the utmost seriousness. These pages, however, are not filled with historical examples supporting the reasons why criticisms of just war thinking are themselves justified and reasonable. I accept as a given the claim that wars are horrible, much to be avoided, and seem inevitably to end up as "unjust," even those that may begin with reasonable claims to being "just."

4. This book is sensitive to cultural differences and notes that some things pushed to the background in one society or cultural setting will be brought forward in another. This phenomenon of cultural life lends some apparent support to the idea that societal differences and the cultural divides we have constructed and know so well require us to see ourselves as morally disconnected from one another. Some of this will be sorted out in the upcoming discussion of cultural versus moral relativism, but at the outset the reader should know that in this book I do not regard the idea of "human nature" or the possibility of a "moral community" transcending cultural difference as chimerical. I will hold in these pages—even though this is not discussed at any length—that those ethical theories that deny human nature or discount an ethic grounded in reason and the human capacity for reasonableness are themselves flawed in this sense: they are detached from insight into those values common to reasonable people of goodwill and thus fail to help us understand human action and even the deeper moral meaning of being human. Those values common to all, which I shall refer to as "goods of life," are what I mean by "human nature" in the relevant moral sense.

5. Careful readers may detect some conceptual slippage in the way I use the term "experience" in the pages ahead. There is both a normative and a descriptive meaning for the term, and I cannot dispense with either. The concept "experience" may refer in a *normative* sense to the way we live and ought to live our lives as reasonable persons of goodwill who, in community, are concerned for human flourishing and thus for the welfare of ourselves, others, and our world. The more *descriptive* sense of "experience" refers to the way people actually live the moral life, and I attend to this sometimes backward-looking, historical sense of experience because it is evidential support for the ethical approach I am advocating. So, just as one example, I argue in the discussion of physician-assisted suicide that in constructing their legislation, the authors of Oregon's Death with Dignity Act actually employed this mode of moral reasoning—the law itself is evidence for this descriptive claim. But I will also argue that they did well in doing so (normative), for the Oregon

legislators exemplified the use of the ethic I am advocating here, acting as they should to face a difficult moral problem as reasonable and responsible people of goodwill concerned with human suffering and end-of-life decision making. My hope is that context will make these two uses clear.

6. I defend here the idea that an ethic *behind* just war actually transforms how just war thinking should function and what just war might mean *as an ethic*. I claim just war thinking is not, as a list of criteria, an ethic, and I make the moves that I believe resituate the criteria of just war in a moral context where they serve a basic normative principle concerning the use of force. To make the case that this transformation acts as a serious constraint on the use of force, I go not to historical examples of purported just wars but to Gandhi and King, each of whom appealed implicitly to this ethic in developing their action steps for nonviolent resistance. So constraining is this ethic on the use of force that even they—Gandhi and King—run into problems with justifying the force used in nonviolent resistance. This move is not meant to discount or even criticize Gandhi or King, both of whom I admire greatly, but to show that the ethic behind just war is demanding in ways we have not come to grips with in our typical public deliberations on the uses of force. If just war puts a check on Gandhi using nonviolence, how much more of a check will it put on those pursuing a preemptive military incursion where horrible violence is unleashed and thousands of innocents are killed?

7. Part of my reason for writing this book and reconstructing just war think-ing in the context of a broader "common agreement ethic" is to take just war tools out of the hands of policy makers who want to use just war for nation-alistic, self-serving, and, as it turns out, destructive political purposes. Just war ideas have been used to seduce public opinion into the illusion of moral justification for all kinds of misadventures where force is used to achieve political or economic ends. The ethical reconstruction of the ethic behind just war presented here may not stop that from happening, but at least it might raise awareness about just war ideas so that there might be a more vigorous public conversation where challenges are issued to—and through—the moral justification process itself. If the argument about the common agreement ethic behind just war gains a hearing and finds acceptance, future policy deci-sions presented for public acceptance on the basis of just war ideas will have to look elsewhere for their justification. If those policy moves are motivated by national, political, or economic self-interest, they will have to base justi-fication on self-interest and bypass the kind of deep moral justification often claimed by the appeal to just war ideas. The ethic behind just war will prove an obstacle to such efforts at justification, rather than providing the stamp of approval that puts a moral patina on a self-serving and self-interested policy. Just war, I suggest at one point but do not develop—this is something I leave

for readers to contemplate—can actually serve as a basis for endorsing a practical pacifism without committing one to the incoherencies of theoretical pacifism.

The ideas in this book have been tested in several different forums, and some of the ideas here have appeared before in print. I have had the good fortune to explore some of the ideas in this book in various scholarly settings, including three global conferences on "Making Sense of Dying and Death" held at Oxford and Salzburg; a meeting of the International Society for Universal Dialogue in Hiroshima; a conference on "The Morality of the Death Penalty" at Catholic University Law School in Washington, DC; an international interdisciplinary conference on "Religions and the Politics of Peace and Conflict" at the Irish School of Ecumenics, Trinity College, Dublin; "The Annual Gandhian Nonviolence Conference" in Memphis, Tennessee; the "Unequal before Death Conference," at Columbia University in New York; and the Hampshire College–sponsored conference, "From Abortion Rights to Social Justice: Building the Movement for Reproductive Freedom." I was honored to have received an invitation to deliver the Han O. Tiefel Lecture in Religious Ethics at the College of William and Mary as well as an invited lecture in the Leon S. Peters Lecture Series at California State University–Fresno, where, in both instances, I developed some of the ideas that appear in this book. My thanks to Michael Daise at the College of William and Mary and Andrew Fiala at CSU–Fresno for their kind hospitality and interest in this work. I am grateful to have received so many opportunities to present the ideas in this book and am humbled by generous colleagues and conference participants who engaged with me and this work as it was developing. I truly appreciate comments from anonymous reviewers of the manuscript who offered constructive suggestions for improvement.

Because some portions of work included in this book have appeared in print, I wish to acknowledge and thank the following publishers for permission to use some previously published material. A version of chapter 6 originally appeared in "The Ethics of Patient Non-Treatment," in *Re-Imaging Death and Dying: Global Interdisciplinary Perspectives*, Dennis R. Cooley and Lloyd Steffen, eds. (Oxford: Inter-Disciplinary Press, 2009), 211–24; a version of chapter 5 originally appeared in "The Ethics of Physician Assisted Suicide: A New Approach," in *Mortality, Dying and Death*, T. Chandler Haliburton and Caroline Edwards, eds. (Oxford: Inter-Disciplinary Press, 2008), 183–205; and a version of chapter 8 originally appeared in "The Death of Innocents: Noncombatant Immunity vs. The Divine Fetus," in *Layers of Dying and Death*, Kate Woodthorpe, ed. (Oxford: Inter-Disciplinary Press, 2007), 97–106. All of these articles were published in conference proceedings and have been revised and significantly expanded for this volume. A revised version of chapter 7, originally published as "Stop the Killing: The Protections of 'Just War' on Non-Combatants," in *Unequal before Death*, Christina Staudt and Marcelline Block, eds., is published here with permission of Cambridge Scholars Publishing; and portions of chapter 2 have been drawn from two previously published articles, "Gandhi's Nonviolent Resistance: A Justified Use of Force?" *Journal of Philosophy and the Contemporary World* 15, no. 1 (June 2008): 68–80 and "The Presumption of Peace: Where Just War and Non-Violent Resistance Meet (and Diverge)," *Conflict and Conciliation: Faith and Politics in an Age of Global Dissonance*, Jason Daverth, ed. (Dublin, Ireland: Columba Press, 2007), 20–38.

Work leads to gratitude and gratitude to a sense of indebtedness. I am indebted to the many friends and colleagues who have lent a patient ear as I have talked about the ideas in the book over the years. I am most grateful for the kindness that has been shown me by the gift of engagement and critical response. And while I cannot name all those friends and colleagues here, I must single out Thomas P. Kasulis, Thomas G. Poole, Andrew Fiala, and Paul Lauritzen for special mention since they discussed at length with me at various times some of the ideas that appear in this book. They of course are not responsible for my mistakes or for viewpoints presented here to which they may have objected. I do want to name—and thank—Emmajane Finney, my spouse—talk about patient—who made sure that this sabbatical project did not interfere with a memorable trip to Paris in the fall of 2010; and I want to thank my three sons, Nathan, Samuel, and William, just because they are who they are. This work is dedicated to them—*gaudium patris* indeed.

Introduction

The subject matter of ethics can be teased out of a few important questions: "What is the good life?" "What kind of a person should I be?" "What should people do to live well?" These are timeless questions. Thoughtful people, in whatever time or place, by asking these questions, enter into that domain of inquiry we call ethics, and at stake is something more than an argument on abortion or whether a particular deception can be justified. The questions that prompt ethical reflection pertain to the creation of meaning and the possibility of human fulfillment.

The subject matter of ethics is more basic, more far-reaching, and more integral to being and becoming human than some might at first suspect, for ethics is the training of reflection on our lives as persons in relation to one another. Ethical reflection is concerned to analyze and understand what we do and who we are in the world of moral relationships. The decisions we make, the freedom and the constraints on freedom we experience, and the relationships we form with ourselves and with others are all grist for the ethics mill. Ethics is concerned with our aspirations to be persons of a certain sort—happy, engaged with projects, reflective, respectful of others, caring and cared for, flourishing. And the work of ethical reflection inevitably directs attention to our publicly observable actions as well as to the inner processes that inform and direct those actions, such things as our choices, decisions, motives, intentions, desires, emotions, wants, aims, purposes, passions, character, virtues, values, volition—in short, all those inward aspects of our lives that we engage to become the persons we become and to craft our many ways of creating meaningful human existence.

The branch of philosophy that we call "ethics" includes descriptive ethics, normative ethics, applied ethics, and meta-ethics, but for all the complexity of what ethical inquiry can be, the basic questions that address the good life and how to live well serve as the below-the-surface rudder that steers ethical inquiry. By describing these questions as "timeless," we take note of the startling fact that ethics is not friendly to innovation. Although changes can and have occurred in the way we theorize ethics, as happened, for instance, when Enlightenment thinking in the West shifted the Age of Faith foundations of ethics from divine revelation to reason, the basic questions at issue in ethics—those questions about what is required to live well and achieve fulfillment as human beings in relationship with others—have not—and will not—change. What constituted "the good life" in Aristotle's Athens in the fifth century BCE may not precisely correspond to our ideas of the good life today, but even with all the changes that would separate us from that time and place, the basic question that preoccupied Aristotle as an ethicist—the question about the good life—is still with us.

Ethics has not experienced any kind of paradigm shift equivalent to Copernicus's in cosmology or Einstein's in physics: it was wrong to break promises, cheat, or steal in Aristotle's Athens and in Confucius's China, and so it is today. Ethics is not a field of investigation like physics, where whole conceptions of the universe and the forces that govern it can be turned upside down (or inside out) with new discoveries. When, in the nineteenth century, John Stuart Mill argued for a utilitarian ethic that would determine goodness on the basis of a rational calculation of action consequences, he would make no claim to being revolutionary. Rather than emphasizing what was new in his approach to ethics, he made sure to underscore continuities with the ethics traditions he had learned and obviously respected, connecting his utilitarian ideas with the most enduring of his own culturally cherished ideals of human behavior: "In the golden rule of Jesus of Nazareth," he would write, "we read the complete spirit of the ethics of utility."[1] Ethics addresses enduring questions about goodness, right action, and moral character, and moral philosophers are not inclined to entertain even the possibility that a new discovery could suddenly transform the moral universe, rendering it unrecognizable.

The timeless and enduring character of the basic questions involved in ethical inquiry contributes to the irony of picking up a book in the "recently published" section of the bookstore and seeing that it is classified as a work in "ethics." The irony, of course, is that every book written in the field of ethics proposes to say something new about matters that are, as just mentioned, very old. This book is no exception. This book will attend to classic ethical issues about moral thinking, including the best ways to determine right and wrong action, the processes whereby reasonable people establish defensible justifications for their moral viewpoints and their decisions to act one way rather than another, even why moral disagreements occur and people of goodwill wind up taking opposing sides on issues of moral controversy. But another issue will press for attention in the pages to follow, and it too has been around a long time and seems ever to want our attention: how are we to reconcile our moral thinking and ethical theories with our lived moral experience?

Lived experience and thought: if reconciliation is not achieved between them, the result could be purposeless action devoid of meaning on the one hand or an unsatisfying work of "theory" that simply lacks practical significance on the other. Practical significance is not important in some areas of inquiry, but in ethics, the charge that practical significance is lacking amounts to a devastating criticism. "Practical" is a key word in ethics, for not only does "practical" refer to *practices*—the things people actually do or think they should do (morals), which are then subject to philosophical reflection and analysis (ethics)—but moral philosophers accept the idea that there is a particular form of reason—*practical reason*—that comes into play whenever people make decisions about how to live, how to act, and how to establish relationships with others. Ethics invokes a practical mode of rationality, and it is practical reason that enables us to do the work of ethics: to analyze action, to address ethical problems or dilemmas, to argue positions, to construct answers to ethical problems, to evaluate justifications for acting one way rather than another, to decide in a context of freedom how best to live well with ourselves and with others—and then, finally, to act. In our moral experiences of ordinary daily life, we constantly make decisions that address our own well-being and that of others, and ethics not only helps us to understand why we do what we do, but it guides the process whereby we evaluate justifications for why we choose to act one way rather than another and why we would commend a particular action or moral viewpoint as preferable to another. Normative ethics is just this: a branch of ethics that inquires into the supports people provide for their moral viewpoints. Normative ethics seeks to establish reasons for action while determining which viewpoints ought to be accepted.

The project of this book is to inquire into the adequacy of certain ways of "doing" ethics—yes, ethics is itself an activity that is subject to scrutiny and evaluation. If one way of doing ethics reconciles our ethical theories with our moral experiences better than another, then we ought to choose that better way. Practical reason would insist. In ethics courses students are exposed to different kinds of ethical theories, and those theories are usually presented as discrete and incommensurate options that cannot logically intersect or aid one another in the effort to explain how we ethically justify our decisions to act. This book will suggest that matters are more complicated than our standard presentation of theories would suggest, that features of different theories actually can intersect, and that for all the difficulty of making that case, the more important claim may be descriptive and empirical—people actually do, at different times and under varying circumstances, think differently and even inconsistently on the theoretical level as they address the issue of trying to live well in the world as moral persons. What is fascinating is that those inconsistencies may not actually be impediments to living well; they may not really affect our ability to flourish as moral persons. The point, rather, is that any chasm that opens between our thinking about the moral life and our experience of flourishing as moral persons points to a problem worthy of attention. That problem is that our theories can be inadequate to the task of accounting for the way we actually live the moral life; our theories can fail to reconcile moral experience, which is to say that they are inadequate to the task of explaining how we live and flourish as moral persons, imperfect though we all are.

ETHICS CONSIDERATIONS IN THE BACKGROUND

This book makes the practical assumption that people in their life projects are working to advance those things they recognized as good for themselves and others while avoiding wrongdoing and actual evil. Moreover, this project assumes that moral persons—reasonable people of goodwill—engage with others to create a better, more just and humane world around core values that on some level all people of goodwill, in whatever culture or social setting, share. Despite the differences to be found in the way ethical theories themselves are constructed, all of them in one way or another point back toward a simple question prompted by practical reason, the question of ethics itself, "What is the good life, and why do people do what they do in their efforts to attain it?"

Those who hold the view that ethical judgments are nothing but personal opinions are usually surprised to find out that the ethics question, "Why do people choose to do what they do?" can actually be answered. What is even more surprising is that the answer does not amount to a hodgepodge of subjective opinion. On the contrary, an actual consensus has settled around the answer to this question, the "answer" being that ethics, however formulated theoretically, is centered on the practical issue of goodness—recognizing and promoting goodness, working to realize goodness in one's life and work and in one's relationships. People do what they do because they think what they are doing is good.

This statement should not be controversial, but it is important for what will follow that the claim here is understood. Do we not choose to act one way rather than another based on judgments about what the good—the best—thing to do is in this case and that situation? Do we not justify our actions, even actions that turn out badly for one reason or another, in the frame of goodness, offering what we believe are the best reasons for our actions? The appeal to goodness is found in both sinners and saints—and everyone in between. Even the worst wrongdoers and the vilest criminal offenders act in relation to some idea of goodness that they believe they are advancing by acting one way rather than another. They may of course be mistaken or self-deceived, but there is little doubt that on some level their commitment to ideals of goodness affects their deliberations and is integral to their choosing, even if, in the end, we wind up saying what the grail-protecting knight said to Indiana Jones, "He chose poorly." Do saints and the law-abiding as well as the miscreant and the criminal not offer reasons for their actions? Do they not all believe that their actions are justified and that their justifications are based on the strongest reasons available, which are the best reasons and thus must be accounted good reasons even if in some situations they are not technically good reasons (i.e., the least bad options)? Is it then any wonder that people commend their ethical ideas, as well as particular views about moral behavior, to others, thinking that others should or ought to act likewise? Ethics is not like nondirectional counseling, free of values and judgments. Ethics involves evaluations, interpretations, and finally judgments—"should" and "ought" language is common, even necessary, in ethical discourse.

So people do what they do, and believe others should as well, for various reasons related to ideas of goodness, and these reasons are gathered up into theoretical systems of justification. The test of an ethical theory is how well it reconciles the theory with our moral experiences in the common life, thereby guiding us in confronting—and resolving—ethical problems.[2] A theory that fails to take account of the complexity of moral experience as people live it in their everyday lives or that fails to guide reasonable people of goodwill through reflection on moral perplexities may be fairly said to be inadequate.

The inadequacies of major moral theories are often noted, but it is not always clear what the noting of deficiencies in a moral theory is supposed to mean or what effect an awareness of those deficiencies is supposed to have on our readiness to employ the theory. Every ethical theory seems to have problems. Let us consider briefly two examples, Kantian, or deontological, ethics and utilitarian, or consequentialist, ethics.

The deontological, or duty-based, ethic of Immanuel Kant (1724–1804) asserts certain principles that establish the rational basis for good and right action. Kant proposes a two-part categorical imperative. "Act on that maxim through which you can at the same time will that it should become a universal law"[3] is the first formulation of this ethic, and it is followed by a second: "Act in such a way that you always treat humanity, whether in your own person or in the person of any other, never simply as a means, but always at the same time as an end."[4] These principles, which we could shorten as the "universalizability" principle and the "respect for persons" principle, are formal reason-based action guides that encapsulate important aspects of moral thinking. They also reconcile moral thinking to many aspects of our lived moral experience, for we can easily grasp that if something is right for me to do, it should be right for another person similarly situated to do. This idea of universalizability seems to accord with our basic idea of moral living. Furthermore, the idea that persons should not be treated instrumentally as a means to an end but as ends in themselves, where personhood designates an inherent dignity deserving of respect, giving rise to rights, as in a right not to be killed or even interfered with as a matter of basic liberty, is likewise an idea easily accessible to moral understanding and worthy of being practically enacted.

But Kantian ethics has problems, and these are often noted in the ethics literature. It is often noted, for instance, that it is not clear how the Kantian is to deal with a moral dilemma or even problematic situations where duties conflict. John Stuart Mill goes so far as to say that Kant's universalizability principle allows for the possibility of bad, even immoral things happening: a criminal wanting to be set free could universalize that all persons in that situation should be set free, and thus the formal test is passed, but the result would certainly be undesirable. And other problems attach to Kant. In refusing to allow a person to be treated as a means to an end, Kant opposes using the body as a means to an end. This may seem reasonable, but it leads to conclusions beyond a moral condemnation of body piercing and tattooing. In the medical ethics context, it leads to a prohibition on organ transplantation.[5] Furthermore, Kant opposes suicide on the grounds that killing oneself to improve one's situation is contradictory, thus irrational, since one would be trying to improve one's situation by an action that would make it impossible to experience the improvement sought by the action. Kant himself then dismisses the possibility of rational suicide, an idea that in the world of contemporary medicine many reasonable people of goodwill do not find so contradictory.

Although Kant's ethics exerted a profound influence over Western ethical thinking, scholars often note that despite the clarity Kant achieved through his rational proposals, such clarity does not always equate with moral correctness or moral sensitivity. In fact, the worst aspect of Kantian ethics is the move into ethical absolutism. Absolutism in ethics does achieve the end of clarity, but it does so at the expense of imposing rigidity when two maxims (rules) actually conflict or people of compassion, sympathy, and a willingness to engage complexity find themselves reluctant to assert "the answer" imposed by the categorical imperative, which, if it gives way to absolutism, may allow for a rigidly asserted "one correct response per situation" perspective.[6] Kant was right to assert that rational constraints on moral action exist, that moral rules ought to be binding and consistent, but the moral life is real life—it is complex and at times morally ambiguous, and people can be placed in terribly difficult situations where invoking the categorical imperative does not dissolve perplexity, relieve anxieties, or provide comfort. Reasonable people may not know how to actually formulate a rule in accordance with the categorical imperative. For instance, should the Nazi who asks whether you are hiding a Jew in your attic be told the truth because of a categorical (absolute) duty we have to tell the truth no matter what the consequences? What about the duty to protect an innocent life? Is the solution to create a universalizable maxim to this effect: telling a lie to save an innocent life is always the right thing to do?[7]

Kant did not have to deal with organ transplantation issues, but he did attend to things such as lying and suicide, and he does not make it easy to see how two duties, say, to protect an innocent life and to tell the truth, are to be adjudicated when a conflict arises. It could be argued that the categorically proper solution—telling the truth—must be followed because one is not responsible for what the Nazi might do: you cannot really know for certain the consequences of your lie, and the categorical imperative insists that consequences be ignored. But lying to save a life, which appears to be universalizable, does not rationally square with a "never tell lies" maxim; and never telling lies is out of sync with our experience of the moral life, where sometimes lies do seem to admit of some justification due to situation and circumstances: that is the whole point of the Nazi pursuer example.

If thought and moral experience are to be reconciled, this classic textbook ethics case exposes how conflicting duties make such reconciliation difficult. And this is a central problem in classic Kantian ethics. Another problem has to do with the tendency toward moral absolutism—the idea of "never" doing this or "always" doing that as if there cannot be exceptions due to circumstance or situation. To the extent that Kantianism endorses a moral absolutism it can be said to be deficient for a reason any absolutist appeal is deficient: absolutes as a logical matter entail their own contradiction—for that is by definition the nature of an absolute. We see this even when considering the ultimate absolute—God—for when considered to be absolute, all knowing, and all powerful, God must assume responsibility for the presence of evil, or in mythic language, for having created Satan. Kant demands a rational ethic that is consistent, universalizable, and noncontradictory, but absolutism negates that demand. And although it is worth noting that some philosophers have explicitly argued that it is possible to work in Kant's ethical framework without accepting the idea of absolute rules,[8] absolutism is a possibility and a pressing problem in Kantian ethics.

Utilitarianism, on the other hand, does take account of consequences, and it too operates by a principle, though it does so, ironically, by in general eschewing principles. The principle of utilitarianism is this: that act is good, right, and fitting to do that maximizes utility and minimizes disutility for the greatest aggregate number. So in this ethical approach, calculation becomes the rational mode of determining the good thing to do, and foreseeing the consequences of action is what determines how utility and disutility are to be weighed and calculated. Utility, or the idea of "usefulness," can mean different things, and the content of utility has meant different things to particular utilitarians. Jeremy Bentham defines utility as "the property in any object, whereby it tends to produce benefit, advantage, pleasure, good or happiness" requiring "an account of the *number* of persons whose interests appear to be concerned."[9] John Stuart Mill asserts that utility refers to the greater happiness only human beings can experience due to the exercise of reason ("better to be a human being dissatisfied than a pig satisfied," he famously writes)[10]; and for the Christian act utilitarian Joseph Fletcher, author of *Situation Ethics*, utility is love—the good, right, and fitting thing to do is that act which is most loving and yields the most loving consequences. Whatever the content, utility identifies some value that is to be maximized for the greatest number.

In thinking about the problem of reconciling theory to experience, we must ask whether we ever run calculations of possible consequences to determine what is good and right to do, and I think there is no doubt but that we resort to utilitarian thinking many times in the course of our daily lives. If Kantianism establishes a principled firewall against, for instance, lying, the utilitarian, who does not oppose lying on principle, will justify a lie that would maximize utility and yield the greatest good for the greatest number. It is safe to assume that if asked about the moral correctness of lying, most people would respond in a general way and say that on principle lying is wrong, thus siding with a Kantian approach to the question. On the other hand, if we were to investigate people's behaviors to determine whether they lie in their daily lives, we would be justified in concluding that the Kantian firewall does not actually function as advertised. And if the categorical imperative does not actually prohibit and thus eliminate lying, what we discern again is the gap between theory and experience. On the utilitarian side, evidence that people do lie in their daily lives would allow us to infer that people also justify their lies, and utilitarian consequentialism would provide the theoretical basis for the justification. All a potential liar need do is weigh consequences and determine that more good than evil or benefit over harm for a greater number would result from the lie, and a utilitarian justification is in place. Lying becomes a justified and thus allowable act in a particular situation.[11]

But an empirical question looms, one that goes to the heart of the problem about the relationship of theory to experience, and since we have raised the issue of lying, let us continue with that example. Is lying and being lied to in fact a part of our daily experience, and is it the case that in fact we often disregard the very principle against lying that is commonly accepted? A news article recently reported this:

> Researchers at the University of Vienna, Austria, have found out that men lie more than women.
> Up to 200 lies per day are required to cope with reality. Men lie for example about career matters, women mainly about shopping.
> Lying helps surviving in a tough society with a lot of competition. It is "as essential to life as air and water" (according to the researcher Professor Peter Stiegnitz).[12]

Steignitz, a social psychologist at the University of Budapest and author of *Lying, The Spice of Life*, conducted surveys that show that people lie "simply to avoid trouble," with 41 percent of lies covering misbehavior and about 14 percent being the "white lies" that "make social life possible." And Steignitz says that lies have "to do with everything from wanting to be loved to sheer laziness and, in most cases, the lies are harmless."[13] The word "harmless" is the researcher's evaluation of the lying, which is purely utilitarian-conse-quentialist: little, if any, harm results from the lie, so the lie is evaluated as morally permissible. Appeal to harmlessness is undoubtedly the justification for lying in the minds of the survey respondents: that is, the harmless lie is easily translated into a "good" act since it yields positive benefits that clearly outweigh harms. Lies, then, "make social life possible," so on that interpreta-tion lies can be justified, maybe not all, but, as the survey reports, many—up to two hundred a day.

This study about lying is worthy of consideration because it challenges the Kantian claim that the categorical imperative directs rational people irresist-ibly to the rightness of truth telling and establishes the clear wrongness of lying—regardless of the consequences. The Stiegnitz report shows that lying is common and that it serves the purpose of being a survival mechanism of sorts in modern life. Attending to the consequences of the lie is obviously an important consideration for those who lie as well as to those who, like Stiegnitz, evaluate the lie.

Few people would simply deny that lying is wrong. Empirical evidence from research on lying, however, suggests that lying is common, and what can be inferred from this is that it is common because people do not really believe it is wrong. It constitutes a kind of psychological necessity in modern life, even a way to negotiate relationships, which is to say that in the calculus of utility, lying can yield positive benefits.[14] The Kantian moral theory cannot account for this—the utilitarian theory can. When weighing the consequences of actions it is simply a fact that people justify doing things that ill conform to the strictures of the Kantian viewpoint so that utilitarianism, an ethic that determines goodness and right action by calculation of benefits and burdens, is often, even commonly, used. It is even sometimes dictated, as when the United States federal government insists that a calculus of benefits and burdens be used by the institutional review boards that evaluate the protections of human research subjects. Much as a potential juror who opposes the death penalty will be excluded from a case that requires by law a "death-qualified" jury, Kantians are in a practical sense excluded from serving on institutional review boards—at least they would be ill fit, since some research might involve intentionally misleading a subject's beliefs, the classic definition of deception, which for the Kantian could not be justified.[15]

The lying research example simply illustrates that people commonly resort to utilitarian ethics in daily life. Whether or not the two hundred lies per day is precisely accurate or even if the research showing that men lie for profit and ego and mainly about their careers and women mainly to protect their children or friends, the important issue for present consideration is this: the Kantian firewall may be commonly acknowledged as a moral guide, but it is not always engaged, not on the question of lying, for people tell lies maybe several times, even scores of times every day, no doubt believing they are justified in doing so. Utilitarianism does close the gap between an ethical theory and moral experience—at least it appears to do so on the issue of lying.

But utilitarianism is itself fraught with difficulties. Lacking any articulation of a principle of respect for persons, it does not accord persons "inalienable rights" or what we might today call human rights; it insists that people act in ways that maximize the aggregate good, even at one's own expense, which in many cases conflicts with ordinary prudence; it does not, arguably of course, lay down a foundation for justice, for in some situations calculating the greatest good for the greatest number could justify acts of discrimination or what in nonutilitarian circles would be referred to as "human rights abuses" against some troublesome minority. The utilitarian appears to hold that as long as maximum utility is achieved, the justice question of how good and evil are to be distributed is of no moral consequence. These are problems with the philosophy, but utilitarianism also points to a peculiar issue having to do with the people who use the philosophy. They have to be smart—very smart—to anticipate all the possible consequences that might flow from a prospective action.[16]

This last point merits a comment. A utilitarian might have allowed the cloning that made *Jurassic Park* possible on the grounds that this would promote the aggregate happiness or the greater good through an application of a new technology based on cutting-edge scientific research. The point of the novel, however, is that things can go wrong, that things unforeseen may happen ("chaos theory"), and the novel and film chronicle the horrific breakdown of human control over the results of the scientific experimentation. The utilitarian always has to consider and then evaluate prospectively things that might happen in the future as a result of a decision made today—how are we to take into account all the things that could come from acting this way rather than that? For that an incredible intelligence is needed, and it is no surprise that utilitarianism is particularly attractive to persons of high intelligence and confident of their intellectual prowess, persons like John Stuart Mill, one of the founders and most able proponents of utilitarian philosophy who is known for off-the-chart intellectual capabilities.[17]

Utilitarianism is in common use by people throughout the world as the pathway for making decisions and acting, but it is problematic for the reasons given and others besides; and in its refusal to acknowledge a principle such as respect for persons it makes decision making look like relativism—for is it not the case that someone must run and thus control the calculus that determines what constitutes the aggregate good? Who does that? People with influence, authority—power. Ethical or moral relativism, the view that any moral judgment is "purely dependent upon a specific framework and is only valid within that framework" is worthy of more discussion,[18] but let it suffice at the moment to say that as an ethical perspective, relativism is incoherent; it unravels ethics and transforms the ethics project into a "might makes right" ethic, denying any possibility of moral error or any universal standards of right or wrong. Utilitarianism does not lead inevitably to relativism, and on that we must be clear. If one concludes that a particular act is right in one situation and wrong in another on the basis of a utilitarian calculation in each of those situations, this is not relativism but decision making based on the application of a utilitarian principle, which the utilitarian would hold to be universally valid. Still, in the idea that no act is intrinsically wrong if it satisfies the utility principle, utilitarianism can appear to offend against some basic moral intuitions and relativize the meaning of certain actions that offend ordinary moral sensibilities.[19] So in this limited sense, relativism poses a potential challenge for utilitarianism, though not as directly as absolutism poses an actual danger in Kantian ethics.

So two major philosophical perspectives about ethics—the Kantian and the utilitarian, which are taught in ethics classes in colleges and universities around the world and are in use today by people in their daily lives—are beset with problems. Many ethics books and articles take pains to point out the problems with these theories, but the most challenging issue for our purposes is that these theories in critical ways do not square with our moral experiences. The Kantian has a way of establishing principles, say, against telling lies, that people violate without huge pangs of conscience, and utilitarians deny principles pertaining to respect for human dignity or intrinsic rights, for utilitarianism proceeds on the assumption that nothing is intrinsically wrong or immoral. Put another way, anything is potentially justifiable to the utilitarian if the calculus yields the greatest good for the greatest number, even a questionable or morally repugnant act. This may be a consistent view philosophically, but a gap shows again between thought and experience: the idea that there are no intrinsically wrong actions does not conform to the experience of people who live with others and who in fact do, as an empirical matter, hold that some actions are so heinous, so serious a violation of human dignity, that they must be held to be intrinsically wrong.

Noting problems with these major ethical theories leads to this question: Are these problems not significant? Do we note the problems and then simply proceed to use the theories as if they are acceptable despite their defects, allowing thought and experience to divide—someone might buy a car having been told the brakes do not work, but would that person then drive it? At issue is the fact that if our thinking about the moral life is to square with our experiences, then these theoretical problems should not be accepted as inconsequential. Reasonable people would not ordinarily accede to the duty of truth telling if by a deception an innocent human life could be saved; yet neither would reasonable people accede morally to some blatant human rights abuse because the calculation of benefits and harms for the greatest number happened to turn out in favor of allowing the abuse to continue. One of the tragedies of human rights abuses that persist despite efforts to stop them is that the gap between moral thought and experience becomes glaringly apparent. While no doubt politics accounts for ineffective action in the face of such abuses, our moral judgments about such human rights abuses is usually clear: reasonable persons will not on the basis of a utilitarian calculation endorse as good, right, and fitting some abusive practice—say, the summary execution of political prisoners, or the enslavement of women in the sex trafficking trade, or pressing children into the military—as if the good and proper thing to do is to say, "Onward, let the abuse continue."

Utilitarianism and Kantian ethics both present problems not easily resolved within the framework of the theories, and these problems, including the problem that as theories they do not account for our common moral experiences, are not arcane or hidden but widely noted, as any student of ethics comes to learn. The question raised by these shortcomings, however, is whether we should acknowledge them as flaws and then simply proceed to rely on these theories, using them as guides to moral thinking as if they were cars that we knew had failed brakes. By raising this issue, I am proposing that we reconsider *how we think about the moral life* and attend to some other ways of thinking that might avoid these particular problems. We ought to keep our eyes on the objective of reconciling our ethical thought with our moral experience so that the way we think about ethics conforms to the way we live our lives as reasonable people of goodwill in community, concerned for the welfare of ourselves, others, and our world. This leads me to the specific project of this book.

AN ALTERNATIVE ETHICAL MODEL:
A MODEST PROPOSAL FOR A HYBRID ETHIC

Ethical theories provide a framework of standards, principles, and guidelines that allow us to determine what is morally right and what is morally wrong. The purpose of an ethical theory is ultimately practical, since we evaluate possible actions against the theory, determine what would, in light of the theory, constitute the right thing to do, and then act, believing that we understand what it is we ought to do. We have looked at two ethical theories, acknowledged their enormous influence and positive value, but then exposed some standard criticisms and often-discussed shortcomings. Ethics theories do not abound, but there are ethical theories besides utilitarianism and Kantian deontology—axiogical ethics, eudemonistic ethics, commutarian ethics, vices and virtues, W. D. Ross's project of prima facie duty ethics, casuistry, feminist ethics, and an ethics of coherence grounded in John Rawls's model of reflective equilibrium. Serious study of these approaches would reveal various shortcomings and deficiencies in them as well, some on the order of those found in utilitarianism and Kantianism. Most ethics introductions that comprehensively survey ethical theories point out strengths as well as deficiencies in these various approaches, and ethics scholars will often face the challenge of these deficiencies to suggest improved ways of working the ethics field.

In the pages ahead a case will be made that there is an approach to ethics that amalgamates many of the strengths of different ethical theories while reconciling theory with experience. The alternative ethical model to be offered for consideration bridges the gap between theory and experience by approaching the moral life itself in its complexity; and it reconciles this complexity with a "theory" that is neither so pristine as Kantianism nor so clear as utilitarianism. I shall offer a more holistic, or, as I prefer, a "hybrid" approach to ethical thought, one that takes account of duty and principles yet steers clear of absolutism and that attends to consequences but avoids relativism. One of the advantages of this hybrid approach is that people actually use it. People will put it to work in their ethical thinking about problems and in their lives as persons who want to do what is good, right, and fitting. People actually use it; and they do so without making any explicit reference to its being an identifiable theory. We can articulate a theory to explain the content of this ethic, and, more important, we can even show how this approach to ethics has been appealed to, even if implicitly, in an empirical sense as a guide to right action when confronting moral questions, problems, or even dilemmas. That, again, is the test of an ethical theory—how well it helps us deal with practical ethical problems.

This hybrid theory to be discussed is grounded in something very old, much older than the Enlightenment theories of Immanuel Kant or John Stuart Mill—natural law. Natural law is associated with Aristotle and Cicero in the ancient Western world and Thomas Aquinas in the Christian era, and it has powerful contemporary advocates in the philosophers John Finnis and Germaine Grisez. Natural law is at its most basic a theory that asserts that human beings as rational persons have access through reason to moral knowledge and understanding; that our capacity for understanding the universally binding rules of morality is part of our very constitution as human beings—part of our nature; and that being endowed with reason, human persons hold a natural capacity to discern goodness. This capacity is exercised in projects that seek to realize, enjoy, and promote for others the goods of life—those things people "naturally" recognize as good and that human existence would be impoverished without, such things as friendship, practical reasonableness, aesthetic enjoyment, even the good of life itself;[20] and that reason will commend these goods to us as good and thus worthy of moral aspiration.

This hybrid ethic is difficult to identify, and it does not have a convenient name, but it has been expressed perhaps nowhere more cogently than in the tradition or doctrine of what is commonly called "just war" thinking. In "just war" thinking, a model for ethical analysis and deliberation exists that holds possibilities for a "new" way of doing ethics that seeks to reconcile ethical thinking with our moral experiences. Just war is, of course, not new—it is in fact very old, even ancient. The idea of just war and constraint on the use of force goes back in the West to Cicero, and it has been preserved, developed, and transmitted through such figures as Augustine, Aquinas, Grotius, and Vitoria. It is in use today, for military people and political policy planners consult it and attempt to abide by its guidelines. And because the world we live in is so war torn and just war is acknowledged to offer meaningful assistance in figuring out the moral meaning of responses to conflict and war, it is a topic of keen interest today for ethicists, philosophers, and religious thinkers who are writing books, delivering papers, and attending conferences that deal with this central moral problem of our time—the problem of war and the moral justification for uses of force.

The history of just war theory or doctrine is of course worthy of serious study, and scholars have devoted an enormous amount of attention to the meaning and possibilities, both positive and negative, of just war thinking. Invoking the term "just war" will prick at the moral sensibilities of many reasonable people of goodwill, for the idea of a just war will strike many as highly dubious if not oxymoronic, and I will include myself in that number. So noting that just war thinking has its critics could—perhaps should—arouse a concern that a "new" approach to ethics that takes just war as a starting point is defeated from the outset. There are hurdles to jump, no doubt. What can be said at the outset is that appealing to just war thinking as a model for a broader, more inclusive ethic is not the same thing as using just war theory (or just war doctrine) as it is commonly used today in political and military projects. Actually, the idea of invoking just war theory for the purpose of justifying war is itself of limited value for this project. The "new" way of thinking about ethics or doing ethics expressed through the model of just war thinking is not new in the sense that an ethical equivalent to a Coperni-can revolution is in the offing—"new" here is much more modest a notion, referring to a reframing and a reintegration of valuable ethical insights that have long been around, that are today widely accepted, and that function to bridge the gap between our ethical theories and experience. What follows in the pages ahead is a proposal for thinking about the project of ethical inquiry in ways that avoid absolutism on the one hand and ethical relativism on the other, both being viewpoints destructive of the ethics project itself. And at issue is whether this approach has the advantage of reconciling our moral thinking to our moral experiences.

Just war thinking as it is commonly used, I shall argue, is not an ethic, but it certainly appeals to an ethic—a way of ethical thinking. I shall argue that the ethic that lies *behind* just war, once articulated, will prove to be widely applicable to all kinds of ethical issues and quandaries so that this investiga-tion comes to have practical or applied consequences. And that is at it should be. If an ethic lies behind just war, that ethic must have implications *beyond* the particular question of war or the use of force. All kinds of issues must be subject to analysis and deliberations through the ethic, just as Kantians apply their theoretical perspectives to lying and suicide and utilitarians apply their theories to abortion and cap-and-trade environmental policies. Extracting and articulating the ethic—the ethic to which just war thinking itself appeals—is the constructive proposal of this book. Just war is not an ethic itself but rather the exemplification of a model for ethical thinking that lies *behind* just war and has practical significance *beyond* just war. That ethic can actually be used to critique the ethics of war and claims people will make about a just war.

Inquiry into the just war model is relevant to the central focus of this book, which is the idea that people of goodwill the world over share *common agreements*. Certain common agreements underwrite just war thinking as well as the moral life itself, and the expression "common agreements" allows us to focus on those things that bind us together into moral community, into one moral world, while acknowledging all kinds of variation in particulars. Reasonable people of goodwill share certain common agreements on moral matters, by which I mean those things reason identifies as goods of life; and these goods are universally recognized as good and thus worthy of desire, cultivation, protection, and transmission to others even if they appear differently one culture to the next. Such agreements do not pertain to descriptive diversity issues such as one society's preference for forks over another's for chopsticks, but to morally serious and relevant matters such as promise keeping or truth telling or settling disagreements without resorting to force. On the basis of certain common agreements, we find ourselves connected to one another across cultures, even in the face of our extraordinarily complex and diverse world and the inevitable misunderstandings and ethnocentrisms we experience in our engagements with others. However much we may experience difference with others due to cultural divides, social experiences, history, and even reigning philosophical or ideological perspectives, there is reason also to say that human beings share certain moral values and avow common agreements about some very important matters.

The emphasis on the human inclination to goodness found in the ancient Western ethics tradition of natural law, which underwrites just war thinking, provides an ethical resource for grounding this project, and I shall make a case that these common agreements can be extracted and articulated. My case is that doing so allows us to discern the nature of our common moral life—and these agreements are actually integral to our experience of the moral world. We do not live in six billion self-contained moral worlds but in one world, and we encounter this reality in the experience of moral violation—atrocity, genocide, sex trade, child enslavement, mass executions, the oppression of women or children, and even religiously inspired violence. Moral violations appear as the failure of individuals and even whole communities to adhere to our common agreements. The contemporary emphasis on human rights has brought concern for our common moral agreements to a new heightened consciousness, with awareness of these common agreements often arising due to confrontation with human rights violations and violators. Implicit in the criticism of a human rights violation is the positive valence on the idea that there is—and should be—certain "common agreements" that human beings recognize—and insist should be recognized—universally. We experience those common agreements when actions destructive of persons and their communities are at play in the world, insulting the very dignity and moral worth of human persons. And by "persons" here we mean people in any social or cultural context who may be wildly different from one another yet whose diversity is itself a manifestation of how people actually pursue the goods of life in the context of particular situations and circumstances.

Normative judgments about right and wrong are framed within a context of universally shared moral values related to reason's capacity to discern, pursue, and realize goodness; moral decision making about what "ought" to be done finally issues in action that is commended to others as the morally correct thing to do. An ethical theory that supports the idea of *common agreements* functions to reconcile our moral thinking—our ethical theorizing—with our lived moral experience, which means it connects to an applied ethics where at issue are normative judgments that finally yield to action. The actions sponsored by the view that by common agreement certain things are good and right to do are not themselves theoretically controversial in terms of what should be done—the genocide should stop, the refugees should be sheltered, health care should be extended to those who currently do not have it. Practical problems may interfere with swift action to address a moral violation, and reasonable people can disagree about the most effective way to realize morally worthy ends. But our common agreements can be reached beyond our experience of violation or disagreements, and actions based on our common agreements will always express our beliefs and judgments about what we must do to make the world a better place.

The first part of this book will extract the natural law–based and just war–related ethic by looking more deeply at just war thinking, not so much in terms of the history of just war doctrine, which is not my immediate concern and to which I will give only limited attention, but at the ethical meaning and possibilities exemplified by the structures and framework associated with just war thinking. After this look *behind* just war, we shall, in the second half of the book, look *beyond* just war, showing how this ethic contributes to the way we create moral understanding based on common moral agreements. Several contemporary moral issues will be addressed, including physician-assisted suicide, capital punishment, and treatment of severely disabled newborns, as this ethic is applied to actual moral problems, and we examine how it can be—and actually has been—practically appealed to and used. As the book concludes, we shall return to a sometimes overlooked aspect of just war thinking, namely, the meaning of moral innocence and the implications of that for contemporary moral analysis. Two particularly difficult issues will be analyzed in the framework of the ethic proposed in these pages: fetal innocence and its significance for the abortion issue, and the whole issue of noncombatant immunity in warfare.

Part I

ETHICS

The Ethic behind Just War

Chapter One

Just War as an Ethic

JUST WAR: THE SPECIFICS

The just war tradition in the West is based on the idea that war, under certain limited conditions, can serve the interests of justice, defend important values, and promote the common good. Just war has always focused on the idea that restraints must be placed on war and uses of force, and moral thinking about war in the just war tradition—whether advanced as theory or doctrine, tradition or ideas—has evolved and undergone modification over the centuries in response to changing circumstances and historical necessities.

Just war is still in use today as a guide to moral thinking about war, and the content of the theory is invoked in public deliberations about the ethics of war, even if no explicit reference to "just war theory" is made. The moral concerns that people of goodwill raise about war and even the prospective use of force inevitably involve the content of just war thinking. This is the case even though war today is not what it was when just war thinking emerged from its ancient Roman historical setting, where fighting, savage as it could be, involved limited weapons, often for use in hand-to-hand combat, wielded by individual soldiers against clearly identifiable adversaries. Contemporary war involves weapons that, at their most powerful, do not discriminate (i.e., "weapons of mass destruction") and warriors who, as insurgents or suicide bombers, cannot be distinguished as identifiable "combatants." Today, even the language of war is difficult to decipher as metaphorical usage has stretched to include such matters as contraband interdiction ("war on drugs") and even medical research ("war on cancer"). Nevertheless, just war ideas, for all that would seem to count against their applicability in the contemporary world, still provide guidance on moral issues and keep before military leaders and policy makers the idea of restraint in the use of force.

In the pages to follow we shall refer to the just war tradition, just war thinking, and just war ideas. All of these uses are commonly associated with various criteria, which, if satisfied, would justify a use of coercive force to settle conflicts. The criteria are as follows:

- The war or use of coercive force must be sanctioned by a legitimate and competent authority.
- The cause must be just.
- There must be a right intention and announcement of that intention (i.e., achieving a just settlement of the conflict and restoring peace).
- The results of using force and going to war must be proportionate to the end of peace, meaning more good than ill must result—a proportionality requirement.
- Combat or use of force must always be a last resort.
- The war must be undertaken with a reasonable hope of success.
- By resorting to force or going to war one must preserve values that otherwise could not be preserved.

These are a contemporary formulation of the *jus ad bellum* criteria that would be used to establish whether a war or use of coercive force was itself morally justifiable. In addition, two other criteria, reflecting the *jus in bello* tradition, articulate constraints on the actual conduct of a war, guiding action with respect to the means of warfare:

- Noncombatants must be protected from harm (noncombatant immunity).
- The use of force cannot resort to means (i.e., weaponry) that are disproportionate to the end of restoring peace (proportionality).

This listing of "criteria" offers what I believe to be the clearest account of the *content* of just war thinking as it is presently understood and employed. Uses of the term "just war" in the pages that follow refer to this presentation.

MOVING TOWARD THE ETHIC BEHIND JUST WAR

The argument of this book is that just war thinking is itself an expression of a more basic approach to ethics, one that will bridge our thinking about ethics with our moral experience. Just war, I have claimed, is our way into that ethic. But at the outset, this project is facing a serious problem. Just war critic Andrew Fiala writes, "The just war theory expresses our best moral thinking about war. But it is false to assume that since we know what a just war would be, just wars actually exist. In fact there are no just wars. Nor is there any good reason to suppose that it is actually possible for there to be just wars."[1]

If Fiala is right, just war thinking presents one more example of the very problem that we have set out to avoid—the problem of reconciling ethical thought with our moral experience. If the theory of just war cannot be reconciled to our moral experience, if there can be a just war in theory but not in practice, then the theory is of little practical use. The theory may express our ideals, but those ideals remain unrealized and experientially elusive. If that conclusion holds, we should look elsewhere for an ethical model.

Fiala's helpful discussion of what he calls the just war "myth" is not meant so much to completely abandon any role for just war theory—he does, after all, call it "our best moral thinking about war." His purpose, rather, is to urge us to be "cautious and critical," for "The point of calling the just war theory a myth is to force us to be vigilant against the seductions and heartaches of wishful thinking about war."[2] Fair enough. No doubt, just war thinking has for centuries served to justify all kinds of military actions and adventures, many if not most of them morally suspect. In fact, Fiala's claim that there are no just wars, which he asserts as "fact," is probably correct—at least an analysis of any particular war would likely yield ample material to demonstrate that just war thinking has, as an empirically verifiable matter, failed to restrain force as the theory requires. So why do we look toward just war thinking as a model for an ethic if there is evidence that that on the question of war, this particular theory—just war theory—cannot bridge the gap with our experience, for do we not experience war as a destructive evil fraught with all manner of injustices?

We can provide two responses to this important question.

First, just war thinking, as it is commonly interjected into public discussions concerning the use of force, is not itself identical to the ethic on which just war thinking is based, and we shall shortly examine why this is the case. The ethic that underwrites just war thinking cannot be reduced to, or identified exclusively with, any particular moral controversy—not even the issue of war, for an ethic is meant to provide a framework for guiding reflection toward right action on all manner of problems, dilemmas, and decisions that confront people in their moral experiences. So the ethic that lies behind just war thinking functions as does any other moral theory: it guides thought and reflection so as to lead to right action, whether the issue be war, or deception, or abortion, or environmental protection. Furthermore, that ethic can be used not only to guide right action but also to critique actions so that violations of that ethic may be discerned. In the case of war, appeals to the theoretical specifics of the just war theory—the criteria—may appear to satisfy the ethic yet actually fail to do so because those using just war theory for some specific purpose, such as justifying a policy decision for a particular use of force, have in bad faith detached the use of the theory from its ethical moorings.

The second response is related to the first. Just war ideas have become so integrated into public discussions of wars and impending wars that the specific features of the theory—the criteria—have come to be treated as if they have a life of their own. The criteria are often invoked as they were "self-evident truths" that justify particular actions when applied in particular circumstances. Nothing could be further from the truth. The criteria are broad and vague and say nothing about particulars. Everything under just war thinking involves interpretation and argumentation, requiring people of goodwill to work with good and relevant information free from deceit, distortion, and misrepresentation.

This concern, which from another angle also demonstrates how the specifics of just war thinking can become detached from the ethic behind the theory, is most apparent when critics argue that just war thinking provides only a list of items to check off to ensure a prospective war is morally justified.[3] That "checklist" approach to just war fails to direct ethical analysis to the moral foundation that supports and informs the just war criteria, and this would include reference to and direction from a normative principle, action guide, or "common agreement" that is essential grounding for this or any other ethical perspective. If such an appeal to a normative principle is lacking—and the "checklist" approach to just war does lack integrity as a formed ethical perspective—then the claim can be made that just war thinking is being used in a way that is not consistent with its ethical foundations—that it is being misapplied, misused, and even misrepresented *as an ethic*. If the ethic behind just war does not make its appearance in public discussions about war and peace, if those ideas are disconnected from the ethic that gives rise to the specifics of just war theory, or if the criteria of just war are mistakenly asserted as if they were self-sufficient action guides in no need of connection to such morally relevant matters as commitment to some kind of moral principle, then just war ideas will fail to connect to our moral experience of war (i.e., war as unjust). From this detachment comes the idea that any talk of just war is an oxymoron. For if experience tells us that there are, as a matter of fact, "no just wars," then the theory of just war is either terribly flawed, misguided, or just plain wrong, or something is being distorted or misunderstood about the ethical background of just war thinking. We shall proceed on the assumption that the latter is the case. By keeping our attention focused on the need for an ethic that reconciles thought and experience, we can come to a clearer understanding of the value of "just war thinking" while exposing an approach to ethics that has applicability to a variety of moral issues, not only war.

To get to this ethic *behind* just war, we shall need to examine briefly the tradition of just war thinking, then explore how the ethic behind just war directs practical reason to right action on the moral issue at the heart of the just war tradition—the use of force to settle conflicts. We shall examine aspects of the natural law tradition that gave rise to just war thinking, consider briefly some of the history of just war thinking, and then turn attention to the particular issue at stake in just war thinking—war and the use of force. The purpose of this investigation is to explore how reasonable people of goodwill can approach the moral problem of war and the use of force with "an ethic" that provides *adequate theoretical resources* to guide them to right action while taking into account our *experience of war* as an unwanted state of affairs much to be avoided.

NATURAL LAW AND THE JUST WAR TRADITION

The just war tradition is grounded in natural law, and, as John Finnis writes,

> A sound theory of natural law is one that explicitly . . . undertakes a critique of practical viewpoints, in order to distinguish the practically unreasonable from the practically reasonable, and thus to differentiate the really important from that which is unimportant. . . . A theory of natural law claims to be able to identify conditions and principles of right-mindedness, of good and proper order among [persons] and in individual conduct.[4]

Natural law ethics, according to Finnis, emphasizes two things: the natural capacity of reason to identify *principles* of right-mindedness affecting conduct, and the "conditions" of good and proper order among people. The "conditions" of right-mindedness appear in the "criteria" of just war thinking.

The attention Finnis gives to practical reasonableness is vital to the natural law perspective since practical reasonableness constitutes one of the *goods of life*. The goods of life refer to those things reason is *naturally* endowed to recognize as intrinsically good and which people *naturally* seek to realize in the effort to live meaningful, fulfilled, and happy lives. In Germaine Grisez's modern reconfiguration, these goods of life would include life itself, a preeminent good since all other goods rest upon it, and these others: the capacity for aesthetic enjoyment; self-consciousness; friendships; freedom to work, play, and pursue speculative knowledge; physical integrity; a personal identity that reflects a cohesive personality; and "practical reasonableness," which is the good of life that connects being and action and grounds all moral reflection.[5] Practical reasonableness is the good whereby human beings affirm the positive value of peace and harmonious relationships, not as goods of life themselves, but rather as the context and condition necessary if people are to pursue, promote, and realize the goods of life. "The practical reasonableness prescribed by natural law," writes Joseph Boyle, "requires action compatible with a will open to an ideal human community in which all the goods of all people are realized in interpersonal harmony."[6] In its natural inclination toward affirming the value of peace and harmony, practical reasonableness necessarily imposes constraints on the use of force and insists on a nonviolent intentionality whenever a resort to force is contemplated.

As an expression of natural law ethics, just war thinking affirms the capacity of reason to recognize possibilities for realizing goodness even in the terrible conflict situation of war. War may not be a positive good in itself, but it can be undertaken for good purposes such as addressing injustices, protecting vulnerable people, and preserving threatened but defensible values. War can be shaped by the power of goodness to the extent that practical reasonableness guides people to restrain violence and direct themselves—even in the context of war—to the rational and good end of peace. Thus do we derive in the natural law tradition the idea that peace and justice must always be the purpose of resorting to force. As St. Augustine famously says, "War is waged in order that peace may be obtained," sometime translated as "We go to war that we may have peace."[7] Peace in the natural law understanding is not a passive "at rest" or stasis notion but is, as Finnis writes, "synonymous with the ideal condition of integral human fulfillment—the flourishing of all human persons and communities."[8] A social and political situation marked by injustices destroys true peace. Preserving or attaining peace may require a use of force even if resorting to force is itself insufficient to bring about peace, for in the natural law tradition a use of force cannot serve as the cause—in Aristotle's terms the direct or "efficient cause"—of right. So central is peace to human flourishing that the just war tradition developed by refusing to legitimate any intentional destruction of human life. Just war has a long tradition of denying any justification for warfare deaths that occurred because of "an intent to kill." Such an intent is, under just war thinking, forbidden.[9]

In the natural law tradition, justice is integral to peace; and in the Christian natural law tradition, the direct cause of peace is love of neighbor. Affirming the centrality of love of neighbor and the harmonious relationships that obtain from such love led the important natural law Christian theologians Thomas Aquinas (1225–1274) and Francisco Suarez (1548–1617) to discuss war in their writings on love (*caritas*).[10] The significant point to glean from this brief discussion is that just war thinking as an expression of natural law ethics is aimed at serving peace and harmonious relationships. Unjust acts of aggression, coercion, or oppression break the peace and cause disharmony, and resorting to a use of force—war—was conceived as a way of correcting injustices and reestablishing societal harmony. Resorting to a use of force was always deemed regrettable action even if it was also held to be corrective action in service to justice and thus necessary for restoring peace. Regret and necessity are critical aspects of just war thinking. As Augustine writes, "The wise man, they say, will wage just wars. As if he would not all the more, if he remembers his humanity, deplore his being compelled to engage in just wars."[11] War, then, is conceived as a response to the injustices that have disrupted peace, and reasonable persons seeking goodness and continued human flourishing are "compelled" to enter into war in order to restore the peace that if war be contemplated is already shattered.

JUST WAR: AN EVOLVING PERSPECTIVE

In his treatise *On Duties (De Officiis)*, Cicero writes the following: "Although reason is characteristic of men and force of beasts, you must resort to force if there is no opportunity to employ reason. Therefore, wars should be undertaken only so that one may live in peace without wrongdoing."[12] Cicero (106–43 BCE) held that the end of war must be a just peace, that a justified use of force must rest on legitimate cause, and that "no war is just unless it is waged after the government has demanded restitution or unless the war is previously announced and declared."[13] In these reflections of Cicero lie the origins of just war theory. Cicero was committed philosophically to a natural law theory of obligation, which he took from the Stoics and then synthesized with both Aristotle's understanding of the virtues and Plato's theory of duties. The question of war concerned him greatly. Cicero understood Roman law to embody a natural law theory of justice, and war always involved questions of Roman honor. His natural law understanding was that using force should be limited to only such use as justice required. Natural reason, he believed, should lead reasonable people to submit to Roman law without use of force, but he also understood that war could at times be necessary. Resorting to war, however, required a general philosophical justification (*jus ad bellum*); and he insisted on attending to the moral meaning of specific practices in war (*jus in bello*). From this perspective, Cicero could be critical even of Rome's wars. For instance, he condemned Roman cruelty in the sack of Corinth to the point of holding Rome accountable for criminal conduct. As one commentator writes, "Cicero clearly states that evil should never be done, even to save one's country. The gods, or natural law are above the state."[14]

The next significant step in just war theorizing was undertaken by St. Augustine, who advanced three ideas that are still vital to the contemporary formulation of just war criteria: legitimate authority, just cause, and right intention. Augustine hated war as a great evil that unleashed and even legitimized lust and greed,[15] and, accepting the natural law contention that war could not be an efficient (direct) cause of right, held that war could not bring about the justice and harmony to be associated with true peace. Augustine condemned wars that were motivated by "a thirst for vengeance."[16] He believed the defensive wars in his own time that were waged to resist barbarian invasion were justified; he also defended as justifiable biblical wars, such as Moses's "war" against the Egyptians and the aggressive war Joshua led against the wicked people of Ai. These were wars commanded by God and were "just" due to that divine sanction.[17] It was Augustine who refused, for the first time in the West, to associate war with honor, and he offered viewpoints that could support several approaches to war. John Langan writes that "the elements [for the Augustinian writings about war] could be put together in support of a just war position or a holy war position or a pacifist position,"[18] but clearly there are warrants to claim Augustine as a just war theorist.[19] In the transmission of just war ideas through the moral teachings of the Roman Catholic Church after Augustine, just war thinking developed the idea that public authorities have a duty to pursue justice, even at risk to their personal safety, and Augustine himself held that Christians, as an expression of neighborly love, have a special obligation to put themselves between warring parties in the effort to end war.

As it developed in the West in the context of the Roman Catholic Church's own commitment to natural law thinking, just war came to be understood as demanding justice, with charity and love of neighbor integral to the notion of justice itself. In the twelfth century, Gratian's *Decretals* advanced a just war theory around the idea that just war can avenge wrongs and coerce the Church's enemies. In the thirteenth century, Raymond of Pennaforte formalized Augustine's theory and regarded war as what we would today term a prima facie, or presumed, evil. Alexander of Hales (ca. 1185–1245), an Englishman who held a chair of theology at the University of Paris, wrote the first major philosophical treatise on war by a noncanonist. He argued on scriptural grounds that fighting an unjust war is forbidden and then offered the view that the difference between a just and an unjust war depends on six preconditions: authority, state of mind, intention, condition, desert, and cause.[20] John Finnis has summarized Alexander's position as follows:

> The person declaring war must have (1) the right *affectus* (state of mind) and (2) authority to do so; the persons engaging in war must (3) not be clerics, and must have (4) the right *intentio*; the persons warred upon must (5) deserve it (the war must have *meritum*); and there must be (6) *causa*, in that the war must be waged for the support of the good, the coercion of the bad, and peace for all.[21]

In the thirteenth century, Thomas Aquinas adopted Augustine's just war idea that a use of force required right authority, just cause, and right intention, but he moved beyond Augustine by adding what I would call a "grounds-for-action" idea that would later be formalized in the idea of a "just cause" criterion. Wars, according to Aquinas, could be justly waged if they were for the purpose of righting wrongs, which would include restoring what has been unjustly taken away or to punish a nation that has failed to punish crimes committed by its own people. As Thomas wrote,

> In order for a war to be just, three things are necessary. First, the authority of the sovereign by whose command the war is to be waged. For it is not the business of a private individual to declare war. . . . Secondly, a just cause is required, namely, that those who are attacked should be attacked because they deserve it on account of some fault. (Quoting Augustine) "A just war is wont to be described as one that avenges wrongs, when a nation or state has to be punished, or to restore what it has seized unjustly." Thirdly, it is necessary that the belligerents have a rightful intention, so that they intend the advancement of good, or the avoidance of evil.[22]

And Aquinas made another significant contribution to just war thinking. In discussing the permissibility of self-defense in the *Summa Theologica* (II-II, Qu. 64, Art.7)—"Whether it is permissible to kill a man in self-defense?" was his actual question—he introduced the principle of *double effect*. "Nothing hinders one act from having two effects, only one of which is intended, while the other is beside the intention. . . . Accordingly, the act of self-defense may have two effects: one, the saving of one's life; the other, the slaying of the aggressor."[23] "Double effect" thus came into play to emphasize that individual Christians subjected to unjust aggression could justifiably repel attackers with a use of force that could prove lethal but only as long as any killing occurred as an unintended and secondary consequence ("double effect") of the legitimate just war aim of repelling the unjust attack.

The *right intention* and *just cause* criteria of just war have long centered on self-defense and resistance to unjust aggression, and these notions are current today in Article 51 of the Charter of the United Nations.[24] Thomas held that it was natural for individuals to act to preserve their "being" in an act of self-defense, but the repelling of an unjust attack must be proportional and not excessive, and "it is not lawful for a man to intend killing a man in self-defense."[25] Thomas emphasized that a use of force with the specific objective in mind of killing an enemy is not a legitimate aspect of just war and a criterion of *proportionality* developed over the centuries to indicate that a use of force must always be proportional to the end of restoring peace. Hence certain weapons and war activities that violated this sense of proportionality have always fared poorly under just war, from the medieval practice of well poisoning to the more modern condemnation of weapons such as dum-dum bullets or nuclear, biological, and chemical weapons. All of these weapons have an effect disproportionate to the end of restoring peace. Certain weapons cannot confine the use of force to the immediate situation and circumstance but affect noncombatants far beyond the conflict situation in both space and time, so these are practices and weapons that just war guidelines condemn.

After Aquinas, the Spanish Scholastics Vitoria (d. 1546) and Suarez (d. 1617) and the Protestant Dutch theologian Hugo Grotius (d. 1645) offered further developments in the idea of just war. Often regarded as the founder of international law, Grotius held to the view that "war is not in conflict with the law of nature," so the rules of war were naturally binding. His extensive treatment of war in the context of "the laws of nations" included the premise that "By nature all men have a right of resistance against injury" and that this natural right could not be changed, not even by God.[26] This position showed the transforming influence of secularization on natural law thinking. The idea of a Christian commonwealth underwent further serious disintegration due to the Reformation, and just war thinking was affected by the emergence of the nation-state and continued secularizing political and cultural shifts. Just war thinking began to attend to the problem of limiting the destructiveness of war, a development caused by the devastation of the religious wars of the sixteenth century.

In both the Reformation and post-Reformation eras, just war thinking turned attention to the *jus in bello* concerns for means.[27] The moral doctrine of double effect, which had originally offered restricted justification for the unintended death of a mutual combatant, came to be invoked as a moral doctrine relevant to the killing of noncombatants. New attention was paid to the issue of proportionality. The double-effect defense preserved the idea that noncombatants were not morally legitimate targets for a use of force but then offered that such deaths, regrettable as they were, could be deemed morally justifiable if they were not intended and if every effort was made to avoid them. The development of increasingly sophisticated, high-technology weaponry that seeks to avoid civilian casualties, smart bombs, for example, can be traced directly to the just war requirement concerning noncombatant immunity, even as just war concerns about proportionality undermine moral justifications for nuclear, biological, and chemical weapons that inflict disproportionate damage on innocent persons.

Just war thinking increasingly influenced international law and secular thinking in general, and appeals to just war ideas play an important role in international law today, frequently appearing in United Nations deliberations and resolutions.[28] Note that efforts to enact the intent of the United Nations Charter on the issue of war have not always succeeded; the record is mixed if not dismal. Christian ethicist Daniel Maguire points out that Article 51 of the United Nations Charter advances what he terms a *policing paradigm* that "stipulates that any nation planning to attack another military must face not only that nation but all nations coordinated—police style—into an international security force."[29] He quotes international law expert Richard Falk, who writes:

> the UN Charter [was] a multilateral treaty largely crafted by American diplomats and legal advisers. Its essential feature was to entrust the Security Council with administering a prohibition of recourse to international force (Article 2, Section 4) by states except in circumstances of self-defense, which itself was restricted to responses to a prior "armed attack" (Article 51).

Maguire goes on to comment that the United States has "trashed this historic initiative and returned to the vigilante approach to warring."[30]

The UN idea of a just war–related policing paradigm demonstrates how just war has evolved and modified over the centuries to meet new demands and circumstances. Constant in the background of just war thinking, however, is the understanding that war is a terrible state of affairs, much to be avoided, and that even if uses of force are considered legitimate, they must be restrained because of war's destructiveness. Accordingly, just war theory has developed as a practical restraint on violence as well as a theory of resistance to evil. Roman Catholic theologian Richard McBrien writes, "The purpose of just-war theory, therefore, was not to rationalize violence but to limit its scope and methods,"[31] a perspective that opposes any idea that just war functions essentially as a tool of government to use war, military incursion, and violence to serve national self-interest or political goals.[32]

Just war ideas are invoked today in both secular and religious worlds, but the action guides meant to serve the end of peace and the good of justice are not designed to settle any particular issue concerning the use of force in any particular conflict. The criteria provide, rather, the structured guideline for deliberating uses of force, not just in military or police situations but in the moral reflections of critically minded citizens who worry about violence and its use by the state.

Policy makers and state leaders appeal to just war ideas today in contemplation of the uses of force. A US Senate debate over *last resort*—whether economic sanctions had been given time to work—was very much at issue in a close vote to authorize military force in the 1991 Gulf War; and last resort was clearly the issue UN inspector Hans Blix highlighted when he urged American restraint on military force and requested more time to search for weapons of mass destruction prior to the American preemptive strike in Iraq in 2003.[33] Also in 2003, a just war debate took place over *legitimate authority*

as the United States contemplated war in Iraq. The United States sought support for its cause with the United Nations, which was not prepared to give authorization for military action in Iraq—this would have been (and then was)
a first-strike incursion for which the immediate *just cause*—defense against
weapons of mass destruction—proved to be glaringly absent. Just war provides a guideline for moral deliberation on the use of force, and it establishes
those points of discussion over which people come together to argue whether
a use of force is or can be justified—and often just war ideas will lead reasonable people to the conclusion that force cannot be justified. So just war can
serve as an instrument for critiquing uses of force, and I shall say more about
this shortly. Suffice it to say that military leaders in the United States cut their
teeth on just war theory and employ it to frame military action, with the result
that they often find themselves in disagreement with civilian political leaders.

In modern democratic societies, the content of just war thinking frames
debates over particulars when the use of force is being contemplated. The
criteria themselves settle neither questions of strategy nor questions of moral
meaning in particular conflicts. Just war ideas can be used self-servingly,
even cynically, to justify political and military incursions that require the
gloss of moral justification to garner public support. Despite those dangers,
however, the great value of the just war structure lies in its ability to call reasonable persons together to employ a common language within a reasonable
structure designed to assist public deliberation about the appropriateness of
considering the use of force.

ETHICS—AND THE ETHIC RELATED TO JUST WAR

The content of just war thinking consists in a set of criteria, which are broadly
conceived justice-related considerations that serve to guide reflection on the
possibility of a morally justifiable use of force. The criteria make an implicit
appeal to an ethic through their explicit attention to moral concerns such as
justice and intentionality, but these criteria do not, of themselves, constitute
an ethic. If they did constitute an ethic, we would be able to say that they
reconciled our moral thinking with our experience of war. Furthermore, we
would be able to find in them a guide to moral deliberation that advanced and
even promoted the good end of peace and harmonious relations. The criteria
would prove sufficient grounds for opposing those things that undermine the
good of peace—such things as resorting to violence, using coercive force,
and engaging in war itself. The just war criteria, however, do not, I contend,
accomplish these things in and of themselves, so how they can be integral to
ethical thought requires some comment. A few remarks about what consti-

tutes an ethic are in order at this point. We must clarify what is meant by *an ethic* if we are going to also claim that "just war, as a set of criteria, is not an ethic."

In one sense, ethics can refer to the articulated expectations that guide behavior in specific communities, as in the rules that govern the practices of various organizations to which one may belong, including places of employment, and professions, such as medicine, law, or counseling. An ethic, however, can also identify a *system* of guidance for deliberating, analyzing, and prescribing action that is good, right, and fitting. The study of ethical theory will inevitably focus on the systems that give rise to rules rather than on the rules themselves. Thus do we encounter ethical systems in theories that provide a rationale for establishing what is good, right, and fitting: the deontological, duty-based ethic of Kant; the Jeremy Bentham–John Stuart Mill utilitarian calculus; the virtue ethics of Aristotle; the deconstructionist ethic of Jacques Derrida;[34] or various kinds of religiously grounded ethics that move practical reason through religious values and traditions to support action aimed at realizing goodness. All of these ethical systems share certain conceptual features that reflect what is often called *the moral point of view*; and the moral point of view includes the following five features.[35]

1. An ethic will require some notion of universalizability. Universalizability captures the idea that if an action is morally right for one person, it should be considered morally right for any person similarly situated. If a moral rule such as "Help people when they are in distress" or "Do not tell lies" is contemplated, that rule is valid as an ethical rule only if it applies to everyone. If it does not, that rule may be considered relative to time and place and circumstance. Some rules are contingent and do not apply outside a particular social or cultural framework. Not every society drives on the same side of the road, and "Lefty loosey, righty tighty" may not apply universally, although knowing such a rule in a society where the rule holds may go a long way toward helping people tighten pipes and open jars. But the idea of universalizability insists that there are some overarching ideas of what is good, right, and fitting that do apply to all reasonable people of goodwill, which is to say that they apply across the contingencies of culture. The principle of universalizability defeats any claim that moral relativism might make to standing as an ethic, but it also resists the idea of ethical absolutism. Relativism and absolutism both subvert and finally undo ethics as a rational and coherent intellectual enterprise, and a few words on these subjects are in order.

Moral relativism is, first of all, not cultural relativism, which is simply the sociological description of the diversity of the world. People do not all live and think the same, and a cataloguing of differences based on diversity of attitude, culture, beliefs, practices, traditions, and custom all contribute to the descriptive diversity—the sociological relativism—of the world. Moral relativism advances the claim that those sociological differences constitute normative ideas as to what is right and wrong, with no appeal to any standard of right and wrong above the relativities of social setting and group membership possible. Furthermore, relativism will, as an ethic, offer that its relativistic viewpoint be accepted universally—truly a curious contradiction. Ethical relativism—as a universally binding prescription for how to live the moral life—is simply incoherent as an ethic. It endorses the idea that morality cannot and should not extend beyond a group (and by a *reductio* it can finally yield to nothing more than individualistic subjectivism, meaning what is good, right and fitting is simply an individual's opinion so that moral meaning cannot be grasped beyond individual assertion). Furthermore, ethical relativism denies any transcultural or transgroup standpoint from which to critique practices reasonable people of goodwill would hold to be detestable (enslaving minorities or social dissidents, or condoning rape as a legitimate means of conducting war, or sanctioning genocide as an effective way of dealing with those not in one's group), so that moral criticism can only amount to noting that one group does one thing and another group another thing. Ethical relativism also denies the possibility of moral evolution, so there can be no substance to the claim that the society that eliminates slavery has moved to a higher moral plane—all one can do is note that it was right at one time and at another time it was no longer regarded as right. And ethical relativism implicitly endorses a "might makes right" ethic that eliminates the possibility that a dissident—a Jesus or a Thoreau, a Gandhi or a Martin Luther King Jr.—could represent anything but social deviance against behavioral norms determined by a majority. Universalizability, it must be noted, undermines any claim moral relativism might make to reasonableness, and without that inclusion of universalizability, ethics would not be possible, for as an ethic even moral relativism must necessarily propose that its relativism viewpoint be universally accepted.[36]

But invoking universalizability need not led us to the other extreme either. Universalizability does not equate with moral absolutism. Moral absolutism, the idea that a rule is binding and applies without any possibility of exception, creates a moralizing, inflexible, puritanical straightjacket. Absolutism in moral matters prevents practical reason from functioning as a guide for people as they deal with the messiness of life in a world of complex relationships where they have to think about what to do and make choices, that is, exercise practical reasonableness. Absolutism is ideological extremism, and it entails its own contradiction—absolutists will finally oppose themselves.[37] Absolutizing the idea that "life is sacred" and never to be intentionally ended is a preposterous proposition for any who might use mouthwash and deodorant or who willingly submit to cancer-killing chemotherapy, not to mention the antiabortion extremist who, as an absolutist, believes the protection of fetal life justifies—requires—the killing of abortion providers. Absolutism leads to existential and moral contradiction.

Universalizability does in fact counter the egoistic idea that rules are for others and that "I am exempt from this moral rule." And the idea that ethics should accept a basic and formal principle of universalizability does not mean that universal agreement will be forthcoming when reasonable people of goodwill face the problem of deciding the best course of action to take in a particular situation where options for action are many: the best option is not always clear, decision makers face various unknowns, and people must use practical reason to resolve the issue of what to do. Abraham Lincoln once said that if it were always clear what we should do in any particular situation, "we should have no use for judgment; we might as well be made without intelligence,"[38] thus expressing the idea that people of goodwill must use practical reason to decide how to act. Certainly we can accept that as much as people might universally desire wisdom so that they might do the good, right, and fitting thing, no one individual has the corner on wisdom, knowledge, or truth itself, and we must finally make decisions and act in ways that express our best judgment about what is good to do.

Yet even with these qualifications, there is no denying that universalizability is a necessary feature for any ethic. It is a foundational idea for normative ethics as it establishes a principle to be used in moral reasoning, and it is invoked to help discern the rightness of a possible action while also serving as a critical tool to be used in a systematic way to make decisions in real-world situations. Any systematic ethic—be it philosophically or religiously grounded—will appeal to this principle; universalizability is found in every valid ethical theory.[39] Although universalizability is a formal feature of Kantian ethics, utilitarians would want the "greatest good for the greatest number" principle applied universally, and even religious ethics appeals to it, as in the Golden Rule enunciated by Jesus: "Do unto others as you would have them do unto you"; the Silver Rule of Hillel, "Do not do unto another what you would not want done to you yourself"; and the Platinum Rule, namely, "Treat others as they wish to be treated" (because you would wish to be treated that way too). These are informal appeals to the principle of universalizability. In all these formulations the ethical idea advanced is that a common moral sensibility, concern, or point of view underwrites the ethics enterprise, and this commonality holds despite cultural differences, the sociological fact of human diversity, and even the antifoundationalist challenge from postmodernism that there is no common human nature. The principle of universalizability, in sum, is an essential feature of ethics. It will prove crucial to the critique of the just war tradition and to the ethics proposal in these pages that will integrate the broad criteria of just war thinking into an actual ethic grounded in universal affirmations concerning war and the use of force.

2. An ethic will require adherence to the idea of *benevolence*. Joseph Runzo describes benevolence as "taking others into account in one's actions because one respects them in themselves as persons,"[40] thus tying benevolence to the principle of respect for persons, another Kantian notion. Benevolence is a virtue concerned with promoting the positive welfare of others, furthering their interests and increasing their good, even their pleasure, while lessening their pain. As an action-guiding principle, the *duty of beneficence* corresponds to benevolence and establishes an obligation to promote a person's well-being when one is in a position to do so.

"Benevolence" is sometimes used interchangeably with "beneficence," although "benevolence" is more associated, as a virtue-related term, with an inclination or disposition made up of choice and desire aimed at promoting the good of others. The term "beneficence" denotes more the enacting of that disposition. Beneficence has come to play a critical role in contemporary medical ethics since doing good (*bene*) for the patient identifies the physician's primary motive for offering treatment and care. The idea of working to advance the welfare of patients, maximizing benefits while minimizing harms, seems to turn the focus of benevolence more toward utilitarianism than Kantianism, but different as these two philosophical perspectives are, both attend in significant ways to the need for right action that, as duty or as consequence, expresses an other-regardingness conforming to the moral point of view. Cultivating the disposition of benevolence is a critically important concept in religious ethics, being emphasized, for example, in the compassion ethic of Buddhism and the love ethic in Christianity.

3. Maximizing the well-being, the good, or the benefit of the other identifies benevolence itself as a notion concerned with regard for the other. *Other-regardingness*—taking others into account—is critical to the moral point of view. Intending and demonstrating in action attention to, and even care for, the other identifies a central ethical task that falls on all due to the status of the other, who, like oneself, is a person possessed of reason and an agent worthy of being treated with respect. Kant advanced the idea that rational agents as *persons* deserve respect, for persons are by definition rational rights-bearing agents capable of acting in freedom to do what reason bids is good, right, and fitting. As moral agents duty-bound to obey the moral law, persons act to realize goodness by the respect—as well as the care, concern, and even compassion—they hold for others.[41] Other-regardingness is an essential feature of the moral point of view and a necessary component in any ethic.

4. An ethic will necessarily include an idea of *impartial justice*. "Justice" can refer to several different ideas of justice, including the idea of rights-based justice, where persons claim certain rights, such as the right to autonomy, privacy, noninterference, and liberty, and then extend those rights to others. Justice can also mean egalitarian justice, which honors the principle that "equals are to be treated equally." Legal justice is another notion, one in which positive laws are conformed to the moral requirement of justice-related concepts such as equality before the law, nondiscrimination, and fairness. Distributive justice is yet another idea of justice. It addresses the idea of distributing scarce resources according to some scheme of equity or fairness.[42]

Justice is very much a "fairness" notion related to but not necessarily equivalent to equality. So a concern for impartial justice could inspire a society to address inequality in the distribution of basic goods by directing an unequal or disproportionate amount of resources to those who suffer disadvantage as a way of working toward certain justice goals, such as equality of opportunity.[43] And justice is and always has been a virtue. The idea of a just person points to a developmental, characterological, and even psychological attainment whereby persons achieve the ability to be fair and evenhanded in their dealings with others.

Justice conceptions are influenced by social values and cultural orientations, and in the religious realm, a divine creator-judge and the law of karma that repays injustice with suffering constitute two cosmic ideas of impartial justice. But for the purposes of identifying as a necessary condition of an ethic the idea of *impartial justice*, what is required is that due and equal consideration be given to the welfare of others in deliberations about what to do and how to act. In describing what is required to be committed to the moral point of view, Joseph Runzo identifies impartial justice as "the willingness to take into account how one's actions affect others by taking into account the good of everyone equally."[44]

5. Finally, an ethic must include some set of normative moral action guides that articulate what goodness requires. These should take form as common agreements that people of goodwill can understand, accept without controversy, act upon themselves, and recommend to others with the expectation that they will abide by them as well. The Golden Rule's "treat others as you would be treated" articulates such a normative rule, although the Platinum Rule formulation that people *should* treat others as they themselves want to be treated is more sensitive to cultural difference. But even by such a simple action guide as this we find articulated a principle that establishes motivation, directs action, and provides a basis for evaluating outcomes.[45] Action guides can be affected by the contingencies of cultural variation; and normative principles must be subjected to scrutiny to determine whether they satisfy such

ethics requirements as universalizability, beneficence, and other-regarding-ness. Common agreements, which we shall discuss shortly, must themselves be evaluated in light of the universalizability requirement, for it is certainly possible that an action guide widely supported in a particular cultural setting could fail to meet the test of universal application. One might want to possess slaves, for instance, and even claim that the ownership of slaves is endorsed by a socially sanctioned norm that allows enslavement and makes it out to be a good thing. But it is one thing to want slaves but quite another to want to be a slave. No reasonable person would choose to be a slave. Applying universalizability to a normative action guide endorsing slavery as a good does not withstand the most simple kind of ethical scrutiny, for no reasonable person would voluntarily accept enslavement as good, right, and fitting.

Although contingencies and cultural differences can affect the development of social norms and the action guides that support them, an ethic requires the assertion of some normative moral principles or what I shall call *common agreements* grounded in a universal vision of what is good, right, and fitting. And in its details, any theoretical effort to articulate the good, right, and fitting will direct attention to the practical world of experience and human interaction, where the moral point of view will yield ethical perspectives that are expressly concerned to include others and contribute to the flourishing of all.[46]

Ethics, as we earlier noted, is derived from the questions "What should we do?" and "Why should we act this way rather than that?" and we have now extracted the necessary characteristics of *an ethic*. For "an ethic," as we shall use this term, refers to a system of action guides that are conformed to the moral point of view, which is itself marked by five characteristics: universalizability, benevolence, fairness or impartial justice, other-regardinness or concern for others, and commitment to some set of normative principles.[47] When these characteristics join normative action guides regarding our common agreements about what is good, right, and fitting, we have "an ethic."

This discussion has been offered as necessary background for an argument that will now be made concerning just war thinking, the specific focus of this chapter. Ahead lies a critique of just war thinking and a constructive effort to conform just war thinking to the formal requirements of "an ethic."

TOWARD AN ETHIC BASED ON JUST WAR THINKING

The content of just war thinking is a list of criteria. Those criteria appear to be so broad, open ended, and nonspecific that it is difficult to attach them to an ethic as we have just described it. Who determines legitimate authority if someone claims to possess it? Who decides what a right intention is, or a just cause, or when we have reached the point of last resort? Is it not the case that parties on both sides of a conflict will be able to answer those questions and justify what they are doing in accordance with the just war guidelines, doing so by using those criteria? Just war ideas on this reading seem more of a piece with moral relativism—already presented as incoherent from a moral point of view—than to an ethic proper.

Yet just war ideas have been translated by parties in conflict to serve morally worthy ends such as restoring peace and addressing injustice, and the theory is designed to impose restraint. The problem, of course, is that the criteria have also proved to be unsettlingly malleable, restraining force in some situations, yes, but in others hastening destructive war and taking down barriers to aggression and violence by providing justifications to mount the effort to go to war. This manipulation of the criteria of just war thinking has been made possible because *those criteria do not, as criteria, function as an ethic*. Those criteria are open to wildly divergent interpretations, and they do not enunciate an overarching guideline reflecting the characteristics of an ethic expressing the moral point of view: universalizability, benevolence, impartial justice, and especially the assertion of a normative principle concerning war and the use of force. Those who employ just war thinking with integrity do so assuming that the criteria serve an ethical stance, and that stance is related to restraint. But if just war thinking were reconstructed as an ethic, it would do more than that—it would ground the criteria in a normative principle that reasonable people of goodwill would accept universally, what I would here term a *moral presumption* or a *common agreement*.[48] If the just war criteria were supported and informed by such a normative principle, just war would be transformed from a malleable and manipulatable structure into an ethic that articulates what is good, right, and fitting with respect to violence, war, and the use of force in general. The following points are relevant to eliciting such a *just war ethic*.

1. The criteria of just war serve in a most basic way as action guides. They direct reflection to morally relevant concerns, and they assume values and could even be said to implicitly appeal to principles of a sort, such as "the use of force ought to be restrained."[49] Taken together, the criteria can be considered a constraint on the use of force. The effect of applying the nine criteria to particular situations where force is being contemplated is to invite moral deliberation on the possibility of a justified use of force, and just war thinking has, because of its perceived commitment to restraint, served the interests of moral moderation. That is, just war involves a way of thinking that avoids the extremes of absolutism on the one hand and relativism on the other: just war thinking attends to actual conflict situations where injustices arise and urges

reasonable people of goodwill to deliberate about those conflicts as they experience them in the common life. The criteria of just war guide deliberation and then lead to decision making and action, yielding the "moderate" conclusion that some uses of force are morally licit and others are not. The deliberative chore, of course, is to determine which are which. The criteria, then, taken as a whole, guide moral reflection, analysis, and then decision making regarding a use of force. Just war thinking frames action to serve a vision of goodness, and the criteria impose restraint, insisting that force be used only in a way that is proportionate to the end of addressing injustice and restoring peace.

As action guides, the just war criteria are not intended to rationalize war. Consensus has been reached on this point among students of just war thinking. The criteria, rather, serve the end of responding to a confrontation where issues of justice are at stake, where some significant threat to human well-being and the goods of life is posed and concern for justice itself requires that reasonable people of goodwill resist the injustice, even by force if necessary. The criteria guide engaged deliberation about a possible use of force when other means of settling the conflict have proved ineffective; and the limited use of force being considered must be proportionate and used only as a last resort. Just war criteria aim at the rectification of injustice, and, as we have noted, just war should neither be motivated by a "thirst for vengeance" (Augustine) nor, according to Aquinas, sanction any acts of "intentional killing." The just war criteria also connect to benevolence and other-regardingness for they address the suffering of those afflicted by injustice; and the criteria as a whole function with the end in view of restoring peace. Because social harmony is a foundational value in the just war ethic, *peace is the just war ethic's default position.* When confronting conflict over how to rectify injustice, the just war criteria guide deliberation toward a possible exception to the common agreement shared by all people of goodwill that conflicts are best resolved by peaceful means and by not resorting to force.

2. The criteria of just war lack direction and content with respect to the details of any particular conflict. This is an open-endedness that allows just war thinking to exhibit flexibility and responsiveness to a wide variety of conflict situations. The criteria, then, can be said to invite persons into a conversation about empirical particulars. The criteria require that debate and deliberation attend to the full range of empirical concerns involved in a particular conflict. Just war criteria, then, rather than serving to justify or rationalize war, function to frame reasoned discussion and debate.

The specific criteria focus attention on universally valid concerns that would attend deliberations over using force: What cause is so weighty that force should be considered? What is to be the stated intention limiting the use of force? Is there a reasonable hope that using force will be successful in rectifying the injustice and restoring the condition of peace with an "exit strategy" in place? Have all means other than force been considered so that using force is truly a "last resort"? Whether a war or use of force is morally justified will be determined by testing the particulars of a conflict against the theory and then debating the moral meaning of those empirical matters in light of the criteria. And the questions over particulars never stop: Are the three "just causes" given for the American participation in the Gulf War of 1991—to preserve the American oil supply, to provide humanitarian aid to a nation unjustly attacked by an aggressor neighbor, or to create a new world order—all morally equivalent? Do the particulars of the United States incursion into Iraq in 2003 satisfy reasonable persons that right intention and just cause were met, or last resort, or reasonable hope of success, or even legitimate authority? Can nuclear weapons serve as a proportionate means of response to conflict? Can well poisoning or arming police with hollow-point bullets be justified? (Can spanking a child?) Is retaliation a just cause for using military force in the wake of a terrorist attack? All kinds of questions and empirical issues can be brought forward and then discussed in light of the criteria, and the criteria function to enclose the terms of debate and direct attention to justice-related particulars.

Just war thinking functions as a guide to action and provides a pivot point for analysis and critique. Acts of terrorism, for example, may certainly be motivated by a desire to resist injustice or oppression. Yet the political judgment to describe an act as "terrorist" has profound moral consequences with respect to just war thinking, for terrorist acts are disallowed under just war provisions because terrorism specifically targets noncombatants, thus violating the noncombatant immunity provision of the theory. Acts deemed terrorist will fail other criteria as well in particular instances, but terrorism is defined in terms of a particular feature, namely, attacks on noncombatants, that will never pass just war muster and will always violate that criterion. Just as "murder" identifies a killing that cannot be justified, "terrorism" comes to identify a use of force that cannot be justified. The term "terrorism," then, is pressed into service, just as "murder" is, to point to an act that by definition is wrongful. The term contains within it a conclusion about moral meaning.[50] The difficult issue when using such terms is determining whether the moral performative "terrorism" is the appropriate term to use when describing and interpreting certain events.

Just war requires that every action undertaken in a forceful response to conflict be subject to analysis, and analysis requires information even before it begins the work of guiding moral interpretation. Just war implicitly condemns any effort to restrict information about empirical particulars that would prove relevant to establishing moral meaning. Even more worthy of condemnation would be the deliberate effort to misinform and thus mislead the deliberation process in order to garner support for a proposed use of force. Public officials who are in a position to direct policy can manipulate and distort information, misleading other public officials and the public itself for purposes unrelated to moral deliberation. Should this occur, just war thinking is subverted, for just war thinking as a resource in public discussion must operate in a context of good faith where trust and an honest sharing of information is a necessary prerequisite. Just war thinking well serves a democratic process of open and informed citizen deliberation and debate, and a suppressed premise of just war thinking may be this: that open and honest discussion around an accurate and truthful presentation of relevant facts is itself a weighty restraint on the use of force.

3. The just war criteria are not to be used selectively. All of them must be addressed and satisfied, not just those that are relatively easy or convenient to satisfy. Abuses of just war thinking occur at precisely this point. Government officials often abbreviate matters to make it appear as if a just war requires meeting only a couple of criteria, when in fact there are many. Or the theory is misrepresented by making it appear that to justify a war of indeterminate duration, the theory needs to be appealed to only once—at the beginning. That is to misunderstand the theory and how it works. Just war is to be applied *to any and all uses of force* and can rightly be said to attend a conflict from the moment force is first contemplated and then used to the moment the use of force ceases. Every action in between is subject to analysis under just war, and it is for this reason that so many uses of force that seem to be justified at the start of a conflict fail to meet just war criteria soon after. Particular actions that fail to meet just war criteria, even though they are undertaken in a conflict that had seemed justified, subvert the moral justification as the conflict proceeds. The problem with just war for those who wield political and military power is that just war thinking can establish moral warrants that will justify a use of force one day but deny it the next. And the consequence of removing justification from a use of force is implicit in the theory: a use of force that cannot be justified ought not to be undertaken. Once invoked, the just war criteria are in constant play and remain so as long as force is used.

4. And the criteria are stringent. As just stated, just war thinking is to be invoked any time a use of force is contemplated and carried out, and it demands more than a one-time application. Accordingly, as wars go on and the uses of force escalate, just war presses harder and harder, making moral justification for particular uses of force more, rather than less, difficult. Very few wars can meet the just war tests. They may begin with a justified response to, say, an unprovoked military attack, but wars seem inevitably to push against the

restraint of the theory. The Allied war against Nazi Germany seems to satisfy the just war requirements at the outset, but such actions as, say, the Allied bombing of a civilian city like Dresden violated noncombatant immunity provisions. The Dresden bombing was a deliberate attack focused on a civilian center, and the Allied command, even Churchill himself, constructed such civilian attacks as part of a political "terrorist" campaign designed to break the will of the German people.[51] The purpose was to bring the war to a quick conclusion, but such actions knock the moral props out from under the edifice of an apparent just war.

These four features point out how the just war tradition is enmeshed in moral concerns. While these features suggest an actual ethic, they do not quite clear the ethics bar and allow us to say that we have extracted an actual *just war ethic*. What is required for the transformation of just war thinking into a just war ethic is a simple but very important move, one related to the concern that an ethical perspective must, if it express the moral point of view, assert some normative principle or action guide. The criteria of just war thinking do not themselves provide this, nor do those who appeal to just war ideas in public deliberations. How just war might be transformed to reflect more clearly the ethic behind it is the next point to consider, and this is where we begin to see the ethics possibilities not only for just war as an ethical perspective on the question of war, but for a more comprehensive and inclusive way of doing ethics, one that transcends particular issues and which, by extension, should be applicable to any ethics issue.

OUR COMMON AGREEMENTS

We can begin to extract the ethic that lies *behind* the just war criteria by asking some basic questions: Is there a moral principle to which these criteria are related—and how are the criteria morally relevant? Can we discern some basic moral stance or posture in relation to which the criteria of just war thinking actually serve moral reflection and express normative values?

My answer to these questions is that the criteria of just war cannot function as an ethic if they do not, in the first instance, articulate a normative principle related to goodness, which is in place, operational, and directing action for some morally worthy purpose. I begin by taking it as a given that reasonable persons of goodwill would prefer to resolve conflicts justly and without resorting to war or any use of force whatsoever if that is possible to do. It is this position that establishes the moral platform from which we derive a just war ethic *as an ethic*. The just war criteria are themselves morally meaningful only in relation to a foundational moral affirmation that reasonable people can universally affirm and which, in turn, can be shown to make moral sense out of the just war criteria. Just war criteria, then, become integral to an actual ethic only when we establish some *common agreement* about moral meaning.

The basic moral platform from which the just war criteria derive their standing as morally relevant are these: being justice related, the criteria are grounded in goodness; they are conformed to the moral point of view; and they acquire moral meaning due to a normative action guide or moral principle that is reconciled to our experience of war. In other writings I have termed this underlying normative commitment to a principle governing the criteria of just war a *moral presumption*, which identifies a nonabsolutist statement of moral meaning that reasonable persons can nigh unto unanimously hold to be worthy of affirmation. But a moral presumption can also be thought of, more simply, as a *common agreement* to which reasonable persons of goodwill can and actually do assent. As the moral platform on which the criteria of just war rest, a moral presumption or common agreement will transcend the particularities of cultural difference while expressing the characteristics of an ethic dedicated to the moral point of view. So a common agreement will express universalizability, regard for others, benevolence, and a normative principle, and this agreement must be articulated prior to thinking about devising criteria to justify an exception to it. On the question of war and the use of force, we can articulate a common moral agreement as follows: *The human experience of war compels reasonable people of goodwill to conclude that war is a destructive way to settle conflicts and ought to be avoided; war is not in itself a positive good, and its reliance on uses of force, especially violent force, is damaging to life and subversive to the goods of life and should never be a preferred means of settling conflicts; therefore, ordinarily force ought not to be used to settle conflicts.*

This statement articulates the common agreement or moral presumption relevant to war and to any use of force. These two terms, "common agreements" and "moral presumptions," are interchangeable and will be used as such throughout this book. What is to be noted about a common agreement, like the one above related to war and the use of force, is that reasonable people of goodwill recognize that it expresses the moral point of view: it is reasonable and universally acceptable; it asserts a normative, principled position (on the use of force, namely, that force is undesirable and subversive of goodness itself and thus ought to be avoided); and it is concerned to take others into account (extending benevolence in situations of conflict by advancing preferred nondestructive means for resolving conflict). This position makes no appeal to absolutism or relativism but opens options so that the exercise of practical reasonableness might deal with specifics in all kinds of situations of conflict, and it reconciles thought to the common human experience of war as a state of affairs much to be avoided.

It is in relation to this common agreement that the criteria of just war thinking come to make sense, morally speaking. Just war thinking rests on a common moral agreement that ordinarily we ought not to settle conflicts by use of force, but because the perspective is neither relativist or absolutist, it then proposes the means by which people of goodwill, facing particular situations of conflict, might consider the grounds for making a justifiable exception. Just war as an ethic proposes shorthand justice-related criteria that can be used to deliberate on the wisdom of making an exception to a common agreement in some particular situation or circumstance. That moral meaning is not in dispute: as war is undesirable and using force ought never to be the preferred course of action, reasonable people will not opt to employ force in conflict situations. They will seek to resolve conflict through discussion, negotiation, and third-party arbitration.

Some conflicts, however, are of such a nature that a use of force presents itself as a live option and a reasonable possibility. The just war criteria in such situations come into play as a way of guiding deliberation on the question of the use of force, specifying requirements for justifying an exception to the common agreement. The common agreement that ordinarily force ought not to be used to settle conflicts, however, identifies the moral anchor that holds and should hold whenever circumstances arise in which a use of force is contemplated. And exceptions to this common agreement should not be easy to realize—the moral presumption against the use of force is not effortlessly lifted. It holds until such time as an exception passes moral muster. The point, however, is that a use of force is now to be thought of as an exception to the rule, where the rule is a common moral agreement *opposed to the use of force.* Only in relation to that common agreement and as an exception to it can we proceed to think about a morally justified use of force. This, then, is just war as *an ethic.* It is an ethic inasmuch as it is grounded in a normative principle regarding the use of force and conformed to the moral point of view in its universal applicability. It is an ethic in its concern for justice and in its attention to the welfare of those whom coercive force will undoubtedly harm (benevolence). It is an ethic in that it is asks people of goodwill to employ practical reason to consider the possibilities presented by a conflict situation, including the possibility of an exception to our common agreement. That exception, however, is itself allowed only in limited ways and to the end that the common agreement might be restored to its position as a normative guide to action.

Just war thinking, then, is grounded in our common agreement—an agreement that all reasonable people of goodwill could be expected to support, namely, that conflicts should be settled peacefully and justly and that ordinarily we ought not to use force to settle them. When a use of force is contemplated in the interests of justice, the criteria guide debate over empirical and interpretive matters related to the specifics of a conflict. The just war criteria do not function to "justify" war, as the natural law tradition has consistently maintained. They serve a nonabsolutist ethical stance and guide moral deliberation as people of goodwill consider the possibility of making an exception to our common moral agreement that ordinarily force ought not to be used to settle conflicts.[52]

Our common moral agreements are binding on reasonable people of goodwill, and considering an exception ought to be done in only the most serious and difficult cases. Those cases would include those in which noncoercive means of addressing an injustice have failed and failure to act with force will in all likelihood exacerbate injustices. Approaching ethics through the articulation of a common moral agreement and criteria to guide the process of justifying an exception is a way of doing ethics that is both principled, like Kantianism, and concerned with promoting goodness and achieving good outcomes, akin in some ways to utilitarian consequentialism.[53] It is not relativistic, however, because it is grounded in an explicit appeal to universal normative principles, and it is not absolutist because by definition this ethical approach is in the business of considering the possibility of justifiable exceptions.

The *just war ethic* that can be extracted from the just war tradition is simply this: a common moral agreement or moral presumption to the effect that ordinarily force ought not to be used to settle conflicts is in place as a normative action guide among people of goodwill. In an imperfect world, however, uses of force can sometimes be contemplated as a licit way to settle particularly difficult and dangerous conflicts. Such conflicts might include a self-defense situation where using deadly force may become an option due to one's own life or that of others being put in jeopardy by the unjust threatening action of another, or resorting to force in a humanitarian intervention aimed at stopping genocide. Self-defense and the protection of innocent persons are obvious candidates for *just cause*, one of the criteria of just war, but what is significant for ethics is this: our common moral agreement against using force is a weighty matter, and the criteria, which on the one hand create the conditions for the possibility of an exception, on the other hand function as a barrier to doing so.

The ethic I have been extracting from the just war tradition is, as an ethic, applicable to issues beyond war and the use of force. My argument here is that there is a broader ethic modeled by this ethical construction in relation to which the just war ethic itself is an instance and exemplification. That ethic requires articulation of the broad moral agreements relevant to particular issues to which persons of goodwill can universally give their assent—these constitute our common agreements. These agreements are neither relative nor absolute: they transcend the specifics of group membership and yet are accepted as universally binding. The approach to ethics modeled by this analysis of just war allows that imperfect people in an imperfect world can contemplate overriding or suspending the obligatory force of these agreements for good cause in certain situations, for failure to do so can reasonably be seen as contributing to even greater harm and injustice. This ethic, then, imposes moral restraints on the use of force even as it allows a use of force to be considered a possible action response. Of singular importance is the articulation of the moral agreement that underwrites any application of criteria. What transforms the criteria of just war thinking into an ethic is the inclusion of this articulated agreement as the moral platform for the criteria. The common moral agreement makes the criteria morally relevant. Without it, the criteria do not cohere and present a normative idea about the moral meaning of the use of force under consideration. If a use of force is deemed licit in a particular circumstance, the weight of this common agreement about the moral meaning of the use of force requires that the force be restrained, that it meet justice requirements (criteria), and that the common moral agreement against using force to settle conflict be returned to its operative, normative, and regulative position as soon as possible.

SUMMARY AND CONCLUSION

My task thus far has been to introduce the formal criteria of the just war tradition and to inquire whether these criteria can be deemed an ethic. We examined what an ethic—any ethic—requires, namely, that it be universally applicable; that it include respectful regard and just and impartial treatment of others; that it concern itself with benevolence and promote human flourishing; and, finally, that it incorporate relevant normative principles or action guides. This last point is what opened up a wider discussion about our common agreements—those moral affirmations of commitment and belief that hold the moral community together. Also attention was given to the problems that attend ethical perspectives that endorse both absolutist and relativistic moral guides. Both of these options are antithetical to the requirements of an ethic and can be said to defeat the ethics enterprise. From this point, we returned to the just war tradition to consider whether it functioned as an ethic, a relevant question since the criteria of just war have been traditionally presented as a restraint on force and a structure for deliberating justification for the use of coercion.

The discussion of just war and its relation to ethics has allowed us to conclude that however much just war may appear to be an ethic governing the use of force, the just war criteria themselves do not in and of themselves constitute an ethic. The criteria by themselves can serve all kinds of purposes, and we have noted that some of those purposes do not reflect the moral point of view but such contingencies as national and political self-interest. Without a common moral agreement in place that functions to ground the criteria, the criteria themselves can serve many ends and purposes, some of which may actually violate the just war ethic. Without that common agreement in place, the criteria cannot realize the end of an ethic—any ethic—which is to provide the reflective resources that serve to advance goodness through just and benevolent action aimed at human flourishing. If this defines the basic project of ethics, the just war criteria, in themselves, neither focus explicitly on that project nor accomplish what that project deems essential to ethics. The just war criteria, then, do not constitute an ethic.

However, once the presumptive moral agreement is articulated and reasonable people of goodwill can assent to the proposition that force is not the morally preferable way to settle conflicts, the just war criteria can be reintroduced and their relevance asserted. For if this moral agreement against using force is accepted presumptively and not absolutely,[54] the just war criteria present morally relevant concerns to be addressed if an exception is to be considered in a particular circumstance. The criteria, then, guide the reflection process of conceiving an exception. The common agreement will always make force difficult to justify, and for this simple reason: it is presumptively wrong to use force to settle conflicts. My own view is that the criteria protect the moral presumption against the use of force with a stringency we do not often associate with just war thinking, making it possible to say that a just war ethic actually serves as a rationale for practical pacifism rather than as a rationale for war.

The common agreement that I have identified for the just war ethic is that ordinarily force ought not to be used to settle conflicts. This articulation of the common moral agreement addresses the use of force, not war alone. War involves coercive and usually violent uses of force that are destructive of persons and the many goods of life. But if the *just war ethic* is to have relevance to broader issues related to the use of force, then it must be the use of force itself—not only war—that is at issue. And that is, I believe, the case.

To show how the just war ethic is indeed relevant to broader issues concerning other uses of force, I shall consider another use of force affected by our common moral agreement—nonviolent resistance. Mohandas Gandhi and Martin Luther King Jr. both endorsed nonviolent resistance as a means of addressing social injustice, and they did so quite cognizant that they were using force—coercive force—to do so. It was nonviolent force, to be sure, but still a use of force. Therefore, if the common agreement against the use of force is to have ethical relevance, even Gandhi and King should be subject to analysis and critique through this ethical resource, this "just war ethic." In addition, if this way of doing ethics is as universal and practical as I am claiming, we should find evidence that Gandhi and King observed the constraints and directives of this ethic even as it applied to the use of force they advocated—the force of nonviolent resistance.

And so we shall. Once we have seen more clearly how this ethic works in the case of Gandhi and King, we shall have a better idea of how this method of ethical thinking—this moral presumption accompanied by justice-related criteria governing a possible exception—works; we can then move on and apply this common agreement ethic to a wide variety of other ethics issues.

Chapter Two

Nonviolent Resistance as a Use of Force

"Ordinarily force ought not to be used to settle conflicts." This simple statement recognizes a common moral agreement acceptable to all reasonable people of goodwill. Conflicts arise all the time in the course of human life, and a response to conflict that expresses the moral point of view will insist on such matters as treating one's partner in conflict with respect, proceeding on the basis of a common commitment to resolving the conflict justly and peacefully, and avoiding coercion. Coercion should not, as a moral matter, be used to settle conflicts, not when noncoercive and morally preferable means are available, such as negotiation, arbitration, and fair-minded third-party mediation. An ethic of conflict resolution conformed to the moral point of view will always emphasize the good of talking rather than fighting, the good of laying out the terms of dispute fairly and without distortion, and the good of recognizing human limitations in knowledge and understanding. Even when justice issues are at stake in a conflict, there must be present, as an ethical requirement, openness to reasonable discussion, a willingness to listen to and learn from one's partner in conflict, and a readiness to consider compromise.

In a perfect world, all conflicts would be resolved by such an approach. The problem is that some conflicts have weighty justice issues at stake that are so illuminated by the bright light of practical reason that they cannot be ignored and ought not to be compromised; and the reality is that some conflicts arise in such a way as to put the goods of life—including the good of life itself—in imminent peril. When nonviolent means of responding to conflict though a process of good faith and respectful negotiation fail, practical reason will allow a use of force to be considered. The common agreement that ordinarily force ought not to be used to settle conflicts includes the word "ordinarily" as recognition that the moral agreements we hold may be affected by situation and circumstance. Using coercive force is not the preference or aspiration of any reasonable person of goodwill, but injustices can be so great, and threats to the well-being of persons so pressing, that using force may become the necessary, last-resort means to address injustice. The just war criteria guide deliberation about the moral permissibility of using force in such situations; they also direct that force be applied with restraint so that the conflict might be resolved justly and peace restored.

In the previous chapter the case was made that the just war criteria do not themselves constitute an ethic. Those criteria can be transformed into *an ethic*, however, by resting them on an articulated normative action guide conformed to the moral point of view, namely, the common agreement that ordinarily force ought not to be used to settle conflicts. The ethic that underwrites just war thinking may appear to be focused on the coercive force of violence, but the normative guide against using force applies not only to uses of force that are destructive and violent but to *any use of force*. The claim here is that the moral presumption against the use of force is a common agreement that people of goodwill hold universally. In fact, if the just war ethic I have proposed here is truly grounded on a common agreement that "ordinarily force ought not to be used to settle conflicts," we should expect even the force of nonviolence to fall under that presumption. We should expect the ethic to address uses of force whether violent or nonviolent, for the moral presumption stands as a barrier to *any* use of force, and that barrier can be lifted only for compelling reasons related to opposing injustice and advancing human flourishing. Those compelling reasons are summarized in the criteria, all of which must be met in order to lift temporarily the moral presumption against the use of force. On this account, even nonviolent uses of force are presumptively wrong and difficult to justify from a moral point of view. The ethic, however, is not absolute, and a crack in the normative guideline has been created by that little word "ordinarily." The use of force presents itself as a possibility because the world is imperfect and people of goodwill are directed by "our common agreements" to resist injustice, regrettably at times even by force.

In this chapter I take a look at how the ethic we have been discussing addresses nonviolent resistance as a use of force. Nonviolence—nonviolent resistance—will be considered as a particular way of engaging in conflict. It will be shown to be subject to the weight of the presumption *against using force*, and it will require that the justice concerns to be found in the criteria of just war thinking be addressed and satisfied. I examine relevant aspects of Mohandas Gandhi's and Martin Luther King's thought, not to argue that they explicitly formulated a "just war" response to the conflicts that consumed them in their lives, but to argue that as good and reasonable individuals concerned to respond to injustice, each did so attentive to the ethical requirement that force ought to be avoided when conflicts arise. Both grounded their advocacy of nonviolent resistance in the normative action guide opposing the use of force, and both held that nonviolent resistance could be considered a possible response to injustice if all else failed. Gandhi and King defended nonviolent resistance as a morally permissible use of force that is itself regrettable to employ, as is any use of force, but both came to believe that nonviolent resistance could be used in certain circumstances as a justified exception to the moral action guide to which both were deeply committed, namely, the idea that "ordinarily force ought not to be used to settle conflicts."

THE LANGUAGE OF WAR

The rhetoric employed by advocates of nonviolence can sometimes takes a peculiar turn into martial images and war-related metaphors. Martin Luther King Jr., for instance, writes, "And this is the beauty of nonviolence. It says you can struggle without hating; you can fight war without violence."[1] And King goes on to describe nonviolence this way:

> Nonviolence is a powerful and just weapon. It is a weapon unique in history, which cuts without wounding and ennobles the man who wields it. It is a sword that heals. Both a practical and a moral answer to the Negro's cry for justice, non-violent direct action proved that it could win victories without losing wars.[2]

And Mohandas Gandhi makes similar rhetorical moves. He explicitly calls for the formation of what he terms a "non-violent army,"[3] while declaring: "I am out for battle and am seeking help on bended knee."[4]

The combative tone and use of the confrontational language of "battle," "fight," "power," "weapons," "struggle," "victory," and "winning" appear everywhere in the writings of Gandhi and King, and the explicitness of the rhetorical appeal to war is not to be denied. But is the appeal to the language of war simply a rhetorical trope or does such language suggest deeper conceptual connections to the idea of being at war, even if nonviolently?

The rhetoric suggests that both leaders understood their respective struggles as analogous to war, for both Gandhi and King conceived of nonviolent resistance as a "force" to be used in conflict, a "weapon" as King says. Furthermore, both advocated a careful and constrained use of this powerful force; both identified adversaries and engaged them, seeking to defeat them with superior power; both believed success was possible and demanded in the ranks of followers a discipline akin to that demanded of soldiers in the military; and both defended nonviolence as the most practical and effective means of achieving victory.[5] Both understood nonviolence as a mode of action consistent with the end they sought, which was the restoration of peace and the creation of a just community.

Gandhi and King interpreted the concept of "nonviolent resistance" in terms of power. Its employment constituted a use of force—both are very clear on this point. The appeal to force is what most likely gave weight and relevance to the martial metaphors they employed. The metaphors are worth pondering, but more important is the concept of force at the core of nonviolent resistance.

Nonviolent resistance is widely considered to be a form of pacifism, but both King and Gandhi were clear that it was not the kind of pacifism associated with the "nonresistance to evil" perspective of, say, Leo Tolstoy, which is sometimes referred to as pure pacifism or absolute pacifism.[6] Gandhi allowed translation of *satyagraha* as "passive resistance" but then also distanced himself from any form of pacifism that does not actively engage and resist evil: "Non-co-operation is not a passive state," Gandhi writes. "It is an intensely active state—more active than physical resistance or violence. Passive resistance is a misnomer."[7] And King also dissociated himself from the absolutist pacifism of nonresistance, writing, "I am no doctrinaire pacifist. . . . I see the pacifist position not as sinless but as the lesser evil in the circumstances."[8] Admitting to being influenced by Reinhold Niebuhr and then corrected by Gandhi, King goes on to say:

> True pacifism is not unrealistic submission to evil power, as Niebuhr contends. It is rather a courageous confrontation of evil by the power of love. . . . My study of Gandhi convinced me that true pacifism is not nonresistance to evil but nonviolent resistance to evil. Between the two positions, there is a world of difference. Gandhi resisted evil with as much vigor and power as the violent resister, but he resisted with love instead of hate.[9]

Nonviolent resistance, then, as we have it from Gandhi and King, is active engagement in conflict and confrontation with injustice; it aims at effecting social and political change by the application of force.[10] It provides a strategy for the forceful opposition to injustice yet adopts means of directing and applying force that are consistent with restraint. The restraint goes so far as to embody attitudes of noninjury toward others. Nonviolence, then, aims at addressing injustice and restoring peace through an application of force that is itself peaceful. Reasonable people of goodwill considering this particular use of force can rather easily conclude that it is morally preferable to modes of conflict resolution that resort to violent coercion. In the moral life, we subject force—any use of force—to moral analysis and look for ways to discern and analyze moral meaning. The just war ethic, now that we can see it being grounded in commitment to a normative principle that "ordinarily force ought not to be used to settle conflicts," illuminates the moral meaning of the non-violent resistance Gandhi and King advocated.

My contention is that a just war ethic is presumptively opposed to using force—any kind of force. The common agreement that the use of force is to be avoided if at all possible creates a powerful barrier to proceeding with a use of force, for doing so is presumptively wrong. That barrier is not absolute, as we have noted, and a use of force is always a possibility, for injustices in particular circumstances can drive people of goodwill to consider various action responses, including the use of force. But the barrier to using force is real and powerful. So in formulating a just war ethic around this common agreement, we find just war ethical ideas now expressing values, normative action guides, and benevolent moral aspirations grounded in harmony and directed toward peace. Those ethical ideals are constructed in opposition to using force and are not serving the cause of war or simply rationalizing violence.

To the extent that nonviolent resistance can be framed as a means for resisting injustice authorized by the just war ethic, just war as a resource for moral analysis will present itself as a friend of peace and even as a partner of sorts with nonviolent resistance. This claim will become clearer as we proceed to apply a just war ethical analysis to nonviolent resistance as it comes to us from Gandhi and King. Translated as an ethic based on a moral presumption against using force to settle conflicts, the just war framework of criteria provides a uniquely valuable ethics tool for analyzing the moral meaning of active response to conflict and injustice. The approach to ethics we undertake here by means of this common agreement ethic of "just war" can be critically important for discerning how we arrive at moral judgments about any particular use of force, even the use of force that lies at the heart of nonviolent resistance.

GANDHI AND KING:
THE IMPLICIT APPEAL TO JUST WAR IDEAS

Just war criteria, as we have argued, create a structure for ethical analysis and discernment. That structure serves to protect the moral presumption against the use of force while also identifying the justice-related concerns (i.e., the criteria) that must be addressed and satisfactorily met when we deliberate and then assess the possibilities for just action in light of the empirical particulars of a given conflict. Unless those criteria—all of them—establish that a use of force is deemed licit, the use of force ought not to be undertaken. How such a conclusion is reached will depend on the empirical facts of a conflict situation and how the conflict opens the door to a possible use of force. Remember that the moral presumption against the use of force can withstand many challenges—that is why *ordinarily* force ought not to be used to settle conflicts. Yet that structure of justice-related concerns (criteria) enjoins citizens and policy makers to enter an arena where differences over data, inferences, and interpretations of facts should be deliberated and may even be disputed.[11] King reflects this concern when he says that the first step in any "nonviolent campaign," as he calls it, is the "collection of the facts to determine whether injustices are alive."[12] Gandhi and King both advocated data collection and truth telling, then entered the public arena to debate the justice of their methods and goals with opponents while seeking to persuade the broader moral community that their cause was just. Each undertook to debate particular injustices, and each organized dramatic and effective responses. For King this involved organizing a bus boycott; for Gandhi it was a march to the sea to oppose the tyranny of the salt tax. Neither appealed explicitly to the just war tradition or invoked in a systematic way the criteria structure involved with just war thinking. Both, however, made an implicit appeal to the specific justice concerns we find articulated in the just war criteria. This is something that happens frequently—inevitably, I would say—whenever reasonable people of goodwill contemplate injustice and then consider how to respond to it. If any single criterion of just war thinking is not satisfied, the use of force ought to be disallowed.

The just war ethic as we have presented it does not serve the cause of war or rationalize violence. As argued thus far, that ethic is aimed at peace and at just, nonviolent resolutions of conflict. We can go further: the ethic to which the just war tradition appeals actually asserts commitment to the good of nonviolence as the most effective—and proportional—means of restoring peace when injustice prompts consideration of a use of force. Just war understood in this way could thus be said to be an ethic of peace, not a means for rationalizing the use of force.

Beyond doubt, nonviolent resistance as Gandhi and King articulated it affirms the common moral agreement that ordinarily force ought not to be used to settle conflicts. The appeal to a common agreement must be distinguished from Tolstoy's absolutist pacifism, which advanced the view that all uses of force—without exception—express the law of violence. Tolstoy held that obedience to the law of love required the repudiation of any use of force. No use of force, Tolstoy held, not even one used to resist a threat to one's own life, can be justified. Tolstoy's nonresistance must not be confused with the nonviolent resistance of Gandhi and King, for in Tolstoy's view, any application of force, even that of nonviolent resistance to injustice, expresses the law of violence, which the law of love, to hold it, cancels, and cancels absolutely.[13] Tolstoy was an ethical absolutist.

The argument being made here, namely, that Gandhi and King use force and appeal implicitly to the criteria of just war thinking, requires that we establish that both thinkers enshrine a deep commitment to the common moral agreement that ordinarily force ought not to be used to settle conflicts. If Gandhi and King both accepted this agreement as normative while conceiving of nonviolence as a use of force, as already argued, then it logically follows that we should find Gandhi averse to employing *satyagraha* and King less than eager to engage in nonviolent resistance. And so we do. We find that both are reluctant to use even the force of nonviolence and consent to do so only when other means of addressing injustice have failed. We shall return to this issue in the discussion of *last resort* below.[14] But let us now turn our attention to Gandhi and King as they involve ideas from just war thinking in their social justice movements, showing how both Gandhi and King appeal implicitly to the justice-related criteria of the just war ethic to justify nonviolent resistance. For both Gandhi and King, nonviolent resistance was a necessary but regrettable use of force, their justified "exception" to the common agreement that ordinarily force ought not to be used to settle conflicts.

GANDHI AND KING:
THE IMPLICIT APPEAL TO JUST WAR CRITERIA

Let me proceed to present the traditional *jus ad bellum* criteria for a justified use of force, connecting the criteria of just war to nonviolent resistance and demonstrating how Gandhi and King invoked these criteria implicitly in their deliberations about using the force of nonviolence.

1. Legitimate authority. The just war tradition locates the licit authority for using coercive force in government. Traditionally, an emperor or king sufficed to meet this criterion in particular, but what is at stake is more than a political or governmental structure claiming legal power to sanction uses of coercive force. Legitimation for using force cannot rest solely in law, for laws can be unjust, and governments promulgating laws can be unjust. King noted this point in his "Letter from Birmingham City Jail," when he famously commented that Hitler, as the absolute source of law in Nazi Germany, did nothing illegal. So if we were to consider this criterion of just war from a legal rather than a moral point of view, the genocide committed under Hitler's authorization might actually satisfy the formal requirement of "legitimate authority."[15] King's comment about Hitler doing nothing illegal shows King concerning himself with the just war question of legitimate authority, and he uses the Hitler example to demonstrate that legal sanctions for uses of force do not settle but actually beg the question about moral authority.

Gandhi and King both addressed the question of legitimate authority in their efforts to justify the use of nonviolent force. The authority sufficient to justify force, both held, was to be located not in positive law, but in conscience, as conscience is itself connected to transcendent sources. Both appealed to religious sources of power for legitimating the nonresistance they espoused. Making this move, it must be said, is not without problems of its own. If we recall that the justice-related criteria invite critical analysis in the deliberations about a prospective use of force, we must offer that resting legitimate authority in religious sources can be highly problematic. We can consider an old but important example: Pope Urban II's call to Christian crusade at the Council of Clermont in 1095. The Pope's initiative was explicitly tied to religious authority, specifically in a call to arms derived from the "universal authority of the Pope." Pope Urban II acted as the equivalent of emperor or king, but the power for inciting military action was vested in his authority as the supreme head of the Church, Christ's representative, the Vicar of Christ (*Vicarius Christi*).[16] We can look at a more recent example: the final instructions to the 9/11 hijackers explicitly located the authority for the killing and suicide contemplated that day in the will of Allah.[17]

The problem with invoking religious resources to justify the use of force is that such a sanctioning authority invokes the idea of "holy war." Holy war in a generic sense identifies a call to arms under the sanction of religious authority, and it is morally problematic because it evades moral critique—at least on the part of those who would invoke it. Holy war as a generic idea simply asserts that a use of force is authorized by the divine will. As such those who accept the transcendent source as legitimate do not believe that the authorization for a use of force is subject to outside moral scrutiny. Being without fault or error, the divine will would not be expected to steer human beings in a wrong direction. If God wills it, it is right. To subject the use of force itself to moral scrutiny would be to subject the divine source authorizing that force to scrutiny.[18] That would suggest that the divine authority itself could be legitimately evaluated against some standard of goodness higher than the divine itself, which in the minds of many religious people would be an absurdity, even a blasphemy.

Appealing to religious sources of authorization for using force can give rise to the idea of generic holy war. Yet there is no escaping the fact that holy war itself proceeds from a very clear idea of legitimate authority. This is a point relevant to Gandhi and King, both of whom appealed to transcendent sources of authority for legitimating their use of nonviolent force. "It is not I, but God who is guiding this movement," writes Gandhi: "The only weapon of the Satyagrahi is God, by whatsoever name one knows him. Without Him, the Satyagrahi is devoid of strength."[19] And Gandhi will even make the association to holy war explicit. In his 1918 "Instructions to Volunteers," he makes this astounding statement: "The volunteers must remember that this is a holy war. We are embarked upon it because, had we not, we would have failed in our dharma. And so all the rules which are essential for living a religious life must be observed here too."[20]

King avoids an explicit association to "holy war," but he grounds nonviolent resistance in transcendent sources: "This is a spiritual movement," he claims,[21] and to his followers he writes:

> Your highest loyalty is to God, and not to the mores or folkways, the state or the nation of any man-made institution. If any earthly institution or custom conflicts with God's will, it is your Christian duty to oppose it. You must never allow the transitory, evanescent demands of man-made institutions to take precedence over the eternal demands of the almighty God.[22]

Both Gandhi and King rested legitimate authority for the use of force in transcendent sources, thus appealing their respective versions of nonviolent resistance to the very same source of legitimate authority as those seeking to sanction the violence of holy war. A just war ethical analysis of *legitimate authority* would note the religious sources Gandhi and King relied on to claim authorization for their resistance actions. Both Gandhi and King thought it folly to rest authority for the use of nonviolent force in law and social institutions; both denied that such institutions commanded the transcendent power to authorize love as a practical motivation for politics. And while it is the case that only by an appeal to religious or transcendent authority could these two leaders justify the resistance of nonviolence, a just war analysis will rebuke such a justification as highly problematic, at least *from a moral point of view*, for it is the same move, in a formal generic sense, that was used to authorize crusades in the eleventh century and sanction the suicide-murder attacks of September 11, 2001.

2. Just cause. Just war usually interprets just cause as relevant to self-defense, and King and Gandhi both make such a "just war" move.[23] "I believe that every man and woman should learn the art of self-defense in this age," writes Gandhi, and while "This is done through arms in the West," he adds that "Satyagraha is always superior to armed resistance," since, in Gandhi's view, "It can never be used to defend a wrong cause."[24] Clearly, if *satyagraha* were being employed—and it was—the assumption to be made in virtue of its use must be that it was being used in service to a just cause, since it could not function otherwise.

King addressed self-defense often, mainly because some black leaders endorsed King's methods but only up to the point where they felt a need to defend themselves with force when physically threatened. King would caution, however, "It is extremely dangerous to organize a movement around self-defense. When violence is tolerated even as a means of self-defense there is grave danger that in the fervor of emotion the main fight will be lost over the question of self-defense."[25] King distanced himself from self-defense when it was construed as a justified use of physical violence, but he never doubted the justice of the cause—resisting the injustice of racist social, economic, and political arrangements. King writes about resistance and nonviolence the following:

> It is always amusing to me when a Negro man says that he can't demonstrate with us because if someone hit him, he would fight back. Here is a man whose children are being plagued by rats and roaches, whose wife is robbed daily at overpriced ghetto food stores, who himself is working for about two-thirds the pay of a white person doing a similar job and with similar skills, and in spite of all this daily suffering it takes someone spitting on him or calling him nigger to make him want to fight. Conditions are such for Negroes in America that all Negroes ought to be fighting aggressively. It is as ridiculous for a Negro to raise the question of self-defense in relation to nonviolence as it is for a soldier on the battlefield to say he is not going to take any risks.[26]

For King, then, just cause is to be found in the *conditions* that oppressed people experience. These are the conditions of racial and economic injustice; and seeking to redress these conditions by the programmatic effort to fight racism, advance integration, resist violence, and oppose economic and social inequality puts King and his movement squarely on the side of social justice. King may eschew self-defense but, like Gandhi, he has no doubt that his cause is just, and his implicit appeal to this criterion of just war is clear. He even says in an interview that "the most pervasive mistake I made was in believing that white Christian clergy" would come streaming to his aid "because our cause was just."[27] In offering this as a criticism about white clergy and their commitment to justice, King was once again asserting, for the record, his belief that his nonviolent resistance efforts proceed from a clear determination of just cause.

3. Right intention and its announcement/4. Proportionality of means and ends. Right intention is traditionally cited in just war thinking as aimed at bringing about a restoration of peace after force has been used. Gandhi and King both spoke eloquently about the desire to persuade their enemies to change through nonviolence. "The Satyagrahi's object is to convert, not coerce, the wrong-doer," writes Gandhi;[28] "We will not obey unjust laws or submit to unjust practices. We will do this peacefully, openly, cheerfully because our aim is to persuade," writes King.[29] Both, then, adopted means of action consistent with noninjury and the end of peace, certain that their means were consistent with and would practically achieve the end sought: "If we take care of the means," Gandhi writes, "we are bound to reach the end sooner or later."[30] Their announced intention to bring about peace in a just social order drew on the belief both held that violence breeds only more violence and increases chaos, while nonviolence embodies a "proportional" means of approach that intertwines means and ends. Through their writings, public statements, and uses of the media they articulated their intentions to organize for actions aimed at bringing about the goal of freedom and peaceful community, and both communicated their intentions regarding overall strategy and purpose as well as the tactics to be used in particular communities, as King said, "openly."

5. *Last resort.* It might seem that applying the "last resort" criterion to nonviolent resistance would identify the point where nonviolent resistance diverges from just war. The idea that suggests itself is that at some point in the struggle against injustice, just war advocates determine that the bar to using physical force could be justifiably lifted but that nonviolent resisters would refuse to recognize that this point of "last resort" had yet been reached. This is a plausible interpretation, but it is not actually how either Gandhi or King appealed to the idea of "last resort."

In the effort to stop evil or fight injustice, both Gandhi and King observed a *last resort* criterion by holding to the position that the use of nonviolent force should be a final option when all other means of effecting change and addressing injustice have been tried without success. This is precisely what is supposed to occur when just war traditionalists consider employing physical force. Nonviolent force is not to be applied cavalierly but only after all other means of opposition to injustice have been exhausted and a use of force is deemed necessary to prevent even further evil and injustice.

King, for instance, relates in "Letter from Birmingham City Jail" how the decision to use nonviolence in direct action as a force for change was reached over time and only after other means short of resistance had failed. King decided to mobilize for nonviolent action regretfully and only after he reached the conclusion that there remained before them "no alternative." Then, to keep the use of this force restrained, King took pains to make sure that particpants would be adequately prepared and trained for what was to come:

> As the weeks and months unfolded we realized that we were the victims of a broken promise. The signs remained. Like so many experiences of the past we were confronted with blasted hopes. . . . So we had *no alternative* [emphasis added] except that of preparing for direct action, whereby we would present our very bodies as a means of laying our cause before the conscience of the local and national community. . . . We started having workshops on nonviolence . . . we decided to set our

direct action program around the Easter season, since it was . . . (after Christmas) the largest shopping period of the year.[31]

Likewise, Gandhi's reflection on the use of *satyagraha* involved civil disobedience, which, he said, can be practiced "only as a last resort"; and it was to serve as a means of action only after "we had exhausted all the methods open to us."[32] Erik Erikson noted how Gandhi observed this last-resort just war criterion clearly and consistently:

> The essential preliminary steps in any of Gandhi's campaigns were an objective investigation of facts, followed by a sincere attempt at *arbitration*. Satyagraha must appear to be a last resort in an unbearable situation which allows for no other solution and is representative enough to merit a commitment of unlimited self-suffering. It, therefore, calls for a thorough *preparation* of all would-be *participants* so that they may know grievances as factually true and join in the conclusion that the agreed-upon goal is both just and attainable.[33]

Before the force of nonviolence is engaged, means of resolving the conflict that do not employ force—negotiation and arbitration, for example—must be tried. Using force—even the force of nonviolence—is a last resort, and both Gandhi and King understood that nonviolence as direct action became an option to redress injustice only when all other measures had failed. In their struggles over making the move to active resistance, both leaders demonstrated their commitment to the moral presumption that ordinarily force ought not to be used to settle conflict. It was only after all reasonable and peaceful means were exhausted that Gandhi and King determined, regretfully and as a last resort, to engage in civil disobedience and bring to their respective struggles for justice an actual use of force—the force of nonviolent resistance.

6. *Reasonable hope of success.* Just war requires as a necessary condition that force be used only if there is a reasonable hope of success. Both Gandhi and King saw trouble ahead. Each soberly contemplated that nonviolent resistance could result in the loss of life, which is, again, why discipline among the practitioners of nonviolent resistance was necessary. Nonviolent resisters needed to be trained, prepared, and disciplined so that they might stay committed to the method and principle of nonviolence. Both Gandhi and King avowed the prospect of success in their respective ventures, for both thought that nonviolence provided them with a superior weapon sufficiently powerful to defeat their enemies, if not in the short term, then in the long term. King often remarked on the "long arc" of history and asserted that nonviolence was the appropriate means to defeat evil and injustice: "It is evil we are trying to defeat," King writes: "The method of nonviolence is based on the conviction that the universe is on the side of justice. It is this deep faith in the future

that causes the nonviolent resister to accept suffering without retaliation. He knows that in his struggle for justice he has cosmic companionship."[34]

King could have also appealed to Gandhi's efforts in India to establish historical confirmation that the methods of nonviolent resistance can effect a successful and just outcome. The most telling thing to say about Gandhi on this criterion is to note his belief in probable success based on the idea that "Every worthy object can be achieved by the use of Satyagraha. It is the highest and infallible means, the greatest force,"[35] while also looking at actual history. Gandhi won. In history we actually witness the success of his nonviolence movement. By an appeal to history, then, Gandhi could claim that the belief that nonviolence can achieve political success is, in fact, a reasonable belief.[36]

7. Preservation of values. Just war holds that those who employ force must not sacrifice the very values they are trying to preserve, a notion sometimes referred to as a "lesser evil position." The idea at issue here is that good must clearly outweigh evil when resorting to force. King and Gandhi expressed commitment to this idea in their constant attention to means and ends, discussed previously in criterion 3, and the idea is perhaps exemplified by King's revealing comment, previously quoted, "I see the pacifist position not as sinless but as the lesser evil in the circumstances."[37] Both King and Gandhi insisted that means and ends must conform to each other. The process whereby one seeks the ends of justice and peace requires methods, tactics, and strategies that will embody justice in their performance and thus assure that peace will result. Both believed that using violence to confront violence was an inferior mode of operation that in all likelihood would make things worse than the original injustice. King is, on this point as on so many others, eloquent: "If the American Negro and other victims of oppression succumb to the temptation of using violence in the struggle for justice, unborn generations will live in a desolate night of bitterness, and their chief legacy will be an endless reign of chaos."[38] And committed as he was to the struggle for a life of love, truth, and noninjury to others in a world he recognized as filled with hatred, untruth, and violence, Gandhi would call many times in his writings and speeches for action consistent with the transformative power of love. With love critical to the means as well as the ends, Gandhi envisioned a world where even children would be taught that it is within the power of the soul to "easily conquer hate by love, untruth by truth, violence by self-suffering."[39] What King referred to as the "lesser evil" of pacifism provides the means that accomplish such a transformation, but the end of a just and peaceful society is only reached, according to both Gandhi and King, if the means of action embody—and do not sacrifice—the very values envisioned in the ends sought.

8. Proportionality/9. Noncombatant immunity. Two other criteria of just war theory restrain action in the direct application of force or within war itself, the so-called *jus in bello* requirements. One criterion deals with proportionality—the idea that the force employed must be proportionate to the end of bringing about peace, or, in a Roman Catholic formation, "the evil produced by the means of self-defense should not be greater than the evil produced by the aggression."[40] The other *jus in bello* criterion is noncombatant immunity.

Clearly Gandhi and King thought their methods of engagement were just and proportionate. Any hint of disproportionality in the application of nonviolent force can be located, curiously, in the fact that both believed that the fight with their opponents was not really fair, given that nonviolent resistance was a weapon superior to any that might be employed by their opponents. Both believed that nonviolence would lead inevitably to victory. Nonviolence, they held, was the only weapon that could yield the good result they both sought, which, in King's words, was to be "a community at peace with itself."[41] The use of violence in the struggle for justice would, they both believed, create even more problems and increase the chaos and suffering of all, oppressors as well as victims. In light of this understanding, nonviolence became the only effective use of force (or weapon) proportionate to the end of bringing about the end of peace while not creating an even worse situation of destruction and injustice, which is the inevitable legacy of using violence to resolve conflicts.

The just war concern with noncombatant immunity is a bit more problematic when applied to nonviolent resistance. The program of nonviolent resistance was not designed to inflict harm on the opponent since nonviolent resisters were to take any suffering caused by their actions upon themselves. Thus does Gandhi say that *satyagraha* vindicates truth "not by infliction of suffering on the opponent but on one's self";[42] and King acknowledges the suffering and sacrifice that nonviolent resisters will face, including imprisonment, and "It may even mean physical death," he writes.[43] With these statements, both Gandhi and King acknowledge that from the use of force they advocate, harms may result. This is not inconsequential, since this provides one more reminder that both understood nonviolent resistance to be a force of enormous power, one that ordinarily ought not to be used to settle conflicts. Furthermore, because this force needed to be controlled and disciplined by training and commitment, the prospect always existed that nonviolent resistance could not be sufficiently contained to direct all the harms and suffering back on resisters themselves. Boycotts and other actions of civil disobedience could not help but affect whole communities, and it would be hard to constrain the impact of such actions so that they affected only the resisters or those identified as their opponents.

I conclude that on the question of noncombatant immunity, Gandhi and King advocated actions of resistance and noncooperation that would inevitably cause pain and distress beyond the immediate parties to the conflict. Boycotts and labor strikes are meant to apply widespread economic pressure, and these actions may negatively inflict harm on, say, a community's children. Furthermore, economic sanctions, while not a use of force equivalent to military incursion or bombing, are still considered under international law acts of war, and they can lead to the increase in human suffering, even among those not directly engaged in the conflict. Gandhi, in fact, held that "a summary use of social boycott in order to bend a minority to the will of the majority is a species of unpardonable violence,"[44] and this reality is clearly what led Reinhold Niebuhr to compare the results of some nonviolent resistance efforts to outright violence.

Three different approaches to the question of noncombatant immunity could be used to argue that Gandhi and King did, in fact, satisfy this criterion of just war. The first argument is the obvious one advanced by King and Gandhi themselves, which acknowledges implicitly that nonviolent resistance does cause harms. Advocates of nonviolent resistance understand that this inevitably occurs, so they take such harms into account and strategize to turn the harm away from anyone except the resisters themselves so that the suffering caused by nonviolent resistance is intentionally self-directed. Thus is the point reasserted that the resisters freely present themselves in conflict as willing to take the legal consequences—and any other suffering—caused by their acts of resistance. By directing the harm and suffering caused by nonviolence back on themselves, nonviolent resisters could avoid the charge that they inflicted harm on "noncombatants" not directly party to the conflict. A second approach might be to claim that there are really no noncombatants when the social injustices of racism, discrimination, enslavement, and a denial of dignity to persons are culturally pervasive and involve an entire community or nation. If the entire social and political fabric is stained with racism and discrimination and such injustices are sustained by total communities, not simply military people, or police, or local officials, then the argument could be made that there are no exempt and unaffected noncombatants; and a strategic effort to change the entire community will necessarily address all members of the community and affect everyone. Civil disobedience and noncooperation in opposition to, say, the Indian salt tax or the Montgomery bus system required a strategic response for which the particular situation was simply a local manifestation of a wider, more invidious national injustice that affected everyone.

And a third approach would appeal to a double effect principle.[45] The logic of such an appeal might proceed as follows: nonviolence applies an opposing and corrective force that avoids physical violence, aims at persuasion, and uses patience, sympathy, and love to liberate oppressors from their errors. The peaceful and nonviolent means of action, again, conform to ends that will, in the end, yield a peaceful and just result. The just resolution and peaceful restoration of the community will, as an end, always outweigh any harms unintentionally inflicted on persons not directly involved in the conflict. Such harms as might incidentally or accidentally result could be deemed licit or allowable or justified by an appeal to such a double-effect notion, since foreseen but unwanted consequences of incidental harm would be subordinated to the direct and good intention of achieving justice and doing so by just means that do not contravene the ends sought. In other words, no harm is directly intended and no evil means are employed; no retaliation or vengeance motivates victims of oppression; and no injustice toward oppressors is directly intended as nonviolent resisters insist on recognizing the oppressor in his or her dignity as a human person in a community of persons. Indirect or secondary harms would thus be deemed permissible as foreseen but unintended and unwanted "lesser evils." In this interpretation, any unintended harms visited on noncombatants would be foreseen but unintended, nonviolent and thus non–life threatening. This last point is important since it is then possible to say that restitution to those negatively affected by the nonviolent resistance would be at least theoretically possible—which is different if violence is used and noncombatants are killed. No restitution is possible for the dead. Given the nature of the unintended harms caused by the nonviolent use of force Gandhi and King advocated, the prohibition on harming noncombatants could be reasonably lifted.

EVALUATING NONVIOLENT
RESISTANCE THROUGH THE ETHIC OF JUST WAR

What can we conclude from this application of just war thinking to nonviolent resistance?

First of all, nonviolent resistance and just war thinking as I have presented them are not antagonistic toward each other in their central orientation. That nonviolent resistance is dedicated to justice and sanctions peaceful means is not in dispute. But if just war operates out of a presumption that ordinarily human beings ought not to settle their conflicts by resorting to force, then this presumption, normative action guide, or common agreement about the good of not using force establishes the default position of the just war ethic. This default position renders just war ethical thinking coherent as a program for making possible an "exception to the rule," for the presumption against the use of force articulates the principled ethical norm in relation to which an exception might be made.

The common agreement that ordinarily force ought not to be used to settle conflicts restrains action while also allowing consideration to be given in specific situations to a possible use of force. Some dreadful instance of injustice may provoke such consideration, and an appeal to last resort—explicit or even implicit—would allow a use of force to appear as a live option. Gandhi and King observed a sense of last resort in their programs, refusing to engage nonviolent resistance until all other methods had failed. They do not appeal in any explicit way to just war thinking, but my case is that this picture of just war can be imposed on nonviolent resistance to show how it applies nonetheless. If just war as an ethic is meant to be a rational guide to thinking about how to deal with conflict, and if just war as an ethic embodies values of essential agreement that reasonable people opposed to using force to settle conflicts accept, then Gandhi and King, as reasonable individuals involved in conflict, could be expected to think and act in ways that conform to just war structures and ideas—and I think I have shown above that in fact they do. So the first point is that both just war and nonviolent resistance acknowledge that *ordinarily we ought not to use force to settle conflicts.* If an exception to this commonly agreed-on presumption is considered, the action guide, principle, or rule in relation to which an exception is possible must be present and operational, even if it is not fully articulated. Clearly this presumption against using force is present in the thought of both leaders. As reasonable persons opposed in general to settling conflict by appealing to force, both Gandhi and King accept the moral presumption that underwrites just war thinking. Both Gandhi and King implicitly acknowledge the common moral agreement opposed to the use of force, and both are committed to achieving the ends of justice and peace through the means most consistent with those ends, namely nonviolence.

Second, just war addresses the moral meaning of using force to settle conflicts, and it is clear that nonviolent resistance as articulated, proposed, and enacted by Gandhi and King constitutes *a use of force.* If nonviolent resistance is a form of pacifism, it is a form of pacifism that believes nonviolence is a powerful weapon to be wielded in the fight against injustice. This understanding of nonviolence as a use of force distinguishes Gandhi and King from the nonresistance to evil perspective of Tolstoy, which functioned as a religious ideology disconnected from the work of discerning moral meaning in specific conflicts. Gandhi and King both commit to nonviolence and even speak of being absolutely committed to the method of nonviolent resistance, with neither demonstrating in practice or theory sympathy for Tolstoy's radical and absolutist "nonresistance" form of pacifism.

Third, if just war theory is not about justifying war and violence but about restraining the use of force, then "just war" as a rational framework for discerning moral meaning should be applicable to any use of force, even the use of force involved in nonviolent resistance. My claim has been that this is in fact the case, and I have demonstrated above how Gandhi and King observe in practical ways the criteria of just war and employ them for purposes of moral discernment. They each consider how a particular "battle" should be joined and what "weapons" are permissible to use, so that an implicit idea of "just war"—as I have articulated it—underwrites their approaches even if neither makes an explicit appeal to it.

Fourth, the criteria of just war can be applied to nonviolent resistance in each of the nine particulars. If just war does not itself establish moral meaning but establishes a framework for moral discernment when applied to particular situations, then the criteria establish the terms for reflection on moral meaning. In the above analysis, I showed how Gandhi and King made implicit appeal to these criteria, but that is not the end of the story. If moral discernment is to proceed, then critical reflection and conversation—even debate—ought to ensue, and I have suggested problems the just war ethic might raise, though I did not focus on that part of the process.[46] But we could apply just war ethical thinking as a resource for critically assessing both Gandhi and King. For example, is the King-Gandhi appeal to *legitimate authority* through religious sources adequate for a moral consideration of a use of force? As pointed out, this criterion can also move into the realm of "holy war" justification, and that is a dangerous move. Justifying out of transcendent sources a reason for action and even a program for action provokes a terrible moral quandary: one religious resource might instruct nonviolence, but another declaration of the ultimate will through another religious understanding might just as likely commend violence as the sanctioned mode of action. The appeal to religious resources as a legitimate ground for action in these situations is morally question begging: moral reflection can critique human actions and reasons for action, but religion can be about anything and thus endorse any conceivable action—good or evil—as long as the action is commanded under the auspices of ultimacy and is thus believed to be sanctioned by the divine will. A just war ethical critique would expose this as a weakness in Gandhi and King's ethical position. In a formal sense, when they appeal to God as the ultimate justifying authority for their programs of nonviolence, they make the very move that sectarians advocate in appealing to a divinely sanctioned use of violence, which supports what we have here termed *generic holy war*. Gandhi and King held views that are of course totally different from, say, those of the 9/11 hijackers, but they formally ground the legitimacy of their actions in exactly the same authority and source for moral justification—the divine will.

Other just war questions of moral importance can be raised with respect to nonviolent resistance. King and Gandhi were certainly aware that their methods of nonviolence would incite violence in reaction to them, King even admitting, "It is unfortunately true that however the Negro acts, his struggle will not be free of violence initiated by his enemies."[47] Applying the just war ethic exposes a serious problem. The difficulty rests in the fact that nonviolent resisters seek to achieve their end by *shaming* the oppressor. Both Gandhi and King sought to convert and persuade oppressors by shaming them, but could we not ask whether by such actions they are then forced to create situations and circumstances that invite the oppressor to act shamefully? Would oppressors, in reaction to being shamed, not respond predictably by abusing and degrading nonviolent resisters, submitting them to situations where they risk injury, incarceration, and even death? Nonviolent resisters proceed on the basis of informed consent to what might happen, but the moral question is whether these nonviolent actions actually *provoke* violence (contra King, above) and whether moral responsibility for the violence then attaches to the nonviolent resister's action since the resister aims to persuade and convert, and eliciting shame in the enemy is necessary for that. People cannot be shamed unless they perform shameful acts that can then be understood as shameful. So by acting in nonviolent ways and eliciting from their oppressors actions that can shame the oppressor—acts of abuse and violence—are nonviolent resisters *inciting* violence; and do they then depend upon violence since evoking (provoking?) violence is necessary for creating in the oppressor the experience of shame that is essential if the hearts of the oppressors are to turn? So is nonviolence really so proportionate a response if in fact it is the occasion for inciting violence and even requires violence to achieve its ends?

It may be that nonviolent resistance is not so proportionate a weapon after all, which points to a possible divergence between the perspectives of just war and nonviolent resistance. And what about supposedly nonviolent actions such as boycotts and economic sanctions—are they really nonviolent just because they do not involve military action or physical violence? Do the three possible justifications offered above really allow us to say that certain nonviolent acts of resistance do not visit harms on noncombatants or do so in some way that is morally licit but only because of a peculiar kind of tricky philosophical maneuver (i.e., double effect)?

These questions—all of them—may be easily answerable, but my point is that under the framework of the just war ethic, which includes the just war criteria driven by the moral presumption that ordinarily we ought not to use force to settle conflicts, this ethic underwriting just war requires that we ask such questions, even of nonviolent resistance advocates such as Gandhi and King. *Any and every use of force is subjected to critique*—even the nonviolence of Gandhi and King—because the commonly avowed idea that we ought not to use force to settle conflicts is so morally weighty and so utterly reasonable as a proposition commanding universal moral assent that it governs action presumptively and will not be lifted with ease. From this way of looking at "just war," even nonviolent resistance ought to be considered a failure to observe the moral presumption at issue in just war. Resorting to force—even the force of nonviolent resistance—is, as King said, "a lesser of evils," but an evil nonetheless. The moral point of view would commend to us the idea that goodness is honored whenever justice is advanced by means that do not involve force to settle a conflict.

Fifth, just war is a method of imposing restraint, and Gandhi and King seemed aware that even the force of nonviolent resistance needs to be used with restraint. Gandhi once wrote, "We pretend to believe that retaliation is the law of our being, whereas in every scripture we find that retaliation is nowhere obligatory but only permissible. It is restraint that is obligatory. Retaliation is indulgence requiring elaborate regulating. Restraint is the law of our being."[48] It may seem that just war is itself elaborate regulating, but just war can also be viewed as the articulation of restraint, what Gandhi called "the law of our being." The criteria of just war function to restrain force while satisfying the demands of justice, *but even nonviolent resistance must be used in calculated ways aimed at restraint*, which is why training and disciplined commitment to the principles of nonviolent resistance are so important to both Gandhi and King.

Sixth, if just war and nonviolent resistance emerge from a common presumption that reasonable persons of goodwill could be expected to acknowledge—that ordinarily we ought not to settle conflicts by using force—we can then ask where the theories diverge. Having already argued that *last resort* is not where we should look for divergence, I would suggest that just war and nonviolent resistance diverge in the particulars of proportionality and in considerations of noncombatant immunity. Just war and nonviolent resistance could clearly disagree and part company over the methods and techniques for settling conflicts, with nonviolent resistance holding firm that nonviolence is the mode of action most likely to preserve values, bring about the end of peace, and observe proportionality requirements.[49] Just war as moral critique would question this, as Reinhold Niebuhr did when he noted how the outcomes of some nonviolent actions, such as boycotts, yielded results not dissimilar from using violent physical force.[50]

And a serious question attends the issue of the nonresister who willingly consents to abandoning self-defense and accepting death at the hands of an oppressor. Do resisters who resort in the present moment to a use of physical force to preserve their lives satisfy the proportionality requirement more easily than nonviolent resisters who surrender self-defense and consent to a sacrificing of their lives in the present moment for an outcome to be realized after—perhaps long after—their deaths? The moral concern is that nonviolent resisters whose engagement with an adversary extends to a self-sacrifice that costs them their lives could be viewed as persons who are allowing themselves to be used as a means to an end. Such an act could be viewed as defying the duties of prudential reason and undermining the dignity of the human person. Such self-sacrifice would certainly raise ethical issues relevant to the core values enshrined in the moral presumption not to use force to settle conflicts, which is a common agreement held by rational persons of goodwill—persons of dignity; for allowing oneself to be used as a means to an end identifies a harm to persons and communities.

My final, and I think most important, point aims to *reconnect* just war to nonviolent resistance. Just war theory is a mode of analysis that can be and has been appealed to for centuries to justify acts of violence and military adventurism. And it has often been used perversely. All the criteria of just war must be satisfied when just war thinking is employed, and often governments will pick and choose which of the criteria to haul out to provide justification for a military incursion or police action. But if just war points to a coherent ethic resting on a rational, widely held moral presumption, lifting that presumption is a difficult chore because the presumption is weighty—and weightier than is often recognized. Even nonviolent resistance as a use of force will experience difficulty satisfying the requirements of the criteria, though clearly its mode of operation will make it easier to accomplish than those seeking to justify a use of force involving physical force and violence. From the moral point of view, Martin Luther King Jr. will have an easier time justifying an act of nonviolent resistance in, say, the Montgomery bus boycott under the structure of just war than will, say, the American government mobilizing for a preemptive strike on Iraq.

Just war theory, presented as a coherent theory to justify an exception to a moral presumption that ordinarily we ought not to use force to settle conflicts, is no enemy of peace but an enormously powerful restraint on those who employ force to settle conflicts in the moral world of human relationships. Just war as an ethic is so grounded in a commitment to avoiding force that it will even subject to critical analysis *nonviolent* uses of force. Reinhold Niebuhr's observation that nonviolent force may yield consequences indistinguishable from those of violence merits moral investigation and evaluation.

Nonviolent resistance is a mode of engagement in the world; and it is a resource, method, technique, and tool for fighting injustice to the end of realizing what King called "the beloved community." Just war is—or should be—a framework for moral investigation, reflection, and restrained action.

The criticism could be offered that this presentation of just war in the context of a moral presumption for peaceful resolution of conflicts is untrue to the historical functioning of the just war doctrine in the arena of nation-states. This criticism misfires for the project I have undertaken here. First of all, I am concerned to present a coherent ethical perspective that allows for a critique of issues related to using force to settle conflicts. Second, just war has evolved over the centuries, looking today quite unlike what Cicero or Augustine would have recognized,[51] and if this presentation ill conforms to the Realpolitik use of just war by nation-states and international law today, my defense is that this presentation accepts just war as a mode of moral analysis and thus represents another step in the evolution of the theory. If we can overcome the prejudice that invoking the term "just war" necessarily means that its purpose is simply to justify war rather than to restrain force and preserve the presumption *against using force*, then we might be able to discern that its real purpose as a tool for moral analysis is that it provides a nonabsolutist, thus noncontradictory,[52] mode of engaging moral reflection in the realities of human conflict. The just war ethic bears not a preordained bias for justifying war or violence but serves as a justice related tool that structures what one would hope would be informed moral reflection. The ethic to which the just war tradition appeals is thus to be understood as providing an imposing foundation of commitment to peace and conflict resolution free of force. The just war framework, considered as an ethic, provides an effective tool for the discernment of moral meaning in the confrontation with injustice; and as it is no friend of injustice, neither is it an enemy of peace.

Chapter Three

The Hybrid Ethic and
Its Application

In the effort to offer a constructive proposal for thinking about how to think about ethics, we began by arguing that an adequate ethical theory, one conformed to the moral point of view, must reconcile thought and moral experience. We then noted that serious criticisms have been leveled at some major ethical theories on just this point. The gap between thought and experience can be seen, for instance, in a deontological ethic that might tend toward moral absolutism as well as in a utilitarian ethic that insufficiently attends to the means by which morally good ends might be realized. Neither theoretical option appears to be thoroughly adequate in allowing for the experience of people who face moral problems and struggle with difficult decisions about what to do.

In the realm of experience, people will attend to moral principles and Kantian duty-based ethics to deliberate on the good, right, and fitting thing to do, but sometimes the simple application of a moral principle will seem to morally sensitive people too stringent and not nuanced enough to help resolve perplexities in a particular situation. Morally attuned people inevitably shy away from the rigidities of absolutist ethics. Moreover, reasonable people can actually exercise practical reason and demonstrate just how rational they can be by constructing a thoughtful and defensible exception to a principled rule. On the other hand, right action will sometimes be affected by considering the positive and negative consequences of various action possibilities. But a morally attuned person will not simply give way to a calculation in any and all circumstances. Few people will accede to a process of decision making based solely on a prospective determination of consequences, as if the moral meaning of the act that might yield the best consequence is of no importance. An "ends justifies the means" ethic is fraught with difficulties that ill accords with ordinary moral sensibilities. After all, doing something evil that good might result, as justified as that might be in a utilitarian ethical system, is not how people want to live the moral life. As attractive as utilitarianism might be, it will in some circumstances be rejected because it could authorize action deemed inappropriate or even intrinsically wrong.

This critique exposed a gap between thought and experience in two major ethical theories that are still in widespread use today, and this discussion opened up natural law ethics as an alternative resource that could avoid the extremes of absolutism on the one hand, relativism on the other. This analysis allowed us to consider an ethics alternative, and we turned to natural law and its expression in what is known as just war thinking.

The tradition of just war takes a middle course on the question of war and the use of force and does so "by definition," so to speak. That is because just war reflects a moral understanding that asks people of goodwill to deliber- ate on the specifics of conflict situations and apply justice-related criteria to determine which uses of force are permissible and which are not. The ethics chore is to determine which are which. Just war thinking offers a practical approach to a particular moral problem—the use of force—and as old as it is, just war is an ethics resource still used today.

An ethic, we said, lies *behind* just war thinking. An *ethic*, we said, refers to a system of action guides that express the moral point of view, which is itself characterized by universalizability, impartial justice, benevolence, other-regardingness, and commitment to some set of normative principles. The ethic *behind* just war has been obscured as just war thinking has been reduced to a set of criteria detached from the governing moral agreements reasonable people hold. When those criteria have been pressed into service to justify uses of force and military interventions that serve ends other than re- storing peace and addressing injustice, just war itself has been discredited as a tool to advance national, regional, economic, or political self-interest. Policy makers eager to use force in pursuit of a particular policy will, as a matter of course, consult the just war criteria, not using them as related to an ethic but as a checklist to show that a use of force has been justified, the impression then being given that all the required moral tests have been met. Thus do we witness force being used as if the policies endorsing such uses of force were beyond doubt morally justified. This is a sad state of affairs. The natural law understanding of the criteria is that they serve to direct public deliberation on the possibility of making an exception to some morally principled view concerning force, a principled view we earlier termed the "common agree- ment" or moral presumption that reasonable people of goodwill hold on this issue—the view *that force ordinarily ought not to be used to settle conflict*.

In undertaking to expose the ethic *behind* just war, we argued that the criteria so well known in just war thinking do not, in and of themselves, constitute an ethic. We argued, however, that we can gain access to such an ethic. Reframing and reconstructing the criteria around the central and normative grounding for the ethic, which is the moral presumption or "common agreement"—we used the terms interchangeably—allow us to do that. Once this "common agreement" ethic is extracted and articulated, we can proceed to work with the just war criteria, putting them to work as action guides grounded in a governing common agreement, and we are then enabled to deliberate on questions related to conflict resolution and the possible use of force. And because this common agreement ethic is *an ethic*, it will, as a framework and guideline for approaching moral issues, have applicability *beyond* the specific issue of war and the use of force. Showing how this ethic works beyond just war is our next task.

Nonviolent resistance provided us with a first example of how the ethic behind just war actually works. Just war ethical thinking provided us with a tool that could be used to analyze, assess, and evaluate the use of force King and Gandhi resorted to in their efforts to address injustices. And as admirable as these two extraordinary individuals proved to be, practical reason engaged the particular use of force that they both advocated to provoke critical questions. Applying an ethic—any ethic—will of necessity do that, for in examining the morally problematic idea of applying force to resolve a conflict, something Gandhi and King both did, their justifications for the exception they sought to our common agreement that force ordinarily ought not to be used to settle conflicts is subject to analysis and assessment. Gandhi and King both understood nonviolent resistance to be a use of force, and for that reason it came under the scrutiny of the just war ethic. Both were presented with questions they seem not to have adequately answered—not from the moral point of view, which is, after all, the point of view we are exploring in this project. The reader was left to ponder what it meant that Gandhi and King appealed to the just war ethic, for even though both implicitly found support for their actions in the ethic, the ethic posed some difficult and troubling questions to them as well. If this particular way of conceiving the just war ethic challenged Gandhi and King in their advocacy of the force of nonviolent resistance, one can only imagine the number and severity of the problems a proponent of violent coercion would face from a similar application of the just war ethic.

This investigation into a "new" ethics possibility began by urging consideration of the natural law tradition, which, as we noted, is very old. The natural law ethical tradition, which goes back to Plato, Aristotle, and the Stoics, advanced the idea that universal reason orders the lives of individuals and communities and even the universe itself. In ethics, natural law orders the moral standards that govern human conduct, giving those standards the air of law, even objectivity,[1] and it proposes that such standards reflect our common humanity—those features of our moral ontology each individual shares with all others, our human "nature"—the way things are with human beings. The ethics built upon common moral agreements is meant to reflect the appeal to our common human nature, the idea being that human beings are so constituted that to talk about them holding common agreements on moral matters makes eminent sense both for purposes of theory (thought) and in the moral life as it is lived (experience). Natural law ethics is proposed as a way to bridge the gap that we see open when discussing problems with Kantian and utilitarian ethics.

NATURAL LAW AND THE
POSSIBILITY OF A HYBRID ETHIC

The natural law ethics project we have been discussing is proposed here as a supplement and even a corrective to the Enlightenment theories of Kantian deontology and utilitarianism. But more than that, this ethical proposal asks us to do what those Enlightenment theories say explicitly cannot be done, namely, to view duty, virtue, and even attention to consequences as complementary aspects of ethical thinking rather than as antagonistic terms that logically defy synthesis or cooperation. As the application of the just war criteria demonstrated, the ethic behind just war incorporates duty and consequences, action and virtue. These terms, so hostile to each other and mutually exclusive in the Enlightenment presentation of ethical theory, are here brought into complementary juxtaposition, each having a legitimate, nonexclusive and nonexcluding role to play in illuminating thought about moral experience. What comes into view from this move is in fact a "hybrid" ethic. That is to say, this approach to ethics refuses to pit duty against consequences, character against action—it seeks to find a legitimate place for all of them on this theory: that as our moral *experiences* involve all of these particulars of moral meaning, so, too, must our *thought* account for their complementary inclusion, if, that is, thought and experience are going to be reconciled.

Cicero (106–43 BCE), the intrepid Roman statesman and philosopher, may be our best guide for the kind of "hybrid" ethical thinking I am advocating.[2] We find in Cicero a natural law theorist committed to a framework of ethical thinking determined in the first instance by "the power of nature and reason."[3] He is shaped by a vision of goodness and moral excellences—virtues—such as friendship, justice, and liberality, which are intrinsically good and which he believed we value and pursue because it is in our nature to do so: "Any rules which are to be reliable, lasting and in accordance with natural law," he writes in his major ethical treatise *On Duties*, "can only be laid down by those who consider that moral excellence should be sought solely, or at any rate primarily, for its own sake."[4] Reason is so constituted as to recognize that which is good, and human beings are so constituted as reason-endowed creatures that they pursue those intrinsically valuable goods "naturally."

But within this general natural law framework Cicero takes a further step. Of course, he was not a Kantian duty-based deontologist avowing a first-century BCE version of the nineteenth-century categorical imperative, but he had learned from Plato the importance of duty, and duty was central to his ethics:

> For no part of life, neither public affairs nor private, neither in the forum nor at home, neither when acting on your own nor in dealings with another, can be free from duty. Everything that is honorable in life depends upon its cultivation and everything dishonorable upon its neglect (I, 4).[5]

Virtues are what we cultivate to the end of living honorably and living well, so virtue is juxtaposed with duty at the center of his moral philosophy. In fact, the treatise *On Duties* makes clear that duties have their origin in virtues, for virtues provide depth to any account of motivation for duties:

> The man who defines the highest good in such a way that it has no connection to virtue . . . cannot cultivate either friendship or justice or liberality. . . . Everything that is honorable arises from one of four parts: it is involved either with the perception of truth and with ingenuity; or with preserving fellowship among men, with assigning each to his own, and with faithfulness to agreements made; or with greatness of strength of a lofty and unconquered spirit; or with order and limit in everything that is said and done (modesty and restraint are included here). What holds the life of fellowship and communities together is justice, the most illustrious of the virtues, on account of which men are called "good;" and the beneficence connected with it, which may be called either kindness or liberality.[6]

Cicero held that the highest good is to be associated with a virtuous life. Cultivating and even attaining the virtues of wisdom, justice, liberality (generosity), modesty, and restraint—all of which mark strength of spirit and character—cannot be separated from the duties that the virtuous individual accepts, including the duty to meet obligations faithfully and thus keep promises made. Cicero included in his natural law ethic duty and virtue. And he insisted, good politician that he was, that in the moral life we must attend to consequences of our actions in determining right action. The argument is sometimes made that consequentialist utilitarianism, which seeks to maximize happiness (or pleasure) and minimize pain for the greatest number, can have no place in a natural law–based ethic since such an ethic would derive right action from the natural biological states of sensate pleasure or pain:

"All ethical theories based on pleasure and pain fail to ground any obligation and are antithetical to virtue," writes Montague Brown.[7] Cicero explicitly repudiates any attempt to construct an ethic on pleasure and pain: "There can certainly be no brave man," he writes, "who judges that pain is the greatest evil, nor a man of restraint who defines pleasure as the highest good."[8]

But just as Cicero included duty without committing to all we associate in the deontological ethics of Kant, especially its absolutist tendencies, so too does he appear to pay attention to consequentialist thinking without committing to the idea that pleasure or some other notion of utility is the highest good. Could we not also say that there is present in Cicero a natural attending to consequences in the moral life, and allow this without also having to accept that what Cicero means by consequences must of philosophical necessity mean what the Enlightenment thinkers Bentham and Mill meant when they formalized the pleasure-pain based ethical theory of utilitarianism? If Kant's is an uppercase Duty ethic, Cicero's is a lowercase version; and the same holds on the utilitarian front. Cicero writes:

> The great difference between man and beast, however, is this: the latter adapts itself only in responding to the senses, and only to something that is present and at hand, scarcely aware of the past or future. Man [*sic*], however, is a sharer in reason; this enables him to perceive consequences, to comprehend the causes of things . . . to compare similarities and to link and combine future with present events; and by seeing with ease the whole course of life to prepare whatever is necessary for living it.[9]

It is the ability to be aware of the future and to use reason to "perceive consequences" that is a defining characteristic of the human being as a rational being distinct from beasts. Cicero is not talking about the kind of attending to consequences that the hedonistic utilitarianism of Bentham encompassed, but he does think that attending to consequences is integral to the moral life and to the life of practical reason. Cicero holds to a lowercase form of consequentialism, one that can be set beside a lowercase form of duty as integral to our thinking about the good life and the life of goodness.

These terms of moral philosophy—virtue, duty, consequences—are, in the context of the natural law framework that invites them in, not antagonistic to one another but complementary aspects of a moral synthesis. And all of them have a role in our thinking as we attempt to make sense of our experiences in the moral life. Duties, virtue, natural law, and consequences: these are the terms of the Ciceronian synthesis, and it is just such a "hybrid" ethic that can be discerned in the natural law ethic of just war. The just war ethic is grounded in principles, the common agreement that we have a duty to observe, namely, that ordinarily we should not use force to settle conflicts. Consider that each of the just war criteria does not simply identify a justice-related concern but announces a duty to be observed. It is incumbent upon those who are acting to lift the presumption against the use of force to make a compelling case that doing so is warranted—and just war thinking insists that this be done. It is the duty of those entrusted with power and authority to make certain that all reasonable efforts have been made to resolve the conflict short of force. And the noncombatant immunity provision—that innocent civilians are not to be harmed—points to a duty-based deontological principle within the criteria themselves, as is the idea of announcing intention and establishing just cause.

The criterion of "reasonable hope of success" relies upon people contemplating the future and dealing with foreseeable consequences, assessing possible outcomes and determining by reason's light what should be done in view of that assessment—will more good than evil result from applying force? The reasonable hope of success criterion makes a consequentialist appeal—an action, even when only contemplated, cannot be justified and then allowed if the burdens or evils appear as if they will outweigh the benefits. Additionally, the criterion of "preservation of values" is consequentialist in its focus on determining which course of action is most likely to bring about the best, least destructive result while not sacrificing important values that need to be preserved. Just war thinking attends to consequences as it asks people of goodwill to draw reasonable inferences as to which course of action is most likely to yield a result where good outweighs evil, an important consideration when the issue is using force. We know from experience and history that applications of force almost inevitably yield harmful results, which is why we share a common moral agreement that ordinarily force ought not to be used to settle conflicts.

Thus far, the focus on Kantian-deontological and utilitarian ethics has subordinated any discussion about a role for the virtues, although we now want to claim that virtue is integral to the successful application of just war ideas when deliberating actual situations of conflict. As noted previously, just war fails if it is not employed by people committed to honesty and forthrightness. Just war ideas can be manipulated and misused, and character issues and a lack of virtue can sometimes be detected when just war deliberations fail or are pursued tendentiously or deceptively. It takes persons of virtue (in Cicero's terms, "honor") to actually work the theory. We noted that insufficient or inaccurate information about the facts of a difficult conflict situation or lying by persons of power and authority about the particulars of a conflict situation can distort just war deliberations. Just war discussions can obviously be directed to ends other than restoring peace and harmony with justice; and the proper role for just war thinking in the political affairs of the day depends upon people of goodwill, virtuous people—just, prudent, honest, and wise people—deliberating in public ways how to best to resolve conflicts. The just war criteria can guide this effort even as the moral presumption against using force offers restraint all along the way.

So before we begin to analyze the natural law, hybrid ethic *beyond* just war, let us recall again Cicero, the true originator of just war thinking, who as an ethicist discussed virtues in a moral treatise explicitly dedicated to duties, and whose life as a practical politician was ever beset with calculating risk, benefit, and burdens as he sought to realize the greatest good while serving the common good. Cicero provides us with our clearest and probably earliest example of a moral thinker who *argues for* (thought) and then *exemplifies in his life* (experience) the hybrid ethic being advocated in this book.

THE HYBRID ETHIC

In the ethic behind just war, duty is not an enemy of consequences, nor consequences of duty; virtue is not antagonistic toward action. Including them together might look incoherent given the oft-noted antagonism between Kantian deontology and Benthamite utilitarianism, but we need not concede to Kant or Bentham that their versions of duty or consequentialism exhaust the meaning of these terms in our moral thinking. Cicero once commented, "An objection is brought against me, and by educated men at that, who ask whether I seem to be acting quite consistently,"[10] and we can take note of that. But if we move our heavily freighted Enlightenment ethics terms away from their uppercase exclusiveness and imperiousness and reconstruct them in lowercase, we can, as Cicero did, meet the challenge of inconsistency.

Contemporary ethics, even in standard accounts that end up in college textbooks, recognizes that ethical theories such as Kantianism or utilitarianism have problems. The question asked in these pages has been whether those criticisms should have no effect on our willingness to employ those theories, making it appear that the ethics chore is to decide which theory is most worthy of choosing. But we cannot claim that these theories are in certain ways inadequate and then use them as if they were not. That would be inconsistent. Yet it seems as if the two theories we have focused on, deontological duty-based ethics and consequentialist utilitarianism, are simply opposed to each other. They were constructed and are presented as incommensurable: duty excludes consequences. Furthermore, these Enlightenment action-focused ethics are often presented as antagonistic toward virtue ethics, which focus on character formation and being: action theories exclude virtue theories. The hybrid ethic we find exemplified in just war thinking and sponsored by the natural law ethic, eloquently defended by Cicero, pushes us to think about ethics in a different way. It asks us to consider the many tools we have at our disposal for thinking about the moral life and the many moral problems people face. Rather than saying, however, "Choose these tools to the exclusion of those," this hybrid ethic says. "Bring them all to bear and apply them using the guidelines practical reason gives us in the articulation of our common agreements. Test them against the standard of good, right, and fitting action discernable in our common agreements. Let practical reason guide persons in their assessment of particular situations when the injustices they face are so serious that they warrant opening the possibility that using force might be an allowable option. Let practical reason establish reasonable justice-related concerns to guide people as they consider lifting a moral presumption for some very good and justifiable reasons."

From the outset our task has been to question how we can construct or derive an ethic that reconciles thought and experience. So let us now consider that in our moral experience, we do not always pay attention to consequences—but sometimes we do, and sometimes we should. And sometimes we do things because we have developed certain predisposing character traits, the moral excellences we call virtues that we express behaviorally—even naturally—because we seem unable not to express them; and we act true to those virtues. Were we to act contrary to these disposing aspects of our character, we would violate some deep aspect of our sense of self and experience moral upset, even to the point of finding it hard to live with ourselves. And sometimes we act in ways that we understand may bring us criticism and opposition—we see negative consequences—but we decide to act as our moral lights require, believing we know the right thing to do. If we really do know, then reason bids us do our duty and act in accordance with our understanding of what is good, right, and fitting. Despite the anticipated criticism, we find comfort in knowing that what we do is what any reasonable person facing the same situation should do.

The moral life is like this when we reflect on human experience. It is complex and multidimensional and requires us to use practical reason to deal with the life we live in relationship with others and with ourselves. A hybrid ethic is not incoherent because it includes seemingly incompatible moral features. *What is needed is an ethic that provides a way of thinking that is consistent with the complexity of our experience.* That ethic should account for the fact that we subscribe to duty, to virtue, and to consequentialist thinking in different ways and combinations and emphases at different times and in different situations. That ethic should also highlight that what we do is aimed at goodness, which it is in our nature to recognize and pursue. The hybrid ethic we find in the natural law moral tradition, which is then exemplified and conveniently available in what we have been calling the just war ethic, meets this challenge for an ethic that reconciles theory and experience. It is not inconsistent or incoherent, not if it accurately takes into account how we actually live and not if it provides us with a way of thinking that makes sense out of that experience and helps guide action to worthy moral ends.

The non-relativistic and non-absolutist hybrid ethic *behind* just war requires that we do the work of the moral life, which is to confront problems and think them through, consult with others, clarify our common presumptions about what is good, right, and fitting, and then contemplate action, evaluating whether what we do is consistent with our best determinations as to what is just and permissible. Always at issue is the question whether our actions and intentions express the moral point of view. We have in the ethic *behind* just war a hybrid ethic; it is a natural law ethic that attends to duty, to consequences, and to virtue. It is to be used in particular situations to examine and assess moral meaning; and it is directed toward the end of promoting goodness. This ethic functions to assist us in thinking about the profound questions we face in our experience, which are interpretive questions about moral meaning that every person of goodwill must assume responsibility to answer.

Questions about using this ethic have no doubt arisen for the reader, and we shall show how this ethic we have associated with just war can be applied *beyond* just war to particular issues such as abortion, physician-assisted suicide, and others. That exercise will be for naught, however, if some of the pressing and certainly valid questions about this ethic are not addressed. So in the next chapter, before demonstrating how the ethic works in practice on concrete moral issues, we shall attend to questions about this ethical approach and make the case that this ethic does reconcile thought and experience. The argument will be made that this hybrid ethic based on "common agreements" is one to commend as a way to think about ethics.

Chapter Four

Using the
"Common Agreement" Ethic
A Critical Evaluation

In the effort to fashion an ethical theory that reconciles thought with experience and reflects the way people actually go about thinking through ethical problems, we have engaged a very old ethical resource—the natural law tradition. In that tradition we find a hybrid model for ethical thinking, one that takes into account virtue, duties, principles, and consequences, with all of these things being complementary rather than mutually antagonistic toward one another. Natural law ethics is grounded in the "natural" human capacity of persons to exercise practical reason, operating, as we have argued, from the foundation of common agreements about moral meaning that reasonable people of goodwill can be expected to affirm. Our common agreements, if this ethic is to work, must be truly common and not the result of a close majority vote. Opposition to a common agreement will necessarily mean one of two things: either the opponent is expressing an aberrant, idiosyncratic, even irrational point of view, or a serious criticism is being leveled that the common agreement is inadequately articulated or in some other way not established, which means work has yet to be done. Once the common agreement is acknowledged, however, it has normative force; it should command assent and regulate behavior universally, which also happens to mean cross-culturally.

So, in the example of war and the use of force, we acknowledge that ordinarily conflicts ought not to be settled by force: that is what we believe, and just as important, that is how we actually live. In the pages ahead we will identify other common agreements, such as the obligation to tender care to handicapped newborns; that ordinarily we do not want the state to kill citizens or doctors to assist patients who may want to kill themselves; or that we want social harmony and a justice system that rectifies wrongdoing and restores societal harmony. Our common agreements underwrite the moral life—they are a bond of unity in the midst of a world that is wildly diverse.

Although an ethic can be simply a set of rules—professions have ethical codes, as do criminal organizations—we have proposed a "common agreement" natural law–based ethic that we have taken pains to characterize as conformed to the moral point of view. The moral point of view advances benevolence and justice, normative principles, and the idea of universalizability, but it does not equate universalizability with moral absolutism, which is ultimately contradictory and irrational. This natural law–based ethic, even while acknowledging that our common agreements are normative and command regulative force over behavior, recognizes that life is complex and at times downright messy. People actually do encounter ethical dilemmas and confront moral problems, and the test of any ethic is how well it helps people deal with actual difficulties. Sometimes a directive that issues from a common moral agreement can appear to lock one into a course of action when moral sensitivity to the complex particulars of a situation and even justice itself require a different, more flexible response. When that occurs, we exercise practical reason to assess, evaluate, deliberate, and then make decisions about the good, right, and fitting thing to do based on empirical realities—the facts of a situation—and we attend to what goodness itself requires, even to the point of contemplating action that would, in the interests of justice, counter the common moral agreement.

So this natural law ethic, not being absolutist, makes some formal room for "exceptions to the rule." What must be remembered is that such exceptions are themselves constrained and guided by considerations of justice. Thus do we derive the justice guides—the criteria—so well known in just war thinking but that are applicable, as we shall see in the following chapters, to a variety of morally difficult issues. In our moral experience we can confront situations where it may be permissible to use force to settle a conflict, or, say, not treat a newborn because of the severity of its medical situation, or imprison an offender who upsets the balance of justice and disrupts social harmony. When justice concerns direct us to consider making "exceptions" to our moral agreements, we are not negating the common agreement but seeking to act justly in light of a moral commitment to do what is good, right, and fitting. Our common moral agreements must be subject to review and analysis; exceptions are possible in light of difficult situations and circumstances, and employing practical reason to deal with such issues is precisely what living the moral life is all about. The moral life is not so much about following rules as it is exercising practical reason in the face of moral problems and dilemmas, for it is then that we pay most attention to the problem of deciding what is good, right, and fitting to do.

When a problem presents itself in such a way that we cannot simply accede to our accepted moral understanding—our common moral agreement—but question what we are to do, we acquire a heightened consciousness about the moral life and our moral commitments. In the face of actual, real-life problems, we employ practical reason to figure out what to do and how best to act. It is one thing to be conformed to a common agreement about, say, not deceiving others or not having an abortion, but it is another thing to find oneself in a situation where a deception may be necessary to save lives or a woman's pregnancy suddenly turns life threatening. The issue is not that our common moral agreements are overturned or without value—it is actually our deep and abiding commitments to the force of these agreements that *creates* for us moral problems and ethical difficulties. Our common moral agreements establish our moral starting place. As we confront ethical problems, we proceed to moral deliberation from this starting place, seeking not only to serve the interests of justice but to act in ways that are conformed to the moral point of view. The ethic we have advanced here avows and articulates our common moral agreements, but it then also devises a system of tests or considerations—the criteria—that guide reflection in the interests of justice and that reason bids must be satisfied if "an exception" to that agreement is to be justly made in a particular situation.

The heart of this ethic is located in the common moral agreement rather than in the criteria that guide making an exception. This is why just war, so well known by its various criteria, has an ethical foundation *behind* it; for we distort the just war *ethic* if we do not bring the common moral agreement about the use of force to the fore and recognize its regulative power. The criteria can suffer distortion or serve malleable ends if unloosed from the common agreement that grounds them in the moral point of view. Criteria unconnected to the presumption against the use of force can lead to cavalier claims about the criteria being satisfied, for the criteria are general guidelines that are open to a potentially wide range of interpretations when applied in specific situations. The moral agreement upon which the criteria rest guides behavior, imposes restraint, and prevents any easy overruling of the moral norm articulated in the agreement. Without the common moral agreement in place directing the criteria back toward the normative force of that agreement, all we need do is go down our checklist—just cause here, legitimate authority there, and so on; given our propensity to self-serving action and even self-deception, we can rather easily accomplish the task of putting a "just war" stamp on a use of force that may have been actually pursued and even justified on other grounds entirely, most likely some form of national or political self-interest. The common moral agreement against using force to settle conflicts establishes the moral grounds for transforming the criteria into a powerful instrument that constrains the use of force while continuously working against any easy justification. And so serious are these constraints that even the use of force most likely to be commended by practical reason—nonviolent resistance—confronts justification difficulties. As we have seen, even Gandhi and King confront challenges of justification when the just war ethic is applied to their use of nonviolent force. Our common moral agreement is that force—any kind of force, even that of nonviolent resistance—is presumptively wrong and ordinarily ought not to be used.

Our discussion of this common agreement ethic, now also recognized as a natural law–based "hybrid" ethic, has undoubtedly raised issues and questions for readers, and for the remainder of this chapter I address some of them. Among the critical questions that can be asked are these:

- If this ethic is universal but nonabsolutist, how can one justify certain actions that seem absolutely wrong, such as murder, theft, torture, slavery, or adultery? (Aristotle in the *Nichomachean Ethics* [Book II, par. 6] had once said adultery is always wrong.) Are there not actions that really are wrong beyond any possible justification, that is, absolutely wrong, and for which it would be odd to claim or even imagine an "exception"?
- Where do these common agreements come from? Does one just make them up?
- Where do the criteria come from? Does one just make them up? Isn't this just another form of relativism, so that what has been offered here is by its own guiding principles a failed experiment?
- How do we actually see the hybrid ethic? Because of the focus on "our common moral agreements," little has been said about the role of virtue; consequences have not been emphasized; and can we really put principles together with consequences in a coherent ethical stance?
- Before getting to classic moral controversies such as capital punishment, abortion, or physician-assisted suicide, what are some other kinds of ethical problems people face where this ethic is actually used? What would be some everyday examples of this ethic being used? If the claim is that people don't go around calculating the maximum aggregate utility for every act they undertake (a classic problem with act utilitarianism), how can the claim be made that people actually use this alternative common-agreement-criteria ethic when it does not appear to be used in any explicit way? We argued that Gandhi and King appeal to it implicitly. This hybrid ethic has not made its way as an ethic into textbooks of moral philosophy or ethics. And isn't this common-agreement ethic complicated and cumbersome, and, be honest, is it not the case that people don't employ criteria to evaluate their action options?
- How is this ethic not simply a more complicated form of rule utilitarianism, and wouldn't it be easier just to use that, since it would give us some

guiding principles in its reliance on rules yet also attend to consequences as those moral rules are devised? Is this "hybrid ethics" really just reinventing the wheel?

- And what about problems raised by the question of abortion—how could one argue that there is such a thing as a "just abortion" if some people base their ethics on religious teaching and the religious teaching forbids—absolutely—abortion? The Roman Catholic Church is the great transmitter of natural law ethics in Western culture, yet the Church does not approach the killing in abortion as in any way equivalent to the killing in war—there is, in that religiously framed natural law tradition, no "just abortion." Doesn't the failure of the ethic in such a momentous and culturally controversial issue show that this ethic is irrelevant and has no contribution to make?

No doubt other questions are worthy of attention, but this list does pose issues regarding coherence, comprehensiveness, and the practicality of this ethic. By any measure, these questions must be deemed serious. As such, they are deserving of response. We shall take them one by one.

MORAL LANGUAGE

Question 1: *If this ethic is universal but nonabsolutist, how can one justify certain actions that seem absolutely wrong, such as murder, theft, torture, slavery, or adultery? Are there not actions that really are beyond any possible justification, that is, absolutely wrong and for which it would be odd to imagine an "exception"?*

Let us take the question and ask directly: Could there be a justified murder? Could this ethic support the idea that murder is presumptively wrong but sometimes might be justified—and then devise the criteria that would allow for a justified murder? Does that not follow the model of nonabsolutist ethical thinking argued for in these pages?

The answer to this query is "no." We cannot create criteria that justify murder, for murder is, indeed, always wrong.

But then, have we not walked away from the claim that this ethic avoids absolutism? One might well argue that to say murder is never permissible or justifiable identifies the very kind of moral absolutism this common-agreement ethic seeks to avoid. My response is that what is at issue here is moral language: how it works and how we use it.

The concept of killing is of course closely related to the idea of "murder," but killing is an action that may or may not be justifiable. When the term "murder" is used to describe a killing, however, what is being conveyed by

the use of that term is a *moral conclusion*, namely, that the killing is wrong
and not justifiable. That is what we mean by "murder." "Murder," then, conveys in the linguistic term itself a moral conclusion. Killings may be justifiable or not—and to determine those that are justifiable from those that are
not would require us to fashion a common-agreement ethic of "just killing."
"Murder," however, is not justifiable—it is the linguistic term we attach to
certain killings to convey the meaning that the killing in question is without
justification. That is why those who interpret as *murder* certain killings over
which there is controversy, such as executions, abortions, or withdrawal of
life support, will be uncompromising and absolutist in their perspectives.
Such individuals have drawn a moral conclusion about the killing and have
determined that that particular killing is not and cannot be justified—hence
they invoke the term "murder" to convey the impossibility of justification.

We authorize our language to perform this way. In our ordinary language,
certain terms do entail a moral conclusion, and we use this language correctly
and meaningfully when by the use of these terms we mean to exclude any
possibility for moral justification. "Murder" is such a term, and when we use
this term we negate the possibility of a justified killing.

Attention to this use of moral language is nothing new. It is as old as Aristotle, who argued that we identify goodness and badness by our use of certain
linguistic terms that admit of no qualification of excess or deficiency: there is
only the goodness or the badness.

> But not every action or every passion admits of a mean; for some have names
> that already imply badness, e.g., spite, shamelessness, envy, and in the case of
> actions adultery, theft, murder; for all these and suchlike things imply *by their*
> *names* [emphasis added] that they are themselves bad, and not the excesses or
> deficiencies of them. It is not possible, then, even to be right with regard to
> them; one must always be wrong. . . . Nor does the goodness or badness with
> regard to such things depend on committing adultery with the right woman at
> the right time, and in the right way, but simply to do any of them is wrong.[1]

So a basic appeal to a language of what we might call *moral performa-*
tives—language that performs the work of conveying a moral judgment by its
very use—formally answers our question. Some actions or attributes of character are always wrong because we have constructed language to convey the
moral meaning of wrongness in the terms themselves. All those Aristotelian
vice-related terms that stray from the mean of behavioral excellence as excess
or deficiency employ linguistic markers that identify in the terms themselves
wrongness, as cowardice is the deficiency of courage, rashness its excess—
both cowardice and rashness convey vice and moral inadequacy or impropriety,
and we convey moral meaning with terms we use precisely for that purpose.

So the answer to the question lies in understanding moral language and how it works. What this answer does not fully explore is how the use of moral language may evolve and change over time. Aristotle himself lived in a time when slavery was deemed a morally permissible institution. For a victorious nation to enslave its defeated enemies in the aftermath of war was accepted practice and raised no serious moral qualms. "Slavery," therefore, was not for Aristotle a morally performative term.

That is certainly not the case today. "Slavery" identifies a condition of enforced oppression, a denial of freedom, and a situation of uncompensated labor that offends against the contemporary understanding of what we mean by the moral point of view. That is to say, slavery is not benevolent or just, and no reasonable person of goodwill would freely assent to being a slave. It is a condition and an institution that cannot be universalized or supported as a moral norm reflecting some essential good of life that requires slavery for its realization. Over the twenty-five hundred years since Aristotle, the meaning of slavery has come to identify *in the term itself* a moral wrong. The fact that slavery still continues in the world today is not the relevant moral question at the moment, for so too are murders still committed. The point here concerns moral language. When human rights violations are exposed, such as the selling of women into the sex trafficking industry or the kidnapping of children to work on cocoa estates, the description of these practices as "slavery" conveys by use of that term moral wrongness. So moral evolution takes place, and this evolution is reflected in our language.[2]

Aristotle's comment about such things as theft and adultery are worth a comment. Could there be just theft? Aristotle is right that the term "theft" or the action of "stealing" conveys wrongness in the term itself. However, it is conceivable that a theft could be morally justified under certain conditions. Consider Jean Valjean's theft of bread in *Les Misérables*. Hugo's hero violated the law and for his crime he received punishment, but the punishment was excessively severe and clearly unjust given that Valjean only stole bread because he was desperate and starving. So the question is raised whether we have in this example a justified theft. Let us subject the situation to analysis and determine how it does or does not conform to the conditions we have associated with the moral point of view.

Jean Valjean's theft of bread was prompted by the nearing prospect of starvation. Reasonable persons should be able to agree that for starving people to steal bread that they cannot afford to buy would meet the test of universalizability, namely, that such a theft is actually a justifiable action that is right for anyone and everyone else to do who is similarly situated. An actual theory of "just theft" would require attention to the "similarly positioned" qualification and turn moral attention to the social, political, and economic order that fails to make provision for the essentials of life, since that is clearly what motivated Hugo's protagonist.

Provoking reflection on social justice issues was clearly Victor Hugo's intent, and the question can fairly be asked, "If a social order is so unjust that it creates starving people who need to steal to survive, is the act of stealing any longer a moral offense?" This is to push the question of "just theft" into a broader realm of social ethical analysis, where the moral question about an unjust social order that oppresses people and forces them to steal to live trumps a moral question about an individual act of theft that formally violates a law. If reasonable people of goodwill can condone the theft of bread by a starving man who has no resources to acquire bread except by theft, not only have we moved to the moral questions Victor Hugo wanted his readers to ponder, but we have resituated "theft" as a moral term. The term will still convey inherent wrongness, but it points to the reality that unjust social structures can recontextualize the language of moral meaning to the point where it might not make sense to talk about the wrongness of a theft if the injustices in the social order create conditions that necessitate theft. Social conditions can be so bad that theft for survival trumps the now rather puny pilfering of bread—which is admittedly still a theft—as the relevant moral issue.

Our moral language can change and evolve, but it also has limits and cannot encompass all the morally relevant factors that might require attention if something like "just theft" is to be subsumed by much more serious questions about an unjust social order. Widespread social injustice and the evils it produces can force good people into doing things they ordinarily would not do or ever want to do. The law might isolate the theft from the social context, as it did in Jean Valjean's case, but a moral inquiry would be irresponsible if it focused on the individual theft apart from the context of the social injustice that gave rise to—even necessitated—the "wrongful" act. In any event, practical reason will always support persons in their acts of self-defense—preserving bodily integrity is one of the goods of life—so that a theft of bread to survive in the face of starvation would constitute an act of justifiable self-defense.

Aristotle included "adultery" as a term that carried in its meaning moral censure, and his appeal to the absurdity of justifying adultery on the grounds that one has found "the right woman at the right time, and in the right way" cleverly and convincingly makes his point. Like murder or theft, adultery is a term that carries a negative moral judgment in its use. The term does convey wrongness, but an act of marital infidelity that would come under the aegis of "adultery" may not be so "absolute" as Aristotle understood in his day. A contemporary novelist of popular fiction, the late Dick Francis, once centered a narrative on a male character who was married to a woman paralyzed from polio and kept alive by respirators. The main character's solution to the loss of companionship was to enter into a sexual relationship with another woman.[3] This fictional situation reminds us of the case of Michael Schiavo, husband of Terri Schiavo, the woman who was in a persistent vegetative state for fifteen years. Michael entered into a relationship with another woman while still married to Terri, but only after physicians had convinced him Terri was in a persistent vegetative state and all hope of her regaining consciousness was lost. It was after that point, three years after Terri's collapse, that Michael requested a Do Not Resuscitate (DNR) bracelet for Terri, and this precipitated the objection from Terri's parents, who then took the story to the media. Michael Schiavo did not divorce Terri but remained husband and holder of the decision-making power for Terri's care through the power of attorney. After he requested the DNR bracelet and moved in with another partner with whom he subsequently fathered a child, Michael Schiavo was subjected to exceedingly abusive and hostile criticism. The accusation was leveled against him that he was an adulterer.

This charge added a whole layer of sexual morality complications to the Terri Schiavo case. Both of these individuals, the Dick Francis fictional character and the real-life Michael Schiavo, committed adultery. They confronted, however, a situation Aristotle never imagined. For Aristotle never conceived the possibility that a technology could be devised that would defer natural death indefinitely, and the fact is that the adultery question would have never arisen without the technology of medical intervention. Michael Schiavo was married to a person who had lost the capacity to be a self-conscious subject able to experience the world of interactive relationships. Her personhood was gone, even if she was not technically—physiologically—dead. No such technological interventions existed in Aristotle's day—persons so afflicted just died. Some of the things that occur in society and in culture, such as technologies to sustain comatose life, at least create a complication for an "adultery is always wrong" judgment. Of course, one can wonder why Michael Schiavo did not simply divorce Terri, but that provokes even more difficult issues since Michael Schiavo displayed the commendable virtues of loyalty, commitment, and an involved sense of responsibility toward Terri until medical professionals convinced him that the prognosis was futile.

"Adultery," like theft, still carries the notion of an inherently wrongful act, for it is an act of unfaithfulness to a promised commitment of sexual fidelity. The point is not necessarily to move toward creating a "just adultery" scheme, though it is possible to do so; on the ethical model advocated here, we could say that unfaithfulness in a relationship where faithfulness was promised is presumptively wrong. Moral presumptions are ordinarily binding, and one never proceeds to act as if the exception were the rule. The criteria we should offer as possibly "justifying" a break in that faithfulness would be highly restrictive. Were we to examine the Michael and Terri Schiavo case to come up with criteria justifying "adultery," we might turn to a criterion that was obviously the "marriage breaker" for Michael Schiavo, namely, the fact that the partner to whom he made a promise of life-long fidelity and sexual exclusivity was determined by medical authorities to be so debilitated that she could not be a subject of experience and in any way experience or reciprocate affection. For one who met such a criterion, a marriage vow, we could reasonably say, no longer holds.

We could claim in such situations to have the experiential foundations to justify a theory of "just adultery." If we want to understand Aristotle's point about language performing the work of moral performatives, however, we could simply accept that view and turn toward a consideration of the complexity of the situation demanding our attention. Applying the term "adultery" to the Michael Schiavo situation is a decision we make, but does the term "adultery" actually fit the situation? Was Terri Schiavo betrayed if she was unable to experience the pain of betrayal, something we associate with ordinary instances of adultery? This is where language can fail us. If a theory of "just adultery" seems preposterous, applying the term "adultery" to a case like that of Michael Schiavo also seems inadequate, simplistic, and lacking in moral nuance. "Adultery" may still be relevant in a legal framework, but was it adultery in a moral sense if there was no subject of experience capable of being hurt by the lapsing of a pledge to be faithful?

The ethic we have advanced here helps us sort out these issues, reassert our common agreements about moral meaning, and then query whether a particular situation actually offends against that agreement and may qualify as a licit exception. It may be that in certain cases where we apply a judgment-bearing language—a *moral performative* as we have called them—we do so mistakenly. That is not so much a criticism of the ethical theory we advance here as it is an exposure of the limitations of moral language itself, for in a relevant moral sense, that language does not always apply as we assume it should. A moral analysis could easily reveal, as suggested here, that Michael Schiavo did not commit adultery, any more than would a widow or widower who found a new companion after the death of a spouse. The concept of "adultery" in such a case does not apply, at least in Aristotle's judgment-bearing sense, which denied the act of adultery any possibility of justification. If moral language works the way Aristotle assumed it did, then that conclusion is right and makes sense.

But what if we confront situations not covered by so conclusive a judgment? Either adultery language is not like murder language and does actually admit of possible exceptions (i.e., "just adultery"), or the situation being presented does not conform in relevant ways to the concept "adultery." I think the latter is the case. If that is so, then the work of ethical analysis turns toward a discernment of facts, a presentation of moral issues in light of relevant moral presumptions, and an assessment of what is the good, right, and fitting thing to do. Practical reason must determine moral meaning in light of benevolence, justice, universalizability, and normative principles.

To sum up this discussion: Language is a tool we use to do the work of meaning making, and our moral language serves us well. But it does not serve us perfectly. It can convey in the use of particular words moral approbation or moral censure; it can perform the work of expressing and applying moral judgment. But applying a performative term is itself a decision, and judgment-bearing terms can be used in ways that miss the complexity of situations and circumstances. The common agreement ethic will allow moral language to do its work, but that model also attunes us to complexity, circumstance, and possible qualification. That model urges inquiry about moral meaning beyond the decision to employ a judgment-bearing moral performative to describe a situation, for use of the particular term conveying judgment may inadequately embrace the circumstance and lead to an insensitive moralizing, even a kind of totalizing of meaning due solely to the language employed and the actual choice of words.

We have considered two moral performatives, "theft" and "adultery." The issue is not so much that we have to generate a theory of just adultery or just stealing. Moral language can perform judgmental tasks, with linguistic terms themselves performing the work of conveying moral wrongness. This is what Aristotle was arguing. The issue, rather, concerns the limits of language and whether it is always adequate to our interpretive chores and meaning tasks. The moral question is whether unqualified use of terms such as "adultery" or "theft" can be descriptive of the complex situation faced by someone like Michael Schiavo, whose wife is dead to him, or Jean Valjean, stealing bread to avoid starvation. Approaching these issues with the moral resources of the natural law ethic we have been advocating requires us to evaluate the facts of a situation and circumstance in light of the relevant moral presumption governing behavior and then to consider the justice issues relevant to the situation as well. Adultery and theft are "names," as Aristotle put it, that convey moral wrongness, and that is now not in question. But there are moral issues alive in the context surrounding discrete episodes of behavior where the moral language we choose to use inadequately conveys moral complexity. The bigger moral issues in the cases we considered go to the problem of an economic and social order where persons to survive must steal bread, or to questions about breaking a promise of reciprocal faithfulness with a partner whose personhood has been catastrophically destroyed and who cannot reciprocate affection or experience any mutual relationship. Employing the moral language of "theft" and "adultery" in these cases misses a crucial moral dimension that an ethic, if it is to reconcile thought with experience, must pursue in the interests of moral meaning and even moral truth.

THE MORAL IMAGINATION

Questions 2 and 3: *The question fairly arises, how do we derive common moral agreements and criteria for possible exceptions? Where do they come from? Do we just make them up? If so, have we not slipped into the worst kind of relativism, the kind that reduces ultimately to individualistic subjectivism, so that you have your idea of what a common agreement is and I have mine?*

We have been considering the basis for an adequate ethic, one that reconciles our moral thinking with our moral experience. So we have turned to the natural law tradition, which is the foundation and locus for just war thinking, to offer the view that just war thinking as ordinarily presented is inadequate because the ethic that lies behind it is not articulated. That oversight vitiates the moral force of the criteria of just war, for the criteria are morally relevant and applicable as action guides only in relation to an operative moral norm or common moral agreement. Moreover, we offered that once this ethic behind just war thinking was articulated and conformed to the moral point of view, we could then investigate how this ethic applies to issues beyond just war. Although critical of just war in many ways, we have maintained throughout that just war thinking is a wonderfully useful access point to the ethic *behind* it, an exemplification as well as a model for applying this ethic to other moral problems.

How do we derive *our common moral agreements* and where do the *criteria* come from? The answers to these questions lie in three considerations: practical reason, the moral imagination, and empirical reality.

Practical reason, we have said, is that use of reason we employ in deciding what to do. It is reason addressing questions about how to act. In a natural law context, practical reason operates in accordance with nature, with the natural order of things, which is the good and universal condition of human existence. Aristotle wrote in his *Rhetoric*, "Universal law is the law of nature. For there really is, as everyone to some extent divines, a natural justice and injustice that is common to all, even to those who have no association or covenant with each other."[4] The idea that we are all as human beings possessed of reason and goodwill and thus endowed with a sense of natural justice is the source of our common agreements. Again, these agreements do not pertain to culturally relative things such as whether to use chopsticks or forks, but to those things we identify as goods of life, which are universally recognizable as good and intrinsically good, meaning not dependent on something else to give them their worth and value—friendship, bodily integrity, practical reasonableness, the ability to work, play, and enjoy aesthetic experiences, life itself. Practical reason directs us to reflect on what we should do—what is good to do, what is best to do in particular situations—and we invoke presumptive ideas that are universally applicable and grounded in that sense of "natural justice" Aristotle believed was "common to all." So our common moral agreements or moral presumptions articulate ideas related to action, values, and decision making, and practical reason is the engine that drives the effort to articulate them. Practical reason functions as human agents form their action plans in response to what practical reason recognizes as the "common agreement."

Practical reason tests situations against moral presumptions and inquires whether the guidelines for action derived from our common agreements can hold in certain troubling circumstances. The evaluation of moral meaning in troubling cases identifies the arena where practical reason works. Those who accept a rule of behavior and never find cause to question it in the face of problems people face in real life may have an "ethic" to be sure, but such certainty about action is not practical reason engaged in the work of *reasoning*. Moral problems are in need of figuring out, and practical reason guides the process of evaluation and presents justice concerns that need to be addressed if one is to lift a moral presumption in a particular case and allow an exception. Practical reason is the source of both common moral agreements and the justice-related criteria that might beg an exception to them.

The moral imagination is also at work. To conceive of a "common agreement" that is acceptable to and then applicable to all reasonable persons of goodwill requires us to exercise our moral imaginations. The moral imagination conceives a moral community larger than one's personal sphere of interest and larger than one's own ethnocentric community—it must conceive of humanity, with all of its diversity, connected by some bonds of unity around the question of moral meaning. Common agreements are derived from the imaginative work of conceiving humanity as a moral community. It may not be fashionable to present such a view in a world of postmodern skepticism, where such bonds of unity are criticized as an illusory project. But people of goodwill cannot help but connect to this community experientially when they see it offended, when they are able to see suffering due to injustice in the face of an individual or a community afflicted with "human rights abuses." The ability of people of goodwill to say an injustice inflicted on one is an injustice inflicted on all depends on an act of imagination, for such a statement is not a verifiable empirical truth—in truth, it is just the opposite. Yet such a statement is not without meaning, and it is a profound meaning in that it connects people together in a transcultural moral community. The characteristics of the moral point of view—universalizability, benevolence, impartial justice, and normative principles—all require an imaginative conceiving in order to apply to all persons, regardless of cultural difference and even in the face of the way diverse societies will foreground in one culture some value backgrounded in another, which can make moral discernment difficult. Despite the fact that the imagination is constrained by practical reason and by empirical realities, it is possessed of the capability to conceive of a moral community guided by a common concern for benevolence, justice, and the universal applicability of certain moral ideas or guidelines. So imagination is required to articulate a common moral agreement and to devise criteria of justice.

And respect for empirical facts plays a critical role in the construction of common moral agreements as well as in the articulation of criteria governing exceptions. The just war model, as we have pointed out, never tells what to do in a particular situation—it is a guide, presenting a foundation of moral commitments and justice concerns that are to be applied to particular situations. Those particular situations are to be measured against the moral standard set by the ethic, and everything depends on an accurate description of the facts of a case. If this ethic is, as we have argued, morally moderate, some wars and uses of force will be permissible, others not; some instances of imprisonment will be justifiable, others not; some abortions will be permissible, others not; and so on. We cannot tell which particular situation will be justifiable without attending to the facts of a given case, which is where this ethic is to be applied. And if it is applied with integrity, it must insist that the relevant facts of a case be brought to light before making a determination about how the criteria apply. The problem with the 2003 Iraq War and the just war ethic is that decisions were made not only on the basis of inadequate information but also on what may very well have been an intentional distortion of facts, which then misled policy makers. If practical reason is going to guide decision making and the moral imagination is going to conceive of a moral community where presumptions are applicable to all persons, a healthy respect for garnering relevant facts is essential if the natural law ethic we have been discussing is going to work in particular situations. Moral presumptions and justice criteria must ultimately be applied to actual situations and cases. The most accurate descriptions of the cases—the empirical facts and their honest presentation followed by candid deliberation about the moral meaning of those facts in light of the presumption and the criteria—are necessary in this ethical approach. This ethic may seem to be a form of casuistry, but it is not. Casuistry derives principles from examples, but the action guides of this natural law ethic are derived in the first place from practical reason, the goods of life, and the requirements of the moral point of view—it is thus not in any formal sense a casuistic ethic.

So the answer to this question about where the presumptions and criteria come from may be answered like this: they are derived from practical reason's effort to discern and structure moral concerns that all reasonable persons of goodwill could be expected to avow. They are derived from the effort of persons of goodwill to conceive of a universal moral community though an exercise of moral imagination. Finally, they will be universally valid at the level of theory as well as useful at the level of experience. For the presumption and criteria are to be brought to bear and applied to particular situations where decision making is required because some problem has presented itself to practical reason. That problem, whatever it is, will require an honest and thorough presentation of relevant empirical data relevant to the particular circumstance.

THE HYBRID ETHIC

Question 4: *What are the components of the hybrid ethic, and why has so little attention been given to the role of virtue?*

We have presented our natural law–based ethic as a hybrid ethic inclusive of principles, duties, consequences, and virtues. Often these terms are deemed in moral philosophy to be mutually exclusive: the Kantian duty-based ethic is defined around intentions rather than consequences; utilitarianism is concerned with consequences and thus with outcomes rather than intentions—and never the two shall meet; and both of these action-based ethics are contrasted with virtue ethics, which is concerned about character rather than decision making—the person of virtue will act virtuously, so the moral problem is not with action but with being—and becoming—a person of virtue.

We have seen that Cicero, a natural law moral theorist and the real originator in the West of what developed into just war theory, paid attention to all of these moral considerations, and our argument here is that we should too. Why? Because we live as ethical persons out of all three of these concerns—duties, consequences, and virtues: they are integral to our moral experience. What is then needed is thought—a moral theory or an "ethic"—that captures these different aspects of our moral commitments and our actual life together in the moral community. We do not live as pure utilitarians never concerned with the moral worthiness of the action we are performing; we do not follow ethical rules so strictly that we could be said to hold them absolutely, as if there were never a case for an exception; and we acquire habits of character but still stop to consider what to do in particular situations.

The problem is that some of the standard accounts of the ethical philosophies we have at our disposal seek to encapsulate practical reason itself, to make practical reason a slave to a theory rather than seeing practical reason as the source for thinking about action and character. The great contribution of Cicero in this regard is that he put practical reason first—natural law is the law of reason itself—and never invested a principled duty with absoluteness, or a consequence with relativism; neither did he exempt character from considerations of action or divorce action from character. This is unlike the ethical theories we have inherited from the Enlightenment, which transform ethical thinking into "uppercase" theories that reign without any possibility of other partners contributing to moral governance. The Ciceronian move is far more humble, for it puts practical reason, rather than a theory, on the throne. Moral governance, if we may use such a metaphor, is shared; the ethical theory that results is hybrid.

In the ethic advanced here, our common moral agreements embody principles, which it is our duty to subscribe to and enact behaviorally. We have required that this ethic conform to the moral point of view. This was not a redundant move if we recall that the term *ethic* in a general sense can describe a set of rules governing a community, which need not be the moral community—criminal organizations, we noted, can have rules, an ethic. The moral point of view, as we put this forward, includes commitment to a set of normative principles; and we find in the very idea of a moral presumption or common agreement a stress on principles governing behavior and moral ideals expressing reason's recognition of, and desire to realize, the goods of life. In the case of just war, we identified a principle concerning the use of force—that reason bids force not be used to settle conflicts. That principle is abiding and is not to be offended except for reasons related to extraordinary circumstances, and even then it must be controlled and conformed to principles of justice—the criteria. We find principles appealed to in the criteria we devise. For instance, last resort operates as an action guide—a principle—in just war thinking, the idea being that we ought not to use force except as a last resort. The last resort criterion functions as a principle to restrain the decision to use force in the first instance, and it commends itself to us in the "oughts" and "shoulds" of principles language.

Consequences deserve attention when applying this ethic. Again, keeping focused on just war because of its familiarity, the criterion that directs attention to "reasonable hope of success" asks us to look ahead to the result and avoid uses of force where force will not result in resolution of the conflict. Peter Singer makes use of such a criterion in his discussion of humanitarian interventions.[5] If an intervention to bring about the result of a greater aggregate good cannot be organized, Singer holds, it is best not to pursue such an intervention even in the face of terrible human rights abuses. The just war ethic will include such attention to foreseeable consequences and demand that "reasonable hope of success" be satisfied before permitting a use of force. Whenever people use this common agreement ethic they will inevitably pay attention to consequences. We shall see in the pages ahead that medical staff attending a severely disabled newborn, faced with a concern for pain and distress and a hopeless prognosis, made a difficult decision to discontinue treatment. Consequences will be very much at issue as well when we consider the possibility that physician-assisted suicide will lead to exploitation of the disabled, or that an economic boycott will cause hardship for innocent civilians. We have already noted how even nonviolence has effects that cannot be confined solely to one's antagonists in a protest against injustice. Consequences will play a role alongside duty-binding principles.

And the question of virtue is important as well. It may be that the question of virtue is the most important ethical element in this natural law–based ethic, but it is clear that it is the most offstage ethical consideration. The reason I say this is that the common agreement ethic is a tool or resource that human beings use to make decisions about what to do and how to act, the interest being to advance goodness and promote human flourishing. When applied to a particular issue, such as "just war," "just punishment," or "just physician-assisted suicide," the ethic requires that persons of character work with the empirical data and the ethical resource, do so honestly and with integrity, and not mishandle the particulars of the ethic (i.e., the criteria) for nonmoral or purely self-serving or self-interested ends. What does this mean? We have suggested that because the ethic is a structure to be applied to a variety of situations with the possibility of many kinds of results, those who come together to deliberate the questions posed for the ethic, say, the question of war and peace or physician-assisted suicide, must attend to the binding force of the common agreement, reassert commitment to the governing moral presumption, and then examine the facts of a case—the political and military situation, for example, or the medical situation—and discuss what is known and not known with honesty and integrity. The great weakness of this ethical theory is exactly the weakness we have seen in many contemporary appeals to just war thinking, namely, that persons can distort facts, perhaps even lie, in the effort to conform the theory to a tendentious presentation of a factual situation. What persons of honor and integrity should be seeking are ways to avoid using force and to resolve conflict without force; and if the theory is used correctly, that is how they will proceed in the work of ethical analysis. They will proceed showing due respect to the power of the moral presumption that is in general opposed to using force to settle conflicts.

This theory invites people into the public sphere to debate the great moral issues of our day—abortion, capital punishment, war and peace, medical ethics issues, and so on. It then relies on those who have relevant information to be honest and open with what they know and what they do not know. Deliberation needs to proceed the same way, with honest questions being asked, with deliberation being respectful of other interpretive points of view, and with an understanding that basic moral agreements do bind reasonable people together. Deliberating moral problems should involve persons habituated to honesty and to treating others with respect, and the points of agreement—the common agreements—should be clearly articulated: that all of us as reasonable persons of goodwill, as persons of virtuous character, want to settle conflict peacefully, for instance, or do not ordinarily want physicians to assist patients who might want to kill themselves. The starting point must be clear even if, in the face of moral quandaries, actions may be taken in the interests of justice that constitute an exception to the moral presumption. For the theory to work in an optimal way, however, those who employ it need to be committed to those things we associate with virtue—especially honesty, integrity, cooperativeness, reasonableness, civility, courage, fairness, moderation, justice, conscientiousness, compassion, and a benevolent concern for the well-being of others and of the community. These virtues need to be exercised in a moral community with others likewise committed to seeking justice through wise action, with people offering their own points of view courageously while also listening and evaluating the meaning of information they did not have, showing a willingness to change their minds in the light of new evidence or new morally relevant realities.

We live in a time when it is common to criticize almost unmercifully public figures who take positions on issues and then change them as if an inflexible ideological stance were the hallmark of virtue. The ability to change positions, however, in light of new and more complete information or even better arguments, is the mark of reasonableness and even wisdom. The inability to change, the rigidity of ideological posturing, is, on the contrary, the mark of closed-mindedness, perhaps even cowardice if one refuses to change one's position for fear of criticism when doing so is defensible and justifiable.

Our natural law, common agreement hybrid ethic includes principles and duties, attention to consequences, and reliance on the character of reasonable people of goodwill to forge the ethic into the instrument of democratic public deliberation on difficult and important questions of moral meaning.

OTHER EXAMPLES

Question 5: *What are some other kinds of everyday ethical problems people face where this ethic is actually used? And do people really use it?*

The serious issue posed by this question is whether the common agreement ethic advocated here reconciles thought and experience in ways that people can both acknowledge and actually use. The Oregon Death with Dignity Act will be examined in order to show that legislators working on a difficult political and moral issue and wanting to ensure moral restraint implicitly invoked this very kind of moral resource, as do physicians and nursing staff contemplating withdrawing treatment from certain severely disabled newborns. Gandhi and King reflected on the legitimate use of nonviolence as a use of force—that is in the record even if their attention to justice concerns relevant to using the force of nonviolence was not explicitly attached to a just war ethic. And we shall attend in the pages ahead to the fact that the United States Supreme Court has invoked the spirit of this ethic when deliberating execution exceptions. So even if executions have been affirmed in law as morally warranted and persist as the will of the people for certain offenses, banning the execution of the intellectually disabled can be demonstrated through practical reason to be a needed exception. All of these examples provide evidence that people actually do employ this ethic in the effort to determine the good, right, and fitting thing to do. People do actually use it.

But what about other kinds of relevant issues? Because we have already in previous pages discussed moral issues related to lying and deception, let us consider them once again as we inquire into the adequacy of the ethic we are advancing. We may begin by noting that a common agreement exists that deception and lying are subversive of the moral life and ordinarily ought not to be employed—the language of "lie" and "deception" carries a linguistic moral valence of negative judgment. It is wrong to tell a lie. The reasons for this are many, beginning with the fact that lying and deception do not appear to conform to the moral point of view—acts of lying cannot be universalized; they are not usually interpreted as benevolent; they are not constitutive of acts of justice; and normative principles would actually hold up lying as a wrongful act. Acts of deception and lying do not advance goodness but actually cause harm to those lied to—to the liar, and even to society given the fact that "lying and deception undermine trust and thus undermine the possibility of cooperative behavior."[6] To deceive a person, to mislead another's belief, is to treat persons as if they were not worthy of being told the truth, which is to say, to treat them disrespectfully. Persons of virtue, who cultivate the habit of honesty and truth telling in communications, do not lie or condone lying, and even utilitarians, who do not judge lying to be an inherently wrongful act, cannot ordinarily justify a lie or deception because of the deleterious consequences that follow in the wake of such behavior, such as subverting society's respect for truth. So we can affirm lying and deception as prima facie wrongs and acknowledge a moral presumption against lying and deception. Doing so is not controversial.

On the other hand, the moral presumption against lying and deception is not an absolute prohibition. People who lie will often claim that they had good reason to do so, and we can think of lots of examples of deceptions that we give approval to, even consent to, sometimes mutually, as when attending the theater in hopes that the actors will prove convincing in making us believe something that is not the case. The ability of the artist to deceive—to mislead belief—is the mark of his or her artistry as an actor. But the more interesting moral issue has to do with the thought-reconciled-to-experience issue we have referred to so often, and we will focus attention on lying—the deceptive act whereby people utter direct statements intending to mislead the belief of others by giving information they believe to be untrue. We noted earlier in these pages that lying is a rather common behavior that traditional moral theories simply fail to prevent, despite the fact that such ethics luminaries as Augustine and Kant argued that lying was absolutely wrong, with Aquinas holding out that "jocose lies," lies told in fun, and "officious lies," helpful lies, were pardonable.[7] People actually do lie, and this is an empirically verifiable fact; and they do so rather often, given some of the sociological evidence we cited earlier.[8] If that is the case, then we need to inquire into why people are making the decision to lie and how they are justifying their decisions. Are people in some way appealing to an implicit theory of "justified deception" or "justified lying," meaning that they encounter situations in life where deception and lying are morally preferable to truth telling?

Any attempt to justify a lie would have to acknowledge in the first instance a common agreement that lying is ordinarily wrong. Lying subverts our efforts to realize the goods of life, and it negatively affects the goods that pertain to personal and social relations, such as friendship, practical reasonableness, and the development of a personal identity that reflects character and the cohesiveness of personal integrity.

So in order to create an exception to this presumption against lying, several conditions would have to be met.

The first condition would have to attend to reasons for the lie, a "just cause" notion. We can imagine lying for a grave cause, such as to save a life. One might lie with just cause to a person about to commit murder in order to save an innocent victim, or to save someone, oneself included, from death or serious harm, if in fact a lie would accomplish this feat. Certain threatening situations, especially crisis situations, might so affect one's ability to deliberate on alternatives that the reach for a lie will seem warranted or excusable. There can be situations of oppression and injustice where telling a lie may be necessary for survival. Death camp survivor Victor Frankl tells how he planned to participate in an escape from Auschwitz, but when a fellow prisoner confronted him, he lied and denied it, for "everything that was not connected with the immediate task of keeping oneself and one's closest friends alive lost its value."[9] In such a situation, even truth telling could lose its value, although Frankl relates that he later went back and told the man the truth and then decided to abandon his escape plan and remain behind with him. Lying to protect innocent persons from harm or injustice would appear in a general way to meet the just cause criterion.

A second criterion would focus on intentionality. A justified lie would entail no intention to harm another person.[10] In fact, the intention of a justifiable lie would be to shield another from harm and even to benefit another. This in fact defines "white lies," which are lies involving morally trivial matters told with no intention of harming anyone. White lies are told to spare feelings, and they are usually expressions of opinions we hold rather than an appeal to some objective reality or publicly observable fact we would be distorting. "Do I like your new haircut?—Sure." "The dessert was just fine." If I say the eggplant was good when I happen to hate eggplant, that would constitute a "white lie" to the host who has presented this for my dining pleasure, but it is possible others not so picayune about eggplant really do like it. Lies always pertain to some matter we believe to be true but that may not be the objective truth—one can lie by actually imparting accurate information, believing it to be false. We resort to "white lies" in social situations, and our motivation is to extend courtesy, observe social proprieties, and protect persons from criticism and hurt. The fact that we have devised a distinctive linguistically hued descriptor—the white lie—indicates that we recognize a certain kind of qualification on lying that is more akin to a social grace or matter of etiquette than a term of moral opprobrium. Not that a white lie is without consequence, since the eggplant really could be bad, and my approval could mislead the cook into making sure it is offered more regularly; and my willingness to tell white lies could affect how much others actually trust my opinion if I cannot be depended on to offer an honest response but opt to say what is pleasing to my listener. Obsequious persons live on a regular diet of white lies.

A justified lie ought not to have as its purpose malice or the intentional infliction of harm. On the intention criterion, a lie aims at a morally positive purpose—from the morally grave case of saving a life to the morally trivial situation of sparing the cook's feelings. It is invoked because of sensitivities to situations and springs from a desire not to cause unnecessary pain or distress; and if it is true that people tell numerous lies every day, these are undoubtedly the kinds of lies that are involved.

A third criterion is akin to "last resort" in just war. Before any lie could be justified, the case would have to be made that in seeking to realize some good end, all reasonable alternatives to lying have been exhausted. People facing constant crisis situations or living under continual threats to their freedom or survival can appeal to "last resort" lying since at stake may be the good of life itself.

A fourth criterion involves prospective public viewing of the justification. When a lie is in effect, one does not know one is being lied to. The justification for the lie is hidden from public view, and as such it is not subject to the kinds of public deliberation we have been insisting on for other examples of justified exceptions to moral presumptions—just war, just uses of force, just nontreatment of severely disabled neonates. One advantage of the common agreement ethic is that it insists on public deliberation of specific situations since the ethic itself offers only general moral guidelines that do not involve particulars. But when a lie is operational, there is no public access to the particulars available—they are hidden—and deliberation about justification cannot take place. This is a point made by Sissela Bok drawing on concerns articulated by John Rawls. "*Publicity*," Rawls, wrote, is "a formal constraint on any moral principle worth considering."[11] Bok combines the concern for publicity with an appeal to what reasonable persons of goodwill must consider to establish justification for a lie. "The test of publicity asks which lies, if any, would survive the appeal for justification to reasonable persons." Appealing to the Golden Rule, she goes on to say, "We must share the perspective of those affected by our choices, and ask how we would react if the lies we are contemplating were told to us."[12]

Bok thus frames her investigation of the morality of lying in the moral point of view—especially the universalizability concept—and submits the lie to public scrutiny. Public scrutiny would include subjecting a lie to conscience, and, according to Bok, it must then be reviewed by imagined others, then by chosen peers with whom one would consult in matters of critical importance. But because bias cannot be eliminated from one's own justification or that of persons one would select to consult with about a lie, Bok goes on to suggest a third level of justification: "Persons of all allegiances must be consulted, or at least not excluded or bypassed," thus ruling out the "hand-picking of those who should be consulted."[13] Examples of the latter might include societal consultation and discussion of matters such as medical experimentation where deception is required, the use or limits of use of deception by governments, or even public discussions of practices in crime-detection entrapment schemes.

The question is whether such lies can achieve justification, to wit, would reasonable people of goodwill agree to allow a lie in a particular situation? Would they allow the prohibition on lying to be overridden in a conflict among the goods of life, say, that of preserving the good of life itself? On the common agreement ethic advanced here, certain lies might be able to rise to the level of a justified exception to our moral agreement that ordinarily, lies ought not to be told, and an appeal would be made to the moral community—to all reasonable people of goodwill—to subject the secretiveness that covers a lie to review through the test of universalizability. This would be a way to create a surrogate test of publicity, transforming the lie and its hidden motives into a publicly reviewable speech act that can be analyzed and evaluated in terms of moral meaning.

So a formalized presentation of a justified lie might look like the following. On the moral presumption that lies ordinarily ought not to be told, a lie could be justified if it met these five criteria of moral justification:

- Just cause: The lie is motivated by a conflict in the goods of life, so that morally weighty reasons derived from the details of a particular circumstance and sufficient to overrule a commitment to truth telling must be established.
- The lie must not intend to harm others.
- The lie must intend some benefit to others.
- The lie must be a last resort—all other alternatives to telling a lie must have been considered and exhausted.
- The lie must be assessed within the context of universalizability since the motives and action of the lie will be hidden and interfere with a public moral analysis of the act of lying. The lie must be subjected to review by reasonable persons of goodwill—the moral community—not just individual conscience or selected evaluators, to determine whether telling a lie in the particular situation would receive moral sanction. With bias and self-deception always a risk, the test of universalizability provides access to the moral requirement of publicity.

Sissela Bok writes, "It has been argued that although lying might be justifiable on such rare occasions, most of us will, in fact, never encounter a situation where a lie might be excusable. We should proceed in life, therefore, as if no lies should ever be told."[14] This statement is a clear articulation of a moral presumption—an appeal to our common agreements that we ordinarily ought not to tell lies. The discussion Bok offers about possible exceptions conforms this presentation of the morality of lying with our ethical theory.

The lack of publicity integral to the act of lying makes the idea of a "just lie" particularly difficult to frame morally, but we can see that if we take a nonabsolutist approach to lying, our common agreement approach does allow us to reconcile thinking about lying with the experience that people lie and actually justify lying. Some lies may perhaps require a different kind of framing, such as lying as part of social etiquette, because the cause is morally trivial ("white lies"); many more serious lies may not, and in all likelihood will not, meet the criteria for justification. The adequacy of these criteria is subject to review, just as the criteria of just war have undergone evolution through revision and reconsideration over the centuries. I note as a matter of interest that Mark Twain in his delightful essay "On the Decay of the Art of Lying" actually appeals—implicitly of course—to precisely the kind of common agreement ethic we have argued for here when he writes:

> Lying is universal—we *all* do it. Therefore the wise thing for us is diligently to train ourselves to lie thoughtfully, judiciously; to lie with a good object, and not an evil one; to lie for others' advantage, and not for our own; to lie healingly, charitably, humanely and not cruelly, hurtfully, maliciously; to lie gracefully and graciously; not awkwardly and clumsily; to lie firmly, frankly, squarely, with head erect, not haltingly, tortuously, with pusillanimous mien, as being ashamed of our high calling. . . . Joking aside, I think there is much in need of wise examination into what sorts of lies are best and wholesomest, seeing we *must* all lie and we all *do* lie, and what sorts it may be best to avoid.[15]

Analyses of other moral issues would proceed on the tack just followed. If we were to consider an example of justified promise breaking, a justified instance of cheating, justification for the act of withholding or withdrawing medical treatment or determining death so that we could act to withdraw treatment, or justifying certain business practices in a corporate community governed by the morally presumptive values where business is approached not enthralled by attention to "the bottom line" but as "an essential part of the good life, living well, getting along with others, having a sense of self-respect, and being a part of something one can be proud of,"[16] the approach would be twofold. First, we should determine the common moral agreements that underwrite the activity in question and the problem being faced, and then, second, consider what, if any, exceptions might arise. I say "if any" because some of the situations might be such that by applying a certain moral language to the problem—such as "murder," the clearest example—we exclude the possibility of an exception by imposing a moral performative that establishes a wrongness by definition.

"Cheating" may be such a performative term, but if in fact a culture of "cheating" has arisen on college campuses today, how is it justified in the minds of those who do it? To establish that someone has "cheated" is to draw a moral conclusion about some action related to, say, performance assessment: it makes a moral difference if what one is doing is acting to serve one's own interests regardless of who else might be harmed or unjustly put at disadvantage by an act of unfair self-aggrandizement, which is the moral issue at stake when we impose the conclusion, "So-and-so is a cheater." It is another thing to create room for people to work "collaboratively," which is a mode of learning and teaching but which can also be considered cheating. The point is that our common agreement ethics approach will want to inquire into moral meaning by considering relevant moral presumptions and looking at the way thought and experience connect. The language of cheating imposes a moral conclusion about an unjustifiable behavior—that is not in dispute. We have to be clear, however, about which moral agreements are applicable to the problem we are facing. For on the cheating issue, we should consider raising the question of whether we have created a new learning culture with information technologies that have transformed older traditional ideas of both learning and cheating—and perhaps the issue is that our assessment procedures have not adequately adapted to the changes.

Perhaps it would be wise to withhold the imposition of the moral performative at least until we rethink whether there is need to restructure the learning experience—and assessment procedures—in ways that would allow learners in a new technological environment to flourish and pursue excellence in a community dedicated to the advancement of learning through socially responsible behavior. If cultures of cheating are in place on college campuses today, that experience needs to be connected to thought in such a way that the moral meaning of that behavior is clarified. Imposing the language of "cheating" draws a moral conclusion. No doubt this conclusion is warranted in individual situations where learning contracts (syllabi) have been agreed upon, then violated. But if a cheating culture has grown up in which we selectively address individual situations but do not investigate how and why these cheating behaviors have become integrated more broadly into learning and assessment practices, we overlook important questions of moral meaning in the culture. Those important questions would pertain to how students learn, how they deal with preparing materials for assessment, and how those responsible for assessment should be devising appropriate ways of addressing the question of learning. Employing a morally judgmental language can short-circuit moral reflection and stultify an important moral inquiry, and the experience we have with widespread student cheating may be urging us to reconsider how teachers teach and learners learn—and what should be done to make that happen in ways that preserve a morally worthy commitment to "socially responsible behavior."

All kinds of issues are prompted when we approach ethical problems through the common agreement ethic, which necessarily prevents moral absolutism—or relativism—to govern our moral thinking. We have suggested how this natural law–based ethic might assist us in thinking through specific ethical problems, but the significant point is this: if there is an ethic *behind* just war and it is to function as an ethic, it must apply *beyond* just war as well. *Any* moral issue should be subject to this mode of analysis. By giving attention to our common agreements, to criteria of justice devised by practical reason to help us confront moral complexity, and to the limits of our moral language, we find ourselves equipped with an ethical resource that reconciles thought and experience. That common agreement ethic is sensitive to moral realities yet principled and conformed to the moral point of view.

REINVENTING THE WHEEL? UTILITARIANISM AND PRIMA FACIE ETHICS AND HOW THE NATURAL LAW–BASED ETHIC DIFFERS

Question 6: *How is this ethic not simply a more complicated form of rule utilitarianism, and wouldn't it be easier just to use that, since that theory provides some guiding principles in its reliance on rules while attending to consequences as those moral rules are devised? Reinventing the wheel? We might ask the same about an ethic of prima facie duties.*

It might appear that our just war–related ethic is a complicated way of asserting an already established ethic of accepted standing in the literature on ethical theory: rule utilitarianism. Rule utilitarianism, which was first articulated by J. O. Urmson and then given enormous heft by Richard Brandt,[17] asserts the following: *that act is the good, right, and fitting thing to do that conforms to a rule that, if generally followed, produces the greatest aggregate good for the greatest number, everyone considered.* This is a consequentialist ethic that determines that an individual action is morally right if it conforms to rules or to a moral code grounded in the basic utilitarian orientation—the greatest good for the greatest number. Although a critique of the hybrid common agreement ethic in light of rule utilitarianism is not without some point, we must reassert that the common agreement, while it attends to consequentialist features, also provokes the nonconsequentialist, "lowercase" moral realities of duties and principles and a reliance on virtues. The common agreement ethic, then, does not conform to rule utilitarianism; neither can it be collapsed into it. In fact, this common agreement ethic is critical of utilitarianism, and we have noted some of those criticisms. We might here note one more. "The greatest good for the greatest number" is an abstraction that threatens to overrule the individual and the very idea of individual rights against the minority. This deficiency in utilitarian thinking has led ethicist Daniel Maguire to note, "Utilitarianism contains, among other things, the ingredients of totalitarianism."[18]

The natural law ethic we have been advancing may appear to be doing exactly the same practical work as rule utilitarianism because the action guides of the common agreement ethic look similar to the rules so central to this form of consequentialist thinking. Furthermore, the qualifications in the definition of rule utilitarianism—"if generally followed" and "everyone considered"—allow that exceptions are possible within any particular rule itself, so that a rule on the use of force might look like this: "do not use force to settle conflicts except where self-defense and protection of innocent persons are at issue." So a rule utilitarian could devise a rule with an embedded exception (so could a deontologist) rather than work up a list of criteria to be used in generating an exception to a common agreement. In rule utilitarianism, following rules based on consequentialist calculations of good over evil, benefit over harm, or maximum utility over disutility appears to perform the same task as our natural law–based ethic. The ethic of common agreement appears, then, as a complicated and redundant way of generating moral meaning compared to simply establishing rules grounded in a utilitarian calculus.

Rule utilitarianism is distinguished from act utilitarianism, which holds that moral meaning is determined by acting in a way that produces the greatest aggregate good, everyone considered. My first point would be to assert that because both forms of utilitarianism are *utilitarian*, the foundations for rule utilitarianism are, in fact, individual acts—the rules are created on the basis of calculating utility. In individual acts of telling lies or using force to settle conflicts, negative consequences accrue so that one can devise a rule that we should not tell lies or use force to settle conflicts, thereby avoiding the burden—and it would be a real burden—of carrying out a calculation on every intentional action we undertook. I agree with W. L. Reese: "Utilitarians, generally, seem to have had in mind individual actions; but since rules grow from acts, there is no clear line separating Act from Rule Utilitarianism."[19]

The common agreement ethic does not approach moral issues on the basis of a calculation of some principle of utility, which could be many different things, in particular, pleasure (Bentham), happiness (J. S. Mill), or even love, as Joseph Fletcher argued in his theological reformulation of utility in *Situation Ethics*. Our common agreements consist of an articulation of common values to which reasonable persons of goodwill can freely give their assent. The ethic depends on our ability to employ reason to discern and pursue the goods of life and to act in conformity with an ethical system that is itself conformed to the moral point of view. Moral presumptions, via the content of the moral point of view to which our common agreements are conformed—universalizability, benevolence, impartial justice, and a set of normative principles—create room for us to attend to human rights and the obligations of justice. A utilitarian, however, because no act is intrinsically right or wrong, could not simply condemn slavery as intrinsically wrong if, in fact, the calculation of utility concluded that enslaving a minority would actually maximize the overall happiness for the greater number. An approach to ethical meaning through common moral agreements does not use such a procedure of moral reflection nor yield such a result. Slavery, on the ethic of common agreement, violates our idea that individual persons have rights, among other things, and the accusation that utilitarianism inevitably reduces to an ethic in which "the ends justify the means" ill accords with our experience of the moral life. In our moral experience, we know that unjust means often lead to all kinds of further unanticipated injustices, which is why the idea that "do not do evil that good may come" has wide acceptance as a moral principle.

Furthermore, utilitarianism—this criticism is leveled at act utilitarians—does not respect certain relationships based on trust—parents and children or physicians and patients. W. D. Ross writes that "the essential defect of the 'ideal utilitarian' theory is that it ignores, or at least does not do full justice to, the highly personal character of duty."[20] Utilitarianism could perhaps justify widespread physician paternalism with patients facing terminal conditions on the grounds that lying to them about their conditions and making decisions about their treatment without patient consultation might yield a better overall result, but this would violate our need for relationships with physicians to be based on trust.

Justice, however, is the critical problem for utilitarianism, especially in how it is to be distributed. Daniel Maguire makes this point:

> As Rawls says, "The striking feature of the utilitarian view of justice is that it does not matter, except indirectly, how this sum of satisfactions is distributed among individuals." That's the scary nub of it. It opens the door to exploitation, while stressing, with seeming generosity, the good of the nation, or the good of the corporation or the good of the university or the church or the mosque or the goals of the movement. Beware those who are committed to the greatest sum of goodness (in business it is called the bottom line) until you test their commitment to persons. When the greatest good is defined by an elite—and it usually is in church or state, in politics and in economics—the non-elite on the wayside are the losers.[21]

The natural law hybrid ethic we have advanced in these pages does attend to consequences, but it does not make consequences the determinative factor for establishing moral meaning—duties, principles, and virtues are necessary components of moral thought and experience. Our common agreements arise from practical reason discerning those things that are good for each individual because they are good for all. It is an ethic that avoids abstractions and accepts presumptive generalities about moral commitments and values important to human fulfillment. It is a hybrid ethic. We pursue the various goods of life because we are endowed with reason, and the goods are to be realized by all, not just those who end up on the winning side of a calculation of benefit.

One other ethical alternative is worthy of mention, since it more closely resembles our ethic of common agreement. The English philosopher W. D. Ross put forward in *The Right and the Good* a duty-based deontological theory that sought to recognize what Kant did not or could not account for—conflicts in duties. Ross proposed an ethic derived from nonabsolutist, prima facie or conditional duties. His argument was that if a conflict arose between two duties, the duty that most closely attended to the particularities of a circumstance would take precedence. One duty could override the other because the duties were prima facie duties—conditional duties that hold until such time as a particular circumstance requires another duty to supersede it. A prima facie duty holds until such time as a circumstance arises that relieves that duty of its applicability, replacing it with one more stringently applicable. Ross proposed an ethic that identified a variety of duties:

- duties of fidelity (truth telling, promise keeping);
- duty of reparation;
- duty of gratitude;
- duties of beneficence;
- a duty of nonmaleficence;
- duties of self-improvement;
- and duties of justice.

These duties cover much the same ground as the common agreement ethic. Moral presumptions, as we know, govern action but do not do so absolutely. They hold, but exceptions can be made, which apes in significant ways the idea of a prima facie duty. The various duties Ross describes parallel matters we have identified with the moral point of view: duties of self-improvement, for instance, correspond to virtues and the role virtue plays in the hybrid ethic. Duties of reparation and gratitude appeal to a reciprocity that itself reflects universalizability—what I owe I am obligated to repay, what I have received in benefit from another I am obligated to return in kind as benefit to others. The duties of beneficence and nonmaleficence both attend to the other-regardingness whereby persons take others into account and concern themselves with the welfare of others. The duty of justice is concerned with distributing happiness in accordance with personal merit.[22]

This approach to ethics through prima facie duties does seem closest to what we have called for—a nonabsolutist ethic that establishes obligations around common moral agreements, which for Ross are expressed though duties. Ross was concerned as well with conforming thought with moral experiences, since he explicitly sought an ethic relevant to what he called "ordinary moral consciousness." The problem with Ross's ethic is that prima facie duties do not provide a way to actually settle a conflict between duties. Our common agreement ethics does. Although it frames ethical conflict as involving goods of life rather than duties—goods of life could be thought of as duties in the sense that practical reason obliges us to realize them—the common agreement ethic provides in the "criteria" justice considerations that guide the process of deliberation toward making or not making an exception, allowing one good to override another in a particular circumstance, one duty over another. The articulation of a common moral agreement along with the justice-related criteria relevant to a possible exception does guide us toward practical decisions; and what we find in those moral considerations is the foundation for an overall system of moral meaning—an ethic—made possible by our common agreements.

The common agreement ethic clarifies and then allows the relevant moral issues that arise in a conflict to be addressed in decision making. Prima facie duties come close to doing this, but they lack the procedural guidance to help decision making. The criteria that emerge from the work of practical reason in the common agreement ethic establish the guidelines for resolving moral problems, even dilemmas, so that in the end a decision can be made as to which duty takes precedence, which good of life in a conflict of goods over-rules another.

THE QUESTION OF ABORTION

Question 7: No social-ethical issue is more pressing in contemporary American society than abortion, which leads to a final issue: *Could you argue that there is such a thing as a "just abortion" if some people base their ethical position on religious teaching and the religious teaching forbids abortion? The Roman Catholic Church is the great transmitter of natural law ethics in Western culture, yet it would not approach the killing in abortion as equivalent to the killing in war—there is, in that natural law tradition, no "just abortion." Doesn't the failure of the common agreement ethic on such a momentous and culturally controversial issue show that this ethic is irrelevant and has no contribution to make?*

The first thing to say is that there are several great social justice issues where life and death may be at stake, and for the remainder of this book we shall examine how this ethic applies to them. The particular question about the possibility of a "just abortion" theory is a good one, and fortunately, the work of articulating such a theory has already been done. There is no need to repeat that analysis here, except to note that the result of that construction of a common agreement ethic on the question of abortion does yield a nonabsolutist position that supports the basic, morally moderate position that some abortions are justifiable and some are not.[23] The critical moral question is to determine which are which.

The just abortion theory provides a common agreement ethical approach for guiding decision making in those problematic pregnancies where abortion is under consideration. But another problem involved in the abortion question, one often overlooked, is the moral meaning of innocence. Just war thinking preserves through the criterion of noncombatant immunity the principle that innocent persons—civilians in the case of war—must be protected and not harmed. At the center of the abortion issue is what many will often describe as "the innocent fetus." In fact, defending the fetus as "innocent" is a primary reason often given for opposing even the possibility of abortion. What does "innocence" mean? How does the "innocent persons need to be protected" feature of just war thinking, that aspect of a common agreement ethic, figure into our discussion about abortion? How does a common agreement ethic concern for protection of the innocent affect our thinking about violence, war, and military conflicts? We shall, in the final two chapters, take up the question of innocence as a problem raised by the common agreement ethic for moral analysis and thereby gain access to how this common agreement ethic can be applied to very contentious issues.

Before getting to the issue of innocence however, we shall turn to a few provocative ethics issues to consider how the common agreement ethic illuminates moral meaning and helps guide practical reason to solutions and decision making. We shall examine the issue of physician assistance in dying, the nontreatment of severely disabled neonates, and capital punishment and criminal justice. And in that examination we shall have the opportunity to consider how this mode of ethical thinking and analysis has actually been used, how thought and experience have been reconciled as people have worked to fashion moral understanding and promote goodness amid very real value conflicts. These examples are meant to illustrate how this ethic can be put to work and actually applies to specific issues. We move forward on the understanding that if the common agreement ethic is truly an *ethic*, an ethic *beyond* just war, we must acknowledge that this method of moral analysis should be applicable to these particular moral issues and to *any* moral issue.

Part II

EXPERIENCE

The Ethic beyond Just War

Chapter Five

The Ethics of Physician-Assisted Suicide

We have argued that an actual ethic lies behind just war thinking. We observed that in public discussions of just war ideas, exclusive focus on just war criteria has obscured that ethic, but the ethic can be extracted and put to work in constructive, prescriptive, and critical ways to assess moral meaning and guide action. We then illustrated how this ethic would work on the moral question at the heart of the just war tradition—the use of force. And to highlight how the ethic functions, we opted not to use a historical military example of war as our example of a use of force, but nonviolent resistance, which its most prominent twentieth-century advocates, Mohandas Gandhi and Martin Luther King Jr., both understood quite explicitly to be a use of force. We showed how both leaders observed our common moral agreement that force ordinarily ought not to be used to settle conflicts, but also how in the face of great injustice, both appealed implicitly to the ethic *behind* just war thinking to proceed to restrained but forceful action.

If an ethic lies behind just war thinking and it is truly an ethic, that is, if it focuses not on a particular issue but on a general system of principles or action guides that are themselves conformed to the moral point of view, then this ethic must have applicability beyond the particular issue of war or the use of force. The ethic at issue here is a hybrid ethic that takes into consideration duty, consequences, and virtue. It is extractable by a twofold consideration: first, the articulation of our common moral agreements as those are derived through the resources of natural law thinking and conformed to the moral point of view, and second, the identification of reasonable justice-related criteria that allow for the possibility of an exception to the common moral agreement when applied to particular situations of otherwise uncorrected injustices. We began by considering the ethic *behind* just war thinking. Our next move is to show how this common agreement ethic can be applied *beyond* just war thinking. Having begun this effort by examining the issue of using force to settle conflicts, we then examined how this ethic can be applied to so common a moral problem as lying. We now turn to some big life-and-death issues to show the practical applicability of this hybrid ethic as it functions to reconcile ethical thinking with our moral experience. The next several chapters will demonstrate how the hybrid ethic we have argued for, including the formal framework of this ethic as we know it best from just war thinking, can be used to approach ethical deliberation on a variety of troubling and difficult moral problems.

In this chapter and the next, the focus will be on medical ethics issues, first with physician-assisted suicide or physician assistance in dying, and next by a discussion of medical nontreatment of severely disabled newborns.

INTRODUCTION: BEYOND KEVORKIAN

The controversial issue of physicians directly helping patients die came to heightened public awareness due to Dr. Jack Kevorkian. Kevorkian had argued that medical intervention to terminate the lives of people suffering painful end-stage medical conditions was a patient's moral and legal right, and that providing such aid was not a crime[1] and certainly not a moral violation. Justifying his work by an appeal to the medical ethics principle of beneficence, he performed lethal injections on more than 130 willing individuals. Kevorkian unrepentantly pushed for the right of persons to receive relief from suffering, including the right to receive aid in dying, but his efforts came to a dramatic public halt when the state of Michigan arrested him and pressed homicide charges against him. In 1999 he was convicted of second-degree murder and sent to prison. Good behavior and poor health led to his parole in 2007.

Kevorkian brought attention to end-of-life medical and moral issues in a dramatic way, and despite his imprisonment, he sparked a debate that has led to a legalization of physician assistance in dying in the states of Oregon and Washington. Montana legalized physician assistance in January 2010, although as of this writing, implementation has not been worked out. In 2006, the United States Supreme Court upheld the Oregon law in a 6–3 decision, *Gonzales v. Oregon* (546 U.S. 243). Other states have shown interest in legislation to protect terminally ill patients and physicians who aid them in ending life, but to date Oregon, Washington, and Montana are alone in regulating this practice in the United States.[2]

The Kevorkian story sets the stage for the American debate over physician assistance in dying, but behind the issue is a moral question that Kevorkian imperfectly presented to the public. Kevorkian assumed that the issue was not morally controversial and that the only relevant moral question was the patient's suffering. He believed he had a duty under the medical ethics principle of beneficence to alleviate patient suffering, and the patient had a right to exercise autonomy even to the point of requesting aid in dying. Kevorkian also believed that the society that allowed such action was just and that what he was doing as a physician did no harm and constituted benevolent action in relation to the patient.

Kevorkian himself established for his services criteria that had to be satisfied. He set up a three-step review process, which included a noncoercion requirement, attention to last resort, and a psychological evaluation to ensure that persons who requested his assistance would do so freely (autonomously) and without any reasonable prospect of abuse. This in a way supports the kind of approach to the ethics of physician assistance in dying to be argued for here, which is a theory of "just physician-assisted suicide." But Kevorkian also assumed that patient autonomy overrode concerns about the role of the physician who acts in a direct and intentional manner to terminate a patient's life. Kevorkian did not see that his actions to intend the death of a patient and then act on that intention directly conflicted with his professional obligations as a physician—in fact, he thought just the opposite. Kevorkian held controversially that interfering with patient autonomy was a breach of the physician's professional obligation under beneficence to provide medical care and ease the suffering of patients. Kevorkian was blessed with a clarity about the moral meaning of his activities not widely shared by other members of the medical profession and certainly not by the courts or by large segments of American society. Even the laws passed in Oregon, Washington, and Montana only go so far as to permit a physician to provide information and prescribe medications that patients can then use themselves to end their lives. Those laws do not allow what Kevorkian advocated and actually did, namely, directly administering drugs with the end in view of terminating the patient's life. Kevorkian administered lethal injections, and the moral issue was whether the description of what he did as a physician who killed individuals, with their consent, could be deemed justifiable. Doing so is not accepted medical practice and clearly was not protected under Michigan law.

The debate over Kevorkian's direct action to kill a patient provokes issues in some ways more extreme than those at issue in physician-assisted suicide or physician aid in dying. That issue, however, is controversial enough. Kevorkian articulated criteria to guide his actions, and he deemed those criteria sufficient to justify his action. In that effort, however, he acted much as just war proponents do when they assume that the criteria of just war are alone sufficient to justify a use of force. We have argued in these pages that the just war criteria are not in themselves an ethic, and now we can observe that Kevorkian's appeal to the criteria he thought sufficient to justify his actions do not amount to an ethic either: that the patient request for a lethal injection in a terminal situation be uncoerced; that the patient submit to a psychological evaluation; and, finally, that a lethal injection be deemed a "last resort" measure. On this last point, Kevorkian held that if there were means to address pain short of lethal injection, all such pain management methods should be used and exhausted. Kevorkian did not engage these criteria for physician assistance as if they were part of an ethic—he does not articulate any common moral agreement that would underwrite and govern physician activity. On the contrary, Kevorkian proceeded on the assumption that his actions were benevolent and in the patient's best interests—and thus beyond moral questioning.

THE OREGON LAW AND ITS MORAL APPEAL

I wish to consider the issue of physician-assisted suicide (PAS) and subject it to a moral analysis, much as we did the question of the use of force. In what follows, attention will be focused on the Oregon Death with Dignity Act because this law implicitly appeals to the form and structure of the ethic to be found in the common agreement just war ethic. The Oregon law exemplifies how this way of going about the business of doing ethics is in fact an accessible and practical mode of ethical reasoning that attends to the relationship between thought and experience. The Oregon Law demonstrates how people of goodwill—and in this instance, that will include those responsible for legislating and enacting the Death with Dignity Act—implicitly appeal to the approach to ethical thinking we have been arguing for in these pages, this nonabsolutist hybrid common agreement ethic grounded in natural law thinking. The approach to ethical *thinking* we have been exploring underwrites the Oregon law and provides us with evidence that reasonable people confronting a serious moral problem will turn to this way of thinking out of their need for moral clarity and as an expression of their ethical seriousness. The Oregon law reveals the very approach to ethical deliberation we have been advocating in these pages, and it preserves and formalizes it in an actual piece of legislation. The Oregon Death with Dignity Act conforms in structure and presentation to the central formal features of a common agreement ethic we have seen in our analysis of just war. The law presents a highly principled and restrictive approach to creating a legal—and moral—exception to the widely accepted moral agreement that *ordinarily, physicians ought not to participate in the killing of their patients*. Other legal and professional authorities on the issue of physician involvement in patient suicide have made similar appeals, but the Oregon Death with Dignity law is distinctive in its clarity and thoroughness as it establishes on the foundations of a natural law ethic the public policy action guides that reflect moral deliberation, for the law presents—and intends to present—a morally permissible and rule-governed approach to physician-assisted suicide.

APPLYING THE ETHIC EMBEDDED IN THE JUST WAR TRADITION TO PHYSICIAN-ASSISTED SUICIDE

We have noted how the tradition of just war has addressed justification for uses of force while also insisting that uses of force be restrained by attention to proportionality and various other criteria. We have also noted that the criteria of just war are lacking content and provide only a formal statement of the justice concerns to be addressed as persons of goodwill contemplate and deliberate with others a use of force in particular circumstances. The reflective chore is to determine the extent to which the justice requirement identified by any particular criterion has been met or is likely to be satisfied. All of the criteria must be satisfied, not just a favored few. Although the stringency with which the criteria are applied is subject to some interpretive flexibility, it seems reasonable to assert that because the use of force is prospectively so destructive, the criteria should be applied so that it is apparent that justification for using force is difficult to secure.

Reclaiming and articulating the ethic embedded in the just war tradition allows us to see a mode of moral reasoning that attends to concerns for non-absolutist universality, impartiality, benevolence, and ethical normativity. As such, this ethic provides a model of moral reasoning that should be applicable to any issue or problem where moral meaning is at stake, including the issue of physician assistance in dying or, as we term it here, physician-assisted suicide (PAS).[3] My argument is that despite a widely held moral presumption against it, an ethic of "just physician-assisted suicide" can be constructed on the model of just war out of the same natural law resources. Through this analysis and others to follow in subsequent chapters I hope to show that *doing ethics* by building justice criteria around common agreements is both a practical and accessible mode of ethical reflection and engagement. So what would an ethic of "just PAS" look like?

Physician-assisted suicide refers to a physician acting directly to provide equipment or medication or to otherwise inform a patient about available means that would, if employed, assist a patient in ending his or her own life. Physician-assisted suicide is to be distinguished from voluntary active euthanasia, which refers to a physician responding to a patient request to die by directly administering a treatment or medication with the intent to end the patient's life.

Physician-assisted suicide is a morally troubling issue, not commonly sanctioned under the rule of law, and it is an infrequent but rule-governed practice even in those few places where it is permitted. The involvement of physicians in directly assisting patients to take their own lives is exceedingly rare, both in practice and as a matter of legal authorization. That only a few jurisdictions provide legal authorization—for example, Switzerland, Belgium, the Netherlands, and three states in the United States—testifies to its rarity.[4] Moreover, a check of relevant law and professional codes establishes empirically that wherever such physician involvement is authorized, it is highly regulated and heavily rule governed. I mention these facts because they provide empirical evidence that a widely accepted common moral agreement governs physician-assisted suicide. That agreement can be articulated thus: *Physician involvement in helping patients die ostensibly reflects a conflict between a physician acting in the best interests of the patient and the physician's traditional role as healer dedicated to preserving and enhancing the lives of persons. Since the preservation of life is a preeminent, although not absolute, value for physicians, ordinarily physicians ought not to participate in actions that directly lead to the deaths of patients.* In other words, the moral presumption involved in physician-assisted suicide is *against* the practice.

The reasons that the moral presumption articulates opposition to physician-assisted suicide are rather easy to discern. Physician-assisted suicide is, after all, still suicide, and moral prohibitions attend suicide since, as an intentional killing, it negates the good of life. And although suicide is not universally condemned in every circumstance, it is also not an act that can be universalized, so it is generally thought to be a wrongful act that persons of goodwill concerned to promote the good of life ought to prevent rather than condone or encourage. It is also a tragic act that can inflict pain and suffering on loved ones and even the moral community itself, and the act seems to contain a logical contradiction Kant pointed out, namely, that those who commit suicide seek by that act to improve their situation, but then choose a means that eliminates any possibility that they can experience the improvement—so there is no improvement for the agent, and the act is thus contradictory and irrational.

Aside from these general objections to suicide, the most significant reason that PAS runs into formidable objections is that it fundamentally shifts the role of the physician from healer and comforter to suicide accessory or even killer, and critics of the practice have argued that such a shift in role will lead inevitably to loss of trust in the physician. The physician who directly acts to help a patient die by means of PAS undermines the traditional role of the physician and distorts the medical profession's fundamental commitment to preserving life and serving that end by treating and curing patients.

Critics of PAS point to serious changes that might occur in the role of medicine in society if PAS is allowed. If PAS is an acceptable medical option, critics charge that pressures could be brought to bear to encourage people to make PAS a preferred option, especially those least able to resist them: the frail, the disabled, and the poor. The argument that this procedure would relieve family and society of resource-expending and troubling burdens might lead persons in vulnerable populations to opt more readily for PAS, thus rendering the practice discriminatory and devaluing of certain lives. This would breech ordinary standards of patient care. Another objection to PAS that has been voiced has to do with fear of death and pain management. Fear that medications and pain management will fail to provide comfort to patients suffering certain conditions, thus making PAS seem a reasonable solution, has been countered by the objection that pain management is highly developed in modern medicine and that it can be made adequate to a patient's need.[5] Furthermore, some of the mental conditions that might be prompting a terminally ill person to consider suicide, such as depression, could be treated by various medical, psychological, or even spiritual interventions. And another societally based objection is that if PAS becomes an acceptable medical practice, resources that could be used to serve traditional medical needs related to preserving life and treating illness would likely be shifted away from those ends and negatively affect a society's resolve to find and even expand palliative services and resources needed to help gravely ill, even dying, patients.[6]

With such serious and widely accepted objections as these, it is no wonder that most people—and most societies—have refused to sanction physician assistance in dying. And with those refusals we can observe that a widely shared moral agreement against "just physician-assisted suicide" exists as a matter of sociological fact. The widespread, although not unanimous, refusals to sanction such a role for physicians testifies, then, to the prevailing strength *of a common moral agreement opposed to physicians directly assisting patients to die.* Establishing this moral presumption as a normative guide is the first step in devising a "just PAS" ethic.

A moral presumption is not, however, an absolute prohibition, so the next step in constructing an ethic of "just PAS" akin to an ethic of "just war" or "just use of force" is to establish rule-governing action guides, conditions, or criteria that if satisfied would make an exception allowable. Although my concern here is moral rather than legal, I note that appeals to conditions and criteria—reflecting moral concerns—emerge quite frequently in legal cases. Let me note just two examples, and I draw these intentionally from widely disparate cultures to suggest the universality of the ethic I am presenting. My examples are from the Netherlands and Japan.

Holland legalized euthanasia in 2002, making the Netherlands the first country to allow doctors to kill terminally ill patients facing unbearable suffering. In the section of the statute dealing specifically with physician involvement, the law imposed on physicians the following conditions:

a. the physician must be convinced that the patient's request is voluntary, well considered, and lasting;
b. the patient's suffering must be determined to be unremitting and unbearable;
c. the patient must be fully informed of the situation and prospects;
d. the patient and physician both conclude that no reasonable alternative is available;
e. another physician, at least one, must be consulted;
f. the procedure must be carried out in a medically appropriate fashion (Section 293 (2) of Dutch Criminal Code.)[7]

An ethic governing physician involvement in helping patients die would say that the above articulation of conditions and qualifications serves the moral purpose of creating criteria to govern an allowable exception to our common agreement that ordinarily physicians should not be involved in directly helping patients die. In the Dutch situation, the issue at stake is physicians practicing voluntary active euthanasia, an activity quite distinct from PAS, which does not allow such direct physician involvement. The development of moral qualifications on physician involvement in Holland reflects the influence of the moral point of view, which articulates the ethical guidelines designed to protect the patient and guide the physician. This way of constructing a legal authorization seems to depend on an ethical approach we might call "just voluntary active euthanasia," and this is an ethic that avoids an absolutist prohibition on any such activity by doctors; yet it also attends to the moral presumption that this action ordinarily ought *not* to be taken. The ethic then proceeds to say that when such action is considered, it must meet stringent conditions and cannot be allowed if those conditions are not met. This reflects an approach to devising social policy about a difficult life-and-death topic that actually employs the kind of "just war"–related ethic I want to apply to PAS. PAS, as I have just mentioned, does not allow physicians to administer lethal medications directly, as is allowed in the Netherlands, but the Netherlands illustrates how one society generated a public policy on the basis of a moral understanding that reflects the kind of ethics approach I am advocating here for PAS and other issues *beyond* just war. In the Netherlands we find an example of this approach being employed on an issue even more controversial than PAS—direct physician involvement in dispatching individuals who wish to die.

Let us now turn to another example, this time in Japan. A high court in Japan approved passive "medical voluntary euthanasia" in 1962, but in 1995, a Yokohama district court addressed a case involving a physician who helped a terminally ill patient facing imminent death die. In its decision, the court invoked conditions under which active euthanasia, by which is meant direct physician involvement in helping a patient die, would be permitted in Japan:

a. the patient is suffering in unbearable physical pain;
b. death is inevitable and imminent;
c. all possible measures have been taken to eliminate the pain with no other treatment left open;
d. the patient has clearly expressed his or her will to approve the shortening of his or her life.

The judge declared that the doctor in this case did not meet the conditions since the patient had presented "no clear expressions about his physical pain nor about his will to approve euthanasia. The doctor's action *cannot be viewed as euthanasia* and represents illegal termination of the patient's life."[8] The physician received a two-year suspended sentence for murder.

Although these examples are presented in a legal context, both attend to physician and even societal beneficence and to patient autonomy; and in both examples patient initiative is required to begin the legal process involved. The patient expression of a desire for help in dying becomes a critical determinant of intentionality. The occasion for even addressing the issue of physician involvement is the prospect of imminent patient death and intractable suffering. Attention is focused on physician responsibility, and implicit in these cases is the need to keep the moral presumption that physicians ordinarily ought not to help a patient die unless the conditions that would make such an action permissible are transparently—and strictly—observed, which in the Yokohama judge's view was not the case. Failure to meet the criteria for a justifiable physician involvement yields the consequence that action to bring about the patient's death ought *not* to be done. This is a moral conclusion that, in this case, coincides with the legal determination.

JUST PHYSICIAN-ASSISTED SUICIDE (PAS)

The State of Oregon's Death with Dignity Act exemplifies in an extraordinary way how the "just war ethic" model applies—and actually was applied, implicit though it may have been—to an issue beyond war and the use of force. In keeping with the above examples addressing issues relevant to PAS—patient autonomy, physician responsibility, and a grave medical condition—we can proceed to examine the Oregon law to see how it provides a practical illustration of the ethical approach that we have been considering.

The fact that only three of fifty states have legalized physician assistance in dying allows us to infer that in the United States, moral attitudes toward PAS are overwhelmingly negative. The normative moral position that ordinarily physicians ought *not* to participate in a patient's suicide is apparent due to the lack of legal authorization for the practice and in the lack of widespread calls for laws to be changed. The presumption against physician assistance in patient suicide is glaringly present in the nationwide absence of laws permitting and regulating such action by physicians, and the recognition of the presumption against PAS is even apparent in the Oregon statute that does legally authorize and regulate it. The Oregon statute recognizes the presumption against PAS in the large number of restrictive definitions and conditions imposed on patients and physicians. Seventy-two such restrictions or conditions are mentioned in the statute.

Our common moral agreement opposed to physician-assisted suicide explains the nationwide refusal to grant legal authorization for PAS. The presumption against physician involvement in actions leading directly to the deaths of patients can thus be said to be present, widely accepted, and operationalized in legal prohibitions as well as in professional medical expectations and ethics guidelines.[9] Many jurisdictions impose explicit legal sanctions if the prohibition is violated. The high number of conditions and qualifications that must be satisfied before legal authorization of PAS can be granted in Oregon points to the effort lawmakers made to ensure that lifting the presumption against physician assistance in dying is not done easily or cavalierly.

Physician-assisted suicide in the United States is often framed by an absolutist moral perspective that will brook no exceptions, and the law has come to reflect this perception of moral attitude. The prospect of enacting laws based on a moderate moral perspective of "just PAS," where some instances of PAS could be justified and other not, seems remote. Yet Oregon did enact a law on PAS; and in that particular legal jurisdiction, we can make a case that an absolutist view did not succeed in fashioning public policy. An ethic of "just PAS," rather, was devised and then used to create policy, and both the ethic and law reflect a more moderate moral attitude on this particular life-and-death topic.

The actual content of a "just PAS" ethic must be constructed on the foundation of a common agreement or moral presumption *against* PAS. We have indicated how that moral presumption can be recognized and established. The articulation of a "just PAS" ethic would proceed on the acknowledgment that reasonable people of goodwill are open to the possibility that the moral presumption against PAS can and perhaps even should be overruled in certain cases. On the heels of this acknowledgment, we can proceed to establish relevant conditions to fill out the structural justice-related criteria that would have to be satisfied if we were to articulate the content of a "just PAS" ethic. Such an ethic might take form as follows:

The presumption against physician-assisted suicide may be lifted in a specific case if:

1. The patient makes the request fully informed of his or her situation and prospects.
2. The patient's condition is terminal and death is imminent, with a six-month prospect of life being a generally accepted medical time frame for defining "terminal."
3. The patient's request is not prompted by depression, so that a psychological evaluation is necessary.
4. The resources of palliative care will prove to be limited and not provide a dignified death or prove fully efficacious in the final period of the end stage.
5. The patient's autonomy is respected throughout and patients can withdraw the request for PAS at any point in the process.
6. The physician who participates is willing to participate and has no mental reservations about involvement. There must be no coercion placed on the physician or patient by relevant or interested parties: family, the state, other medical authorities, or insurance companies.
7. The actual means of dispatch is swiftly acting and painless.
8. Laws protect the physician who follows these guidelines from any prosecution for wrongful death, and the family of the patient is protected from those who would seek to benefit from PAS, such as an insurance company that will not pay a death benefit in case of a suicide.
9. PAS is approached as a "last resort" that is designed to preserve the value of physician beneficence and autonomous patient decision making in the face of imminent and intractably painful death.[10]

This listing of "criteria" to create an exception for an instance of just PAS could be done differently. That is, these general "justice-related" criteria could be modified, edited, and streamlined, with others perhaps included. But in taking a look at what practical reason would insist be included in an ethic of "just PAS," these criteria address relevant moral issues related to physician autonomy and decision making as well as to the possibility of rule-governed physician involvement. This particular version of a "just PAS" ethic reflects the general justice-related headings under which the seventy-two different qualifications, restrictions, authorizations, and conditions in the Oregon statute could fit. That the Oregon law yields a "just PAS" ethic in the relevant sense I have been discussing could be made most explicit by simply listing the seventy-two conditions, but this would lead to an extremely cumbersome ethics tool. The significant point is that the Oregon law does attend to the criteria of "just PAS" by stating numerous qualifications, stipulations, and requirements that must be satisfied in order to have claim to a justified exception to the moral (and legal) presumption that physicians ordinarily ought not to participate in their patients' suicides. If those criteria spelled out in the law are not met, the contemplated act of PAS is rendered illicit, and, in this analysis, immoral as well. That law stipulates that only competent adult residents of Oregon suffering a terminal illness that will lead to death within six months are candidates for PAS. It then sets up specific and highly qualified criteria that must be satisfied prior to physician involvement in a patient's request to commit suicide. All of the concerns set out above in the "just PAS" ethic are reflected in the actual statute.

The effect of these qualifications has been to preserve the force of the moral presumption against PAS, allowing it only as a rare but rule-governed procedure. The rule-governed nature of the "allowable exception" contemplated by the Oregon statute can be seen by a perusal of the statute itself, which is readily available on the state's Internet website.[11] But the rarity of its use is discernable in some statistics compiled by the state of Oregon, which are also available on its website. These statistics blunt the idea that PAS, if allowed, will become something other than a rare practice. In the 2010 summary of statistics related to the Death with Dignity Act, the state of Oregon reports that ninety-six prescriptions for lethal medications were written by fifty-nine physicians under the provisions of the law. Of this number, sixty-one patients took the medications and fifty-nine actually died from ingesting drugs; with six patients who had received medications in 2009 actually dying in 2010 from PAS, the total deaths sanctioned under the statute amounted to sixty-five in 2010.[12] This is out of a state total of 30,341 deaths reported by the Oregon Department of Health and Human Services,[13] or a rate of 20.9 deaths per 10,000, a small number indeed.[14] Between 1997, the year the law was passed, and 2006, approximately 270,000 people in the state of Oregon died, assuming 30,000 deaths per year; in that time frame, 292 patients died by means of PAS. This is a rare practice, affecting less than 1 percent of deaths, and this number has, over the years, shown little fluctuation.

The Oregon experience with legalized PAS demonstrates that PAS is heavily rule governed, with the law being invoked infrequently. Statistical evidence confirms that the moral presumption against PAS is firmly in place. Furthermore, PAS has not been subject to abuse or directed toward vulnerable populations, as one might suspect were the numbers of cases by year to begin to increase dramatically. The moral presumption against PAS is observed strictly—although not absolutely—in Oregon. Going back to the proposed "just PAS" ethic laid out earlier, we can say that the criteria for "just PAS" specify conditions that both authorize and morally sanction PAS in those rare situations where the rules governing an allowable exception are satisfied. This of course is possible only if one allows that a moral presumption governs PAS and that PAS is not subject to an absolute prohibition, as would be the case if argued from certain religious or other morally absolutist perspectives that could not entertain any exception.

Recalling the court decision in Japan mentioned earlier, it is worth noting that the just PAS ethic provides not only a framework for justification but also tools for moral analysis. The criteria function to evaluate actual situations and specific cases as well as to critique any act of PAS. In the Japanese situation, the criteria were invoked to determine that in fact the prohibition on physician involvement in a patient's death had not met legal, or, presumably, moral requirements. Such "criteria" of just physician involvement were used in the Japanese case to analyze the situation and to expose shortcomings and the actual failure to satisfy requirements; and although that case involved legal euthanasia, the process of critique would be the same were the issue under consideration PAS. This "just PAS" ethic establishes sufficient backup and bureaucratic reporting on all the steps listed above that failure to meet any of the criteria should put an immediate halt to any PAS project. Furthermore, this construction of an ethic of "just PAS" eschews absolutism, certainly that of a strict Kantian deontologist, yet is sufficiently qualified and conformed to moral constraints in light of a presumption against suicide as well as PAS, that it authorizes PAS only on condition that it be both rare and heavily rule governed. It participates in a basic ethical approach exemplified by the just war ethics model, which would allow that this way of construing PAS could certainly be offered as a universally appropriate way to think about PAS, one that could be offered impartially while aimed at benevolence and patient-centered care. It affirms and asserts a normative view that ordinarily PAS is not something a physician should engage in; and the presumption against such activity can be lifted only if justice criteria are satisfied, which, in the actual Oregon Death with Dignity Act, amount to seventy-two conditions, restrictions, guidelines, and requirements.

CONCLUSION

This way of approaching the ethics of PAS is controversial for those who are opposed to PAS absolutely, the same way a pacifist would object to the prospect of a just war. But if one eschews the possibility of moral purity and considers the moral life to be lived amid complexity, this mode of operation in the ethical terrain of difficult and tragic life-and-death situations opens an approach to ethical reflection, analysis, and evaluation that expresses practical reason in its full engagement. And more than that, the "just PAS" ethic reflects an approach to moral evaluation that articulates conditions to constrain action and preserve the integrity of the normative moral presumption against PAS while offering the possibility that in certain cases PAS might be permissible. This ethical approach urges people into the realm of conversation, even into the public forum, to deliberate the permissibility of this particular criterion or to critique whether a particular criterion can be or actually was satisfied. In this sense, the structure of this approach to moral thinking, rather than resolving particulars, invites deliberation. As a form of citizen engagement, this approach to moral deliberation reflects strengths of democracy rather than debilitating it or shielding persons from moral decision making by the assertion of moral absolutes.

Admittedly, this approach will not convince anyone who is already opposed to PAS on some absolutist principle. But the advantage of taking this approach is that, as the Oregon law shows, a way of moral thinking is advanced that makes the whole enterprise of moral thinking accessible and reasonable. Looking at what the Oregon lawmakers constructed reminds us that people actually do employ this way of thinking and do rely on this way of approaching moral problems, even if the appeal is made implicitly in the course of devising a legal regulation. Thought and experience are reconciled here in a dramatically vivid way. Thinking affects action; moral reflection reconciles experience as consideration is given to the possibility of easing the suffering of certain patients facing a terminal medical situation. The ethic commends a duty to observe our common moral agreement but also to attend to the well-being of patients; it looks to the consequences of the PAS act, not only for the patient but for the family and society as a whole—much attention is given to consequences in the law; and it is assumed that physicians and legal overseers are people of virtue—trustworthy people who look out for the well-being of others and who act courageously and with justice in assisting persons as they come to a decision about what to do. The Oregon Death with Dignity Act demonstrates how this particular law itself came to conform to a moral viewpoint, which in this case happens to reflect the mode of moral thinking associated with a "just PAS" ethic.

The ethical approach advocated here may not be familiar to those schooled in Kantian ethics, utilitarianism, or other theoretical approaches to ethics. Extracting from the just war ethic a more universal and general ethical method, making it available for development around other ethics issues and extending it beyond just war, may represent a new ethical approach for some. For ethical theorists, this common agreement approach to ethics serves as a reminder of an overlooked ethics tool in our traditions of thought, which to ignore or refuse to put to work in our ethics conversations in the public arena impoverishes the attempt to engage practical reason in the creative work of ethical reflection.

Chapter Six

The Ethics of
Patient Nontreatment

Are there ever good and sufficient reasons for deciding not to provide medical treatment to persons because of the severity of their medical condition? The common agreement ethical approach modeled by just war can be applied to this question. In this chapter we shall look at patient nontreatment, an important issue in medical ethics. What would a common agreement ethic of just nontreatment look like, and how would it function?

JUST NONTREATMENT: CRITERIA AND CASES

Criteria

In considering the issue of patient nontreatment, end-of-life and beginning-of-life situations are not equivalent, morally speaking. Adult patients at the end of life can exercise a nontreatment option in ways that are not available at the beginning of life. They can, for instance, simply express their wishes to medical caregivers that they wish to forgo further treatment. They can also prepare advance directives to withdraw or withhold medical intervention as specified physical conditions warrant, and patients can create a proxy process for deciding nontreatment options (both withholding and withdrawing). Given the possibility that individual adult patients possessed of their rational faculties at the end of life can opt for nontreatment as an exercise of personal autonomy, the more difficult cases are those that arise at the beginning of life with severely disabled newborns.

Morally speaking, reasonable people of goodwill can be expected to express common agreement on this basic presumptive action guide: *ordinarily a newborn facing medical difficulties and even disabilities should receive "standard of care" medical treatment, including palliative care in terminal situations.* Medical science can in many cases successfully intervene in neonatal medical problems to preserve life and contribute to the neonate's eventual flourishing as a member of the moral community; so ordinarily we ought not to consider withholding or withdrawing treatment to medically distressed newborns, although there might be good reasons to consider an exception to this common agreement. To justify an exception would require the development, articulation, and application of justice-related criteria akin to those familiar in the just war model.

If, in general, the moral community acknowledges an obligation to treat rather than not treat disabled newborns, and even a proponent of active euthanasia, utilitarian philosopher Peter Singer, gives evidence of supporting this view,[1] the question arises: are there justified exceptions? If so, what conditions would have to be met so that medical help could be withdrawn or withheld justifiably so that the neonate patient is allowed to die? This question is now my focus.[2]

A "just nontreatment" ethic begins with a moral presumption that distressed patients, including disabled neonates, ordinarily ought to be treated. This presumption to treat serves the moral point of view, for it is universalizable; it is a conclusion reflecting impartial justice and nondiscrimination against disabled individuals; it is other-regarding and expresses benevolence; and it draws on a set of normative principles that would hold that we have an obligation to show respect and care for persons by valuing their lives and offering aid and assistance when they are severely disabled or facing dire medical conditions. The possibility of nontreatment arises in the face of particular circumstances only if several reasonable, justice-related conditions are met. These conditions or criteria include the following:

1. The life of the neonate patient is deemed clearly a burden to the infant itself.
2. The intention to withdraw or withhold treatment must be to serve the best personal, social, and spiritual interests of the patient.
3. Descriptions of the patient's medical condition must establish both severity and futility of treatment. The determination must be made that the prospects of enjoying the goods of life, including the very basic good of life itself, is negligible. Reasonable hope that the neonate will flourish as a functioning, interactive human being in relationship to others is not present, and there is little hope that medical intervention will raise the medical condition to even the most minimal level required for flourishing. Medical intervention will, to the contrary, contribute to the burdens the patient must bear rather than relieve those burdens.

4. The decision to withdraw or withhold treatment is patient centered and not determined by the burdens the patient imposes on others—the medical staff, the family, or society at large.
5. The decision must be made by those who represent the various interests of the patient, including family, physicians, medical care personnel, and spiritual advisers.
6. By withdrawing (or withholding) treatment one is trying to preserve respect for the good of life rather than diminish it, and nontreatment will reasonably accomplish this end.

By satisfying these criteria, the presumption that a severely disabled newborn should be medically treated may be lifted, the accumulation of reasons amounting to this: that doing so is in the best interests of the neonate and is ethically justified. These criteria acknowledge a standard of care regarding pain management so that the alleviation of pain, to the extent that pain can be reasonably determined, is addressed even if such an intervention hastens the death of the neonate.

Cases

Several medical conditions might allow for consideration of justified nontreatment. Individual cases must be assessed, but some medical conditions are by their nature so severe that they are likely to provoke consideration of nontreatment in virtue of a diagnosis of the affliction. Let me mention three.

1. Consider a rare skin disease called dystrophic epidermolysis bullosa of the recessive form. Newborns afflicted with this do not live past five years of age, and life is marked by intractable pain that requires heavy sedation, usually with Demerol, which puts the neonate in a stupor. That is the neonate's life and prospect of life: pain or heavy sedation. Babies afflicted with this condition find dressing and bathing excruciating experiences, even screaming in anticipation of such activity. Here is a description from ethicist Richard C. Sparks:

> The quality of life open to this child is either so irremediably pained or else so doped up that should life sustainers be required or treatment become necessary for pneumonia, infections or other curable diseases, one might opt to forgo these efforts in the patient's holistic best interests, hoping for an earlier and easier rather than a belabored and painful dying process.[3]

2. Various cephalic disorders present medically desperate situations, including hydranencephaly, a condition in which the cerebral hemispheres are missing and a neonate has at best a one-year life expectancy. But let us

focus on anencephaly. A newborn with this affliction presents an open cranial vault with no brain present, only remnant brain tissue. According to *Black's Medical Dictionary*, neonates with this condition are "born with defects of skull and absence of brain . . . the brain stem and cerebellum are atrophic. If pregnancy goes to term the infant dies rapidly."[4] A woman can know early in pregnancy that she is carrying an anencephalic baby, and if they come to term, these neonates have "no cognitive activity or relational potential. Death is usually imminent within hours, days, weeks."[5]

3. A third condition, the infant version of amyotrophic lateral sclerosis or ALS (Lou Gehrig's disease), is Werdnig-Hoffman disease, "a progressive, relentless and totally irreversible" condition that creates a "locked-in state" of paralysis that simulates coma while normal consciousness is preserved. Werdnig-Hoffman can cause extreme physical suffering. Neonates require incubation in ICUs, respirators, IV fluids, and feeding tubes. Questions arise about the pain and discomfort level of the afflicted neonate, but clearly the caregivers—parents, neonatal ICU nurses, and physicians—are concerned about any actions that might increase the pain and suffering of the neonate.[6]

These, then, are three conditions that raise neonatal or perinatal[7] patient nontreatment as a reasonable possibility due to the severity of the disorder. Also to be factored into consideration of these cases is this commonplace reality: a serious birth defect is often accompanied by other physical anomalies, and sometimes it is the combination that is at issue, even if individually one defect might not rise to the level of justifying nontreatment.[8]

DISCUSSION

If we apply the six criteria to the three cases listed above, we can see how the criteria guide making a justified exception—or not.

The dystrophic epidermolysis bullosa case as described seems to be so catastrophic, amelioration by treatment so unlikely, and futility so present, that applying the criteria would seem reasonably to recommend justified nontreatment. The description of the disorder given earlier does not fit all possible cases of the disorder, but in this particular description, life itself is a burden to the neonate due to constant excruciating pain on the one hand and being "doped up" in a stupor on the other. Author Richard Sparks suggests that this condition begs the very question of reasonable patient nontreatment. Applying the criteria supports lifting the presumption against nontreatment because the physical condition is so distressingly pain filled and futile. Withholding treatment to hasten death appears to be a course of action in the patient's best interest, and the decision to withhold treatment could be made for patient-centered reasons by those entrusted with the neonate's interests. The value of the neonate's life is in question, and people of goodwill can make judgments about the value of this life, reasonably drawing the conclusion that for the neonate bearing this affliction, life is not a gift but a terrible burden. The decision not to treat is a tragic decision, of course, but the burden of life is so great that nontreatment seems a humane course of medical action.

The neonate with anencephaly presents a severe and futile medical condition that no corrective medical intervention can possibly ameliorate. The neonate lacks the brain structures necessary for the possibility of relationship, identity, and becoming the subject of experience; and although the neonate is a member of the human species, the moral community rightly does not confer upon it personhood. The just nontreatment criteria could be applied and a decision not to treat made in the best interests of the patient. Nontreatment poses no reasonable issue of disrespect for the value or good of life itself, but on the contrary seems reasonably to be in the patient's best interests.[9] This analysis could apply as well to neonates suffering from hydranencephaly and whose brain function involves only the brain stem. The complication with hydranencephaly, however, is that diagnosis is sometimes difficult and symptoms confirming the condition may not show up for some months.

A medical consultation concerning a neonate with Werdnig-Hoffman reveals how a "just nontreatment" ethic can be reconciled with our moral experience. In a journal of clinical medical ethics, Dr. Robert Echenberg, a neonatologist, presented a case study of Werdnig-Hoffman in the context of a perinatal ethics committee confronting the disorder. Echenberg relates how the ethics committee attempted to consider the concerns of the patient, the parents, and the community of caregivers, which included ICU nurses. The nurses, Echenberg reports, bonded with the infant and "became most qualified to assess the neonate's levels of comfort or suffering."[10] Echenberg writes that much was unknown about the nature of pain or suffering being experienced by the newborn—if the newborn could even be said to be experiencing pain due to developmental immaturity and the lack of neurologic integration. Assessing the extent to which a neonate could be meaningfully said to be a subject of experience is an enormously difficult task due to so many unknowns. But traditional ethical theories involving "critical care decisions, logical rules, predetermined principles and commonly trusted beliefs" were not of great help as the care team faced the afflicted neonate. The committee tried to figure out whether nontreatment was the best course of action. Committee members then struggled with how they might best carry out the nontreatment decision once that was deemed medically appropriate. Consensus was sought on the timing and manner of withdrawing treatment.

The committee understood that ethically, the team needed to "be flexible and willing to explore creative, new possibilities." Echenberg writes:

> Through a process of careful interviews and a well-attended committee discussion, we came to a firmer accord in understanding what might be in this child's best interests, as well as in coming to terms with withdrawal of her life support. . . . [T]he critical care nurses . . . played a significant and critical role. We learned, also, that it is desirable to forge a therapeutic and healing process to ease the pain and turmoil of the survivors.[11]

The infant, by the way, had received treatment from the ICU team but later went into cardiac arrest. After consultation, it was decided not to pursue energetic resuscitative efforts as had been done previously. The physicians and nurses in attendance "allowed the baby to die without further intervention."[12]

The Journal of Clinical Ethics, in which the case study appeared, published three responses to the case presentation, and respondents criticized the way the perinatal committee functioned, especially in its call for consensus among caregivers about how to proceed. Specifically criticized was the decision to allow the collective opinion of the nurses to affect the decision making: "We must be skeptical of the assumption that nurses and other caregivers can always be appropriate judges of the patient's best interest," wrote critic Robert Truog, arguing that coercion can be involved in consensus when someone claims authority by appeal to past experience.[13] Another critic, Robert F. Weir, argued that more attention to a benefit and burden analysis might have prevented a technological intervention in the first place, since the physical condition might have sufficed to determine that such intervention was harmful to the patient. Weir asked whether it was not obvious that this medical condition was "interfering with her future interests, impairing her psychological welfare, or was aimless cruelty?"[14] And a third respondent, T. F. Dagi, argued that the emotional needs of health-care personnel ought not to be a focus of moral decision making in such a case. Dagi argued that the crucial ethics chore in this case was making and assessing judgments about the quality of life rather than trying to determine patient pain levels, since pain is a technical issue subject to medical manipulation and control.[15]

All the parties—Echenberg and his critics—paid attention in varying degrees to the centrality of the patient. The committee faced a difficulty determining the extent of the neonate's pain, but all were concerned with it, and none of the author critics disputed the decision to withhold or withdraw treatment: the ethics issues focused on when and how to proceed into nontreatment and who has voice in the consultation. Whereas Echenberg wanted attention paid to the caregivers because of their direct experiential involvement with the patient and because of their attendant grief, he and the committee did address primarily the patient and the patient's welfare. In the face of unknowns about what the patient was experiencing, and having settled the justifiability of nontreatment, the consultation team took a wider view about those entering into relation with the neonate as caregivers. The decision to withdraw treatment was actually clear and demonstrated that an implicit appeal to the criteria of the just nontreatment ethic laid out above were actually invoked, applied, and satisfied. The presumption that ordinarily even a severely disabled newborn be treated was at first observed via medical intervention and resuscitation; but then attention was given to the severity and futility of treatment, and that issue provoked thoughtful reflection on how to determine and serve the best interests of the neonate. Consultation with those representing the patient's interests became a focus, and the role of medical staff then became a specific issue of contention and disagreement. Disagreements did not arise, as I read the case, over the patient-centered decision not to treat the patient—an implicit appeal was made to the criteria of "just nontreatment" in the deliberations and decision-making process, and the determination was made that withdrawing treatment was in the patient's best interests. The attention to the staff's grief makes this case somewhat unusual, but in a sense, even this focus does not stray from the "just nontreatment" criterion regarding consultation, since that is what one is supposed to do with the criterion, namely, examine how the various parties representing patient interest are to be involved. Disagreements can arise about whether and how particular criteria are actually satisfied, but it is the discussion and arguing in public ways that is critically important for the common agreement ethics approach the committee members found themselves using in the face of a difficult situation. Noteworthy in this case are the ways professionals involved in the case made implicit appeals to an ethic of "just nontreatment" not only in the immediacy of the medical situation but also in its aftermath. For a physician attending the patient opened the case to an even wider public discussion by presenting it to a professional journal and thereby inviting colleagues to continue deliberation within the wider professional community.[16]

The formal aspects of the "just nontreatment of neonates" ethic were observed in this case, and conscientiously so. The decision for nontreatment was made in consultation with representatives of the patient's interests and was itself patient centered. The medical prognosis was deemed futile and so grave that life itself was by reasonable inference a burden to the neonate; and the decision-making process showed intent to serve the patient interests, reflecting a continued respect for the good of life. The criteria enunciated above were all invoked and addressed, and applying them to the situation led the consultation team to conclude that the presumption *against* withdrawing treatment of a severely disabled newborn could, in this particular situation, be lifted and treatment justifiably withdrawn.

This case, not only in its presentation but even in the accompanying criticisms of it, demonstrates how the ethic—the just nontreatment ethic proposed here—actually works. People facing moral problems in their everyday work life join others in thinking about those problems and work to find a way to reconcile ethical thought with experience. In this situation, the consultation team accomplished this end not by imposing an ethic—running a calculation irrespective of any duty to treat or ignoring consequences and invoking the categorical imperative—but by fashioning an ethic of "just nontreatment" out of the common moral agreement from which all parties started—that ordinarily treatment should not be withdrawn. Their ethics work led them to conclude that in this situation, an exception—a justifiable exception—was in order. This conclusion was reached as the consultation team considered relevant ethics and justice issues that happen to be articulated above in the criteria of "just nontreatment."

CONCLUSION

I draw three conclusions from this discussion. First, the common agreement ethic proposed here, relevant to the particularities of severely disabled neonate treatment, is flexible and patient centered. The ethic takes into account the duty reasonable people of goodwill acknowledge, namely, that even severely disabled neonates should ordinarily receive medical intervention and treatment. The common agreement ethic, however, is not absolutist. In relation to the moral presumption to treat, the ethic allows that attention should be given to other morally relevant considerations, such practical matters as the severity of the affliction, the likelihood of the neonate's being able to enjoy the goods of life in relationship with others, the prospect of final medical futility, and the intention of decision makers to act in ways that address the total well-being of the neonate. Moral analysis and assessment may lead to the conclusion that a medical situation actually provokes a conflict of duties—the duty to act in the best overall interests of the neonate versus the duty that is expressed in our common agreement that ordinarily we ought to treat even severely disabled neonates. A "lowercase," nonabsolutist notion of duty plays a role in thinking through this just nontreatment ethic, and people of goodwill can very easily experience this conflict and turn to the kinds of justice considerations that would, if satisfied, allow for a lifting of the presumption to treat. The deliberating of medical options in the context of moral decision making was clearly at work in the Werdnig-Hoffman consultation and analysis discussed in the chapter. Caring and virtuous medical personnel, reasonable people of goodwill, can be seen going through a decision-making process that is directed toward serving the best interests of the neonate, and best-interests considerations necessarily involve moral thinking that takes into account foreseen consequences. Just nontreatment is also concerned with the patient as an individual sufferer whose particular situation is deemed deserving of a presumption of care due to a principled moral directive that even disabled newborns deserve treatment due to their status as members of the moral community. Lowercase consequences factor into the decision making, but the neonate is never treated as simply a cipher in a utilitarian calculation. So duty, consequences, and virtue each play a role in the practicalities (experience) that are referred to ethical reflection (thought) for assessment and guidance about direction.

Second, neonatal disability presents specific moral problems related to the good of life and how that good is to be evaluated in relation to other goods. The good of life may be preeminent in any listing of goods of life since all others depend on it (as we said earlier), but it is not an absolute good that must always trump every other good. Were that the case, modern medicine would never recognize futility and would not be able to honor a patient's request not to be resuscitated—mere biological functioning would instead define a "life worth living." The common agreement ethic of justified nontreatment is flexible enough to suggest that the good of life must be placed in an evaluative context with other goods, which is to say that good of life is a good in relation with other goods such as bodily integrity and the capacity for realizing a psychological identity and thus the *capacity* to enjoy the other goods of life (friendship, aesthetic enjoyment, abstract reasoning). When these other goods are catastrophically compromised by physical defect or deformity in particular situations, the good of life can be called into question by applying the justice criteria of the just nontreatment ethic. The ethic allows at the outset that it is possible to determine that not all life is worth living. Moreover, reasonable people of goodwill, exercising practical reason in accord with an ethic like that suggested here, must assume responsibility for acting to advance the well-being of an individual patient whose life may be so burdensome that withdrawing medical care trumps the concern for preserving and promoting the good of life.

And third, a difficult question arises if it is determined that life is a burden to patients themselves. If further treatment appears to increase suffering, cannot the action of dispatching such an individual by means of, say, morphine injection be considered consistent with a standard of care, with the patient-centered action of acting in the best interests of the patient? And should scarce, expensive medical resources continue to be expended on a futile,

medically hopeless patient? These are questions needing further conversation, and utilitarian ethicist Peter Singer is to be applauded for forcing them
into the public arena. But on the ethic proposed here, my view is that the
criterion concerned with preserving respect for the good of life (number 6)
could, in this moment of societal and cultural evolution, be compromised by
physicians acting as "dispatchers." By that I mean to highlight the problem
of physicians allowing their traditional role as healers to be transformed by
assuming the role of a "killer" even as an ethical analysis might conclude
that that a morphine injection that leads to death could also be described as
ultimately a palliative, perhaps even a healing action for a certain patient.

In the United States, we are not ready for this redescription of the physician's role, and the best we can hope for is continued defense of "double-
effect" pain management that brings about death as a foreseen but unintended
consequence. The problem is that in more and more cases, the consequence of
patient death is more than just foreseen—it is actually *intended*. We deceive
ourselves if we deny this, and any reasonable analysis would expose that interpretation. So are we allowing physicians to do what is humane and morally
defensible but withholding a *description* we are not ready to accept? Are we
opting for a deception, even a self-deception, because the honest description
is too painful for us to face? What health education needs to accomplish is a
reorientation that supplants the anxiety of a public fearful of doctors becoming killers with the assurance that doctors will act in concert with caregivers
to operate out of a patient-centered, "just nontreatment" ethic that is committed to a basic common agreement that patients needing medical attention
should receive it. Some situations, however, are so medically challenging that
reasonable people of goodwill can consider lifting that presumption to treat.
In certain extreme medical situations, dying and death are made horrendously
difficult by the intervention of technology, and what is needed is a practical
ethic that seeks to realize goodness by easing off the technological interventions while commending as good, right, and fitting those actions that focus on
the best interests of the patients, including the possibility of a justified course
of nontreatment.

Death can sometimes be in the patient's best interest. Absolutist versions
of a duty-based ethic would deny this by refusing to consider direct action
that would expedite death, for such would be contrary to our duty to respect
persons. Indeed, can one show respect to a person by acting directly to end
his or her life? Utilitarian ethics loses both the individual sufferer and the
caregiver distress in a calculus related to distributive justice, where every individual sufferer is rendered a cipher to be treated as the calculus directs. On
such an account, nothing would prohibit direct killing as wrong per se—*no
action is wrong per se*—but such an approach denies the respect due persons

as persons, which is so important in our moral experience. The difficult social policy issue is whether acting in patients' best interests can, as a matter of "standard of care," include action to directly intend the death of a patient—for the reason that that is the good, fitting, and right thing to do in the patient's best interest. The common agreement "just nontreatment" ethic holds out this possibility.

Chapter Seven

The Ethics of
Execution and Just Punishment

Execution is a direct and intended killing, yet framing a moral debate over capital punishment in the American political context has proved a difficult task, even when most Americans are now aware that capital punishment does not deter crime and the legal machinery and processes involved in execution are known to be highly error prone. Since 1973, 140 individuals convicted and sentenced to death have been exonerated, that is, proven to be actually innocent of the crime for which they were convicted and sentenced to die.[1] American citizens continue to support capital punishment in large numbers, and that support seems to rest on the assumption that any problems that attend the capital punishment system are practical or technical and thus can be corrected. Specific problems, such as wrongful conviction, while acknowledged to be morally provocative, have not led the majority of Americans to rethink their moral assessment of the execution practice and demand of their political leaders an immediate halt to executions. Instead, the assumption appears to be widespread that there is nothing morally problematic about the death penalty per se; and moral controversy has apparently sunk beneath a sea of consensus on this point.

But is there some kind of common agreement that we can point to for guidance on the question of capital punishment? Can we devise a theory of "just execution" on the model of just war, identifying a moral presumption that constitutes a common agreement to which rational people of goodwill could be expected to assent and then consider whether or how capital punishment might be justified as a reasonable exception to that common agreement? And in our effort to reconcile thought and experience, can we demonstrate the practicality of the "common agreement" approach to ethics we have been discussing by finding experiential confirmation that this way of thinking is actually being used and relied upon because it is a useful and practical way to consider relevant justice issues? These are the questions at issue in this chapter. The focus of attention here will be the way the legal system has attempted to fashion policy around what looks to be a kind of "just execution" theory. We shall note, however, by way of critique, that a common agreement "just execution" ethic will direct critical attention to a disparity between thought and practice, so that what "just execution" might make possible on the one hand is taken away by the failure to satisfy the demands of justice on the other. We shall conclude with a consideration of the broader question concerning just punishment, which then has deeper social policy implications. What would a "just criminal justice system" look like were we to evaluate it in light of our common agreement ethic?

JUST EXECUTION

A common agreement ethic concerning "just execution" begins by acknowledging a basic intrinsic good—the good of life.[2] Natural law gives prescriptive force to the claim that life is a basic good, so that it follows that life ought to be preserved and promoted, protected, and advanced, not destroyed. A theory of just execution based on a natural law tradition is committed in the first instance to this claim, namely, that life ought to be promoted and protected and not destroyed.

But the natural law common agreement ethic I am advancing says more than this. Life, as we all know, is messy, and the moral life may be riddled with conflicts. Basic goods can come into conflict with one another; and moral quandaries, even actual dilemmas, can arise. Life itself is a good of life, but it is not an absolute good that is unaffected by relations to other goods of life. If sufficiently strong moral requirements are advanced, a natural law ethic grounded in honoring the basic goods of life may allow the prohibition on destroying life to be lifted, but this is not done idly or without compelling reasons. We saw how this emphasis on developing a common moral agreement functions along with justice-related criteria that might, in exceptional cases, allow an exception to the prohibition on the use of force, or physician-assisted suicide, or nontreatment of severely disabled neonates. We continue to look back to the just war model and to the ethic *behind* just war thinking, even as we look ahead *beyond* just war to another important life and death issue where we are seeking to reconcile ethical thought and moral experience.

If construed as a natural law–based moral perspective wherein reason affirms the goods of life, including the basic good of life itself, a just execution theory in the first instance would affirm that the state ought ordinarily to refrain from killing its citizens. I put the matter this way because this identifies the real moral presumption at stake in capital punishment; and this statement gathers both death penalty supporters and death penalty opponents under a basic reasoned point of common moral agreement. Whatever disputes may arise about particulars, there ought to be no disagreement about the moral presumption behind capital punishment. If states ought ordinarily to refrain from killing citizens and capital punishment is one way states actually do kill citizens, then we must be clear that at the heart of any capital punishment debate is a moral presumption that the state should not resort to a death penalty. Our common moral agreement behind the issue of state-sponsored execution is *a presumption opposing the practice.*

But we note once again that the theory being advanced in these pages and now on this issue is not absolutist. As a moderate theory, the question is legitimately asked: Are there ever circumstances that would allow the state to use lethal force against a citizen? Put this way, examples immediately come to mind, such as the emergency situation where an aggressor is placing innocent civilians in imminent danger of loss of life. Police action to stop such killing, action that as a last resort includes deadly force against the aggressor, would, on the face of it, allow a justifiable lifting of the presumption against the state killing a citizen. So some exceptions to our common moral agreement come quickly to mind, and these exceptions do not seem especially controversial.

But now the question turns to execution. Is capital punishment a justifiable use of lethal force against a citizen? Could it be an exception to the moral presumption that ordinarily states ought not to kill their citizens?

To answer this question, let us construct a theory of just execution on the *model* of just war. Let us say that in order for the moral presumption against capital punishment to be lifted, various criteria would have to be met: The tests or criteria that would constrain the state in the interests of justice yet conceivably permit a use of lethal force would be nine in number:

1. The execution power must be legitimately authorized.
2. Just cause for the use of the death penalty must be established.
3. The motivation for applying lethal punishment must be justice, not vengeance.
4. Executions must be administered fairly, without accidental features such as race, religion, class, or sex affecting administration of the death penalty.
5. The death penalty is to be used as an expression of cherished values, and it must not subvert the goods of life but promote and advance the value of life.
6. Executions ought not to be cruel.
7. Execution ought to be a last resort, with no other response to the offender except execution adequately serving the interests of justice.

8. Execution ought to restore a value equilibrium distorted and upset by the wrongdoing committed by the person on whom execution is visited.
9. Execution should be a response proportionate to the offense committed.[3]

This natural law–based theory of just execution says this: if all nine of these criteria are satisfied, the presumption against the state using capital punishment as a legitimate mode of lethal force against a citizen can be lifted, and an execution can go forward as a morally justifiable act. Having laid out the theory of just execution, what I want now to consider is how this common agreement moral theory has found its way into American law, and to what effect. The point here is not so much to analyze the merits of capital punishment per se but to make the case that the common agreement ethic has actually been used to deliberate issues involved in the death penalty and this way of addressing moral problems is accessible and helpful. People actually use this way of moral thinking and analysis in their lives, thereby connecting thought with experience, and such connection has been a point stressed in this book as a justification for this particular ethics project, which seeks to articulate the hybrid ethic that this mode of analysis expresses. And this way of thinking about difficult social problems can—and has—found its way into legal as well as moral deliberations. The value of looking at the capital punishment issue is that we can see here again that the common agreement approach to ethics helps us reconcile our ethical thinking with our moral experience. Let us begin by examining the question of the moral presumption against capital punishment.

THE APPEAL TO A JUST
EXECUTION ETHIC IN AMERICAN LAW

On the Moral Presumption against Capital Punishment

It is beyond question that the legal debate over capital punishment in the United States is grounded in a moral presumption against the use of capital punishment. Not only opponents of capital punishment but supporters too would affirm this common agreement. The reason for this claim is that in the United States each year there are anywhere from 14,000 to 23,000 criminal homicides. If a simple retribution ethic were in play legally—by that I mean an ethic that said that those who unjustly take a life must necessarily forfeit their own—we should expect to have thousands of executions each year. We do not. We sentence a little over 1 percent of murderers to death every year and execute not thousands, but only a handful. The number of executions comes nowhere near the number of murders:[4] 37 executions out of 14,180 murders in the United States in 2008 (.027%)[5] and 46 executions out of 14, 748 murders in 2010 (0.3%).[6] The American legal system has refused to endorse mandatory death sentences, and it has not called for the expansion of execution to cover every instance of wrongful killing. On the contrary, American law has limited the use of the execution power by imposing on it various conditions and restrictions. It is important to keep in the forefront of the moral debate over execution that the American legal system—through the courts and legislatures and the safety net of executive clemency power—affirms a moral presumption *against* the use of the death penalty. The low number of executions relative to the high number of criminal homicides or other capital crimes establishes this as an unmistakable datum of moral relevance.

But executions are assigned and carried out. American law has devised a system of justice checks that have as their purpose establishing tests of justice—again, the criteria—that must be met and satisfied if state power is going to be used to kill a citizen and if the execution is going to be deemed not only lawful but morally justified. The criteria that are relevant to the idea of just execution articulate restraints on the execution power, and these restraints are publicly exposed in American law. The American legal system accepts that ordinarily states ought not to execute citizens, even for murder, and this common agreement can be discerned in the appeal to statistics—the number of executions divided by the number of homicides. The numbers provide convincing evidence that the very system that claims power to execute—and does execute—also abides by the common agreement that states ordinarily ought not to execute their citizens.

The Nine Criteria for Lifting the Presumption against Capital Punishment

But the state does execute its citizens. From the moral point of view, the simple fact that executions do take place indicates that a theory of just execution is in play, providing a system of authorization and justification for an execution. From a moral point of view, whenever an execution takes place, it does so because good and sufficient reasons have been made to justify lifting the presumption against execution. Would a theory of just execution justify this lifting of a presumption against execution? Before offering a moral critique of the execution practice, let us consider what would be included in the legal appeal to a "just execution" ethic.

On the criterion of legitimate authority: Although the state reserves the right to punish criminal offenders and will neither sanction lethal acts of vigilantism nor condone individual vengeance against criminal offenders, it does not endorse an unqualified execution power. The federal judiciary has ruled that the legitimate authority for execution rests with the states and the federal government. In *Gregg v. Georgia* (1976) the court held that because capital punishment "does not invariably violate the Constitution," legal authorities are free to devise execution laws or not; it then specified legal restraints on use of that power, such things as requiring objective standards for juries to follow in their deliberations about sentencing, requiring mandated appeals, and insisting on jury consideration of mitigating circumstances in assessing capital punishment eligibility. American law certainly recognizes the legitimacy of the execution power, but it subjects that power to oversight so that it conforms to the United States Constitution, which, from a legal standpoint, is the ultimate legal authority for the execution practice in the United States. This first criterion establishes the justification for the state claim to the execution power while also restricting any socially organized use of lethal force against citizens outside the system of legal protections, so that extralegal community execution practices such as lynching are expressly prohibited.

Second, on the idea of just cause: the United States Supreme Court has held in *South Carolina v. Gathers* (490 U.S. 805) the unremarkable opinion that punishment in criminal law is based on an "assessment of [the] harm caused by the defendant as a result of the crime charged." This idea is relevant to proportionality (discussed later in this chapter) but here can be cited as also allowing that criminal wrongdoing is itself a just cause for the legal authority to sanction punishment, one such authorized punishment being the death penalty. Through legislative and court action, the American legal system has restricted the crimes for which execution may be imposed, although the list of crimes has been expanded significantly in recent years.[7] In general, however, the crime for which one may receive the death penalty is aggravated murder. Whether aggravated murder is just cause for invoking a punishment of death has been related to a long-standing legal discussion regarding Eighth Amendment prohibitions on cruel and unusual punishment and how that prohibition is directly tied to the standards of decency held by the American people. The issue has been considered by the U.S. Supreme Court, not only in the *Trop v. Dulles* (356 U.S. 86 [1958]) decision, where this test was enunciated by Chief Justice Earl Warren ("evolving standards of decency"), but even in the landmark *Furman v. Georgia* decision (408 U.S. 238 [1972]), where Justices Brennan and Marshall argued that capital punishment violated contemporary norms of decency. Behind this "evolving standards of decency" test is *Weems v. United States* (217 U.S. 349 [1910]), which acknowledged that "time works changes, brings into existence new conditions and purposes," and ideas of what is and what is not "decent" can be affected as "public opinion becomes enlightened by a humane justice."

If the death penalty were ever declared unconstitutional on the explicit grounds of "cruel and unusual punishment," justification for that change in policy would no doubt be directed to this evolving standards of decency test, with the determination being made, morally, that crimes that had formerly served to provide a just cause for execution now fail to do so.[8] The United States Supreme Court in its decision in *Atkins v. Virginia* (536 U.S. 304 [2002]) acted to prevent execution of the mentally retarded; and it did so making explicit appeal to this legal—and moral—doctrine. Suffice it to say that just cause is ultimately based on a judgment that execution conforms to majority public opinion and a legal opinion about the contemporary sense of decency. When the US Supreme Court struck down as capital crimes rape in *Coker v. Georgia* (433 U.S. 584 [1977]) and kidnapping in *Eberhart v. Georgia* (433 U.S. 917 [1977]), those decisions not only declared execution disproportionate to the crime, but they also invoked a standards of decency test, which execution for these crimes failed. From a moral point of view, execution for these crimes failed to satisfy the criterion of just cause. Aggravated murder, on the other hand, has been upheld as a sufficient and just, though not necessary, cause for invoking the execution power.

Third, the motivation for applying lethal punishment must be justice, not vengeance. As Kant, a great death penalty retributivist, argued, hatred-filled vengeance is a vicious motivation that does not accord with the dispensing of justice,[9] and any theory of just execution will be presented as motivated by a concern for justice. On the legal front, the courts seek to satisfy this criterion when they take action to prevent arbitrariness or inflamed jury opinion from affecting verdicts or when they demand that decisions about imposing death be formed through a rational process of deliberation. Jurors are to reach their conclusions not through passion but by the application of objective criteria.[10] *Woodson v. North Carolina* (428 U.S. 280 [1976]) imposed what the court called "objective standards to guide, regularize and make rationally reviewable the process for imposing a death sentence"—no talk of passions but only of rational determination and judgment. The emotional effect on jurors of victim impact testimony was at first rejected by the Supreme Court (*South Carolina v. Gathers*, 490 U.S. 805 [1989]) but then allowed in so that "the full moral force" of the events at issue in sentencing might be heard. The court wanted juries to proceed in deliberation and "not [be] swayed by mere sentiment, conjecture, sympathy, passion, prejudice, public opinion or public feeling," as Justice O'Connor said. The court had earlier declared itself committed to the necessity of rational deliberation in capital sentencing when it declared, "Capital sentencing decisions must not be made on mere whim but instead on clear and objective standards" (*California v. Brown*, 479 U.S. 538 [1987]).

Fourth, executions must be administered fairly, without accidental features such as race, religion, class, or sex affecting who gets the death penalty. This is, of course, a major justice issue at stake when imposing the death penalty, and the 1972 *Furman v. Georgia* decision, which imposed what turned out to be a four-year halt to executions, was in fact a court recognition that the death sentence had been imposed in an arbitrary, capricious, even freakish manner. All subsequent rulings by the Court were designed to extirpate discrimination and require evenhandedness in death sentencing. The famous case of *McCleskey v. Kemp* (481 U.S. 297 [1987]) raised racial bias issues in a new and dramatic way. My layman's view of this decision is that the court could have granted McCleskey relief only by ruling that the criminal justice system was itself unconstitutional, for the argument in that case was that the criminal justice system *as a system* was shown to deprive black defendants equal protection under the law.[11] That said, the general thrust of American law has been to demand nondiscrimination, and even McCleskey held open the possibility of relief if discrimination could be shown in individual cases. The legal system does *aim* at a system free of unfair, capricious, and arbitrary imposition of the death penalty, however contrary that ideal may be to the execution practice.

Fifth, the death penalty is to be used as an expression of cherished values, and it must not subvert the goods of life but promote and advance the value of life. "Capital punishment is our society's recognition of the sanctity of life," Senator Orrin Hatch says.[12] The courts have acknowledged that standards of decency determine whether or not we have a death penalty, and the idea of killing an offender in conformity to those standards affirms how highly life is cherished, which can be summarized as followed: life is cherished so highly that persons who unjustly take a life risk losing their own.

Sixth, executions ought to be carried out in line with a prohibition on cruelty. Every change in execution method has been advanced as a way of killing more humanely—from the invention of the guillotine to Edison's first electric chair to lethal injection. This criterion has come into play in various incidents, including challenges to the state of Florida over its unreliable and malfunctioning electric chair. The cruelty challenge was stopped by the Florida legislature, which met in special session to authorize what it believed was the more humane option of using lethal injection as the authorized mode of dispatching capital offenders. The legal system has sought to conform to this criterion without doubt.

Seventh, since executions take a life and life is so highly regarded in our moral community, execution ought to be a last resort, meaning that no other response but execution will serve the interests of justice. The legal system seems to acknowledge this criterion in its restrictive application of the death penalty—that there are only certain cases that merit the death penalty, that they are special, and that they are and should be relatively rare. Therefore, the logic would seem to go as follows: those individuals who receive a death sentence do so as a judgment on the part of the justice system that execution is the appropriate penalty, that no other penalty would be adequate and hence, de facto, we satisfy last resort. Last resort seems to be involved in dispensing death sentences against the backdrop of a legal system where different jurisdictions dispense different punishments and open different options for eventual release, even after so serious a crime as murder, which can at times warrant a seven-year—sometimes shorter—prison term.[13] Imposing capital punishment in capital cases where the killing is deemed especially egregious seems to some to have the effect of preventing a particularly dangerous murderer from reentering society and threatening it, so execution could be thought to ensure societal protection—and juries do act in line with this justification, even in jurisdictions where a life sentence for murder means no possibility of parole. This particular appeal to last resort does affect juries, but note that this kind of reasoning points to a problem involving failures of the criminal justice system to assure citizens of protection rather than being a death penalty justification per se.

Eighth, execution ought to aim at restoring a value equilibrium distorted and upset by an offender's wrongdoing. Restorative justice efforts at this point are deemed inappropriate in aggravated murder cases. Retributive justice, however, has been appealed to as the means whereby the scales of justice, upset by the murderer's unjust act, have their equilibrium put back in balance, or so society seems to have adjudged the matter. The fact that laws have been written to allow surviving victims to witness executions is some legal recognition that the law is concerned that the retributive act of execution serve the end of satisfying the victim survivors that justice has been done, so such laws would provide evidence of support for this criterion in the legal system.

And ninth, execution should be a proportionate response to the offense committed. For the sake of argument, we shall adopt a Kantian standpoint and stipulate that execution is a proportionate response to only one crime, aggravated murder. In decision after decision, the Supreme Court has addressed the issue of proportionality, and certain crimes have been proscribed as inappropriate for execution. The court has ruled *against* mandatory death sentences in *Woodson v. North Carolina* (1976) and *Sumner v. Shuman* (483 U.S. 66 [1987]), thus eliminating the idea that death is *always* a proportionate sentence for a certain type of crime.[14] The court's reasoning in reserving to jury discretion the type of punishment is that by this stipulation the actual details of a particular case must be considered and evaluated so that a proportionate response may issue, one that is not excessive for certain types of crime (e.g., rape or kidnapping). *Coker v. Georgia* was a proportionality decision; *Lockett v. Ohio* (438 U.S. 586 [1978]) dealt with mitigating circumstances, and *Godfrey v. Georgia* (446 U.S. 420 [1980]) with aggravating circumstances—all in an effort to weigh relevant factors in a defendant's circumstance so that sentencing might be rendered proportionate to the crime. *Edmund v. Florida* (458 U.S. 782 [1982]) ruled that a party present in the circumstances of capital murder who was nonparticipant and lacking in intent was not liable to be executed; and *Pulley v. Harris* (465 U.S. 37 [1984]) was a proportionality review case in which the court entrusted states to regulate the imposition of capital punishment in accordance with basic fairness. *Ford v. Wainwright* (477 U.S. 399 [1986]) prohibited the execution of the mentally incompetent, calling it "mindless vengeance," and *Thompson v. Oklahoma* (487 U.S. 815 [1988]) banned the execution of persons under the age of sixteen.

In all these matters—in court decisions, in statutes passed by legislatures—the legal system is shown straining to preserve capital punishment as legal action consistent not only with constitutional principles but with moral ideals of permissible action and necessary restraint, especially in light of the fact that at issue in capital punishment is the morally weighty matter of the state acting intentionally and willfully to extinguish a human life. The decisions above appeal not only to the constitution and a legal system but to a moral theory—a common agreement–based theory of just execution, a theory that holds an execution is permissible only if it meets certain criteria of justice.

THE VALUE OF THE THEORY

Noting that the legal system makes an implicit appeal to a just execution theory does not settle the moral debate over capital punishment. The purpose of the appeal to such a theory is, rather, to frame the moral issues and make conversation and debate possible. The value of the theory lies in its articulation of those moral concerns relevant to the notion of justice, which reasonable people can be expected to affirm without undue controversy. The just execution framework structures debate and insists that engagement over moral issues proceed from a common affirmation of moral meaning. And even though contemporary debate over capital punishment does not make formal appeal to the theory *as a theory*, no important conversation about the moral meaning of the death penalty proceeds without appealing, at least implicitly, to the particulars of the theory. The criteria just discussed identify justice issues that guide moral deliberation around a common agreement, namely, that ordinarily the state ought not to kill its citizens, not even by capital punishment. We have identified the empirical warrants that support this claim. Persons on both sides of the death penalty debate can—and do—appeal to just execution criteria in the course of the debate. The criteria appear in deliberations over particular issues in particular cases. And I have broached the theory of just execution though a discussion of the legal system to suggest that developments that have occurred in American law around the issue of capital punishment have not taken place in a moral vacuum. In fact, the law on capital punishment has developed over the years in response to justice challenges to execution practices that fail to meet the "just execution" guidelines, with the 1972 *Furman* decision going so far as to halt executions altogether because of the injustices associated with discriminatory imposition practices. That "just execution" theory, grounded in natural law ethics, can be invoked to explain the review of capital punishment in the American legal system as that system has addressed the serious moral question of capital punishment and the exercise of the state execution power.

In case after case over the course of the past forty years, the law has affirmed the moral presumption that the state ordinarily ought not to kill its citizens. Legal review has also attended to questions about fair imposition and other justice problems in the capital punishment system such that justice-related criteria have developed in the law to govern the execution practice. The legal developments, whether brought about by legislatures or by court review, are fraught with moral meaning, and, as I have argued here, they demonstrate that the legal system itself is seeking to conform to an implicit moral theory—a "just execution" theory grounded in a common moral agreement opposed to the death penalty. The value of pointing out that American law appeals implicitly to a theory of just execution is that once such a theory is articulated and can be seen as the legal embodiment of a moral theory, the theory can then be used as the bar of justice against which the execution practice can be evaluated. *In other words, we can test the American execution practice against the very standards of justice that the practice recognizes as the requirements of justice.* A moral theory, we have been arguing, must be reconciled to our moral experience, and we can investigate the execution practice to see whether the way we actually apply the death penalty is consistent with the standards of justice articulated in the theory and to which the law itself is making implicit appeal. We can then find ourselves in a position to discern the moral meaning of the American practice of execution. The judgments we shall make about the practice of execution in light of that moral theory will not be idiosyncratic or grounded in a religious or political ideology. They will, rather, be framed around the concerns for justice that invite all reasonable persons into reflection, deliberation, and conversation around a commonly accepted structure of moral meaning.

And that is, in fact, how we debate the particularities of justice-related issues relevant to the death penalty. We frame our disagreements over particulars around a structure of value that is itself not in dispute. Take the just execution prohibition on discrimination, for example. Although there is dispute as to whether evidence actually shows that the American execution practice discriminates on the basis of race, class, or sex, debate goes on because both death penalty defenders and death penalty opponents acknowledge that discrimination is morally unacceptable. So there is debate about the facts and even about what those facts mean, but there is not a debate over the criterion of just execution that insists on nondiscriminatory imposition. About that criterion of nondiscrimination both sides of the dispute will agree. Disagreement arises, then, not because human beings hold hopelessly diverse opinions about value questions that are relative and simply cannot be conformed to one another. Disagreements arise over empirical issues and their interpretation, or because of differences in the way we choose to emphasize values in relation to one another. But the point is that in moral debate, disputants enter into the same moral arena to debate the meaning of facts and exercise judgment in light of a structure of moral thinking and system of moral valuation that are not themselves in dispute.

Just execution, like just war or just nontreatment of neonates, is grounded in a broadly conceived and widely accepted presumption about moral meaning. The presumption is not an absolute principle, so the idea that the presumption could be lifted in certain situations or circumstances yields criteria that indicate how that presumption might be lifted in accordance with the requirements of justice. Such a theory is a structure for moral thinking and reflecting—it is not a panacea that can by fiat simply establish moral meaning. And it requires that persons come into the debate educated and informed about the various matters relevant to the justice concerns: Does execution desensitize a society to violence? Is the imposition of death sentences discriminatory? Are methods of execution cruel and torturous? and so on. Opinions are always available on such questions, but debate enabled by just execution theory wants debate to proceed based on reasoned interpretation itself based on knowledge, experience, and substantive information. Impressionistic opinions will not do. Just execution requires disputants to enter into conversation having learned as much as they can about the issue under debate and prepared to offer reasoned interpretations, which will then reflect not only extent of learning but depth of wisdom. In this way of conceiving of ethical reflection, knowledge and its interpretation, not the structure of moral meaning, is in dispute.

If ethics and moral inquiry are nothing but private opinion, this theory is irrelevant. If law defines morality, this theory is irrelevant. But if moral inquiry seeks to find a basis for common moral understanding and reasonable agreement, if it can be seen as the compass directing how the law develops and finds practical expression, then a "just execution" theory establishes the framework to make such developments possible. And the theory can be used to discern moral agreements in spite of all that may be disputed, in spite of all that separates those who oppose the death penalty from those who support it.

We can articulate what some of those areas of agreement ought to be. Appealing to just execution theory, persons could easily assert the moral horror of executing an innocent person. No reasonable person should ever want to support or condone or respond with indifference to the prospect of a wrongful execution. Should the courts be required to hear evidence of actual innocence when petitioners make such claims after their convictions? Federal courts have said no, but if doing so is reasonable, then the decision in *Herrera v. Collins* (506 U.S. 390 [(1993]) comes under tough moral scrutiny at this point. Other agreements can be fashioned as well: the death penalty ought not to be imposed arbitrarily or unfairly; it ought not to be an instrument of vengeance or passion or secured in a case through the use of inflammatory testimony; it ought not to devalue respect for life but enhance it—thus providing critique of every cheer ever uttered outside a prison where an execution has taken place; it ought to be imposed as the most severe penalty for the most severe crime, the unlawful and aggravated taking of human life. (And when it is pointed out that at times some drug offenders in the United States have served more time behind bars than murderers, the question can be raised whether murder is, in fact, the crime society and the legal system deem the most serious offense.[15]) *Just execution provides a framework to enable moral critique of policy and practice.*[16] It will ask how death rows have changed in makeup since the death penalty was overturned in *Furman* in 1972 on the grounds that the death penalty was being imposed arbitrarily, capriciously, and freakishly. What does it mean, morally speaking, if all the legal "reform" that has taken place in American law since the *Furman* decision put a moratorium on executions has not effected change in the execution practice? What does it mean if death rows today look exactly as they did forty years ago, filled, that is, disproportionately with males, minorities, and poor people? A just execution theory will pose this question to the criminal justice system and ask how closely the practice of execution is conformed to the "just execution" moral theory that is implicit in the law.

Just execution theory is structural common ground. Huge debates about the criteria should not be expected, for they are grounded in basic goods of life and function to maintain those goods by restraining the state's power to execute. On the other hand, the criteria offered above should be subjected to critique and changed if deficient. As long as the death penalty exists, every effort must be made to observe not only constitutional safeguards but also the moral requirements laid out in the just execution framework to which that constitutional-legal system appeals. Execution is a killing, and a killing will always require the most strenuous kind of justification process. The moral presumption in capital punishment is against using state power to kill, and tests have been devised—inscribed in law actually—which to meet could lift the presumption against capital punishment. Failure to lift that presumption locates execution in the moral arena of wrongful homicide, even murder.

The ultimate moral question to come out of debate over the possibility of just execution is whether capital punishment is an exception to the moral presumption with which we started—is it ever permissible for the state to kill its own citizens? The question is whether capital punishment qualifies as a particular way of killing citizens that meets the requirements of justice and is thus morally constituted as a justifiable mode of state killing.

My objective here has been to lay out the structure for a theory of just execution that is grounded in natural law ethics but that functions today as a moral theory to which American law has made implicit appeal. I have else-where presented my views as to how well the American execution practice conforms to the moral ideals enshrined in just execution,[17] and although I shall not reiterate them all again here, I will share that I find the execution practice at odds with the theory. Thought and experience do not meet in the *practice* of execution—and it is the common agreement ethic articulated here as "just execution" that exposes this problem. Serious deficiencies can be found when the practice of execution is measured against the action guides of the just execution criteria, and failure at the point of one criterion suffices to deny the death penalty moral legitimacy. There are, I believe, significant issues to raise with all nine criteria, and let me point out how one influential person appealed implicitly to a "just execution" criterion to condemn the ex-ecution practice. Several years ago in a speech in St. Louis, Pope John Paul II condemned the death penalty on natural law grounds.[18] He implicitly ap-pealed to what I have here called a criterion of *last resort*. His comment was that because societies are now able to provide protection against those who engage in terrible criminal wrongdoing, such as aggravated murder, capital punishment is not necessary for such societal protection—we have other means today to assure public safety. We do not need to do this. The pope's remarks provide evidence for the fact that in debates over capital punishment, we inevitably argue over capital punishment at the justice points of the "just execution" criteria. Articulating those criteria, which has been my purpose, may help to facilitate the debate, narrow the moral issues worthy of attention, and result in more informed voices entering into the conversation over the moral meaning of the death penalty.

Just execution theory does not itself provide the resources to answer specific questions about such things as discrimination, last resort, or whether the value of life is enhanced or diminished by execution. What just execution theory does is organize inquiry and establish common ground for engaged conversation and debate. People of goodwill debate this issue, and much is at stake. For this theory holds that if any criterion fails the test, an execution is rendered impermissible. My own examination of the death penalty has led me to conclude that given the strict requirements of the theory, no execution in America as part of the execution system can possibly meet all of the criteria, so no execution is morally justified. What is significant about this statement is that it represents a morally moderate conclusion, since one can oppose capital punishment yet still affirm that there are situations where the state can act to kill a citizen and do so justifiably. The point is that execution does not happen to be a form of state killing that meets the test of moral justification. Just execution theory convinces me that where capital punishment is concerned, the presumption against the state killing its own citizens should remain in place and stay undisturbed.

If the practice of execution is evaluated in light of the moral guidelines of just execution theory, that theory will itself contribute to sounding the death knell of capital punishment. The practice will be exposed as unjust and unjustifiable, for the execution practice will necessarily fail to meet the stringent demands of reason and justice. That end will come about only if we also engage in vigorous debate over the death penalty practice and if citizens enter that debate having become educated about how our legal system operates to put persons to death. That process is mysterious and unknown to most Americans. Yet just execution makes a contribution at just this point, for it calls citizens to take responsibility for engaging in informed conversation about a legal and public policy issue of deep moral significance. Just execution theory, then, this product of natural law that has found its way at least implicitly into American law, is a spur to citizen education; and the increase of educated citizens is finally the best evidence we have for avowing the reality of an "evolving standard of decency"—that moral ideal embedded in American law.

A JUST CRIMINAL JUSTICE SYSTEM

Having now used the just war–related ethic to examine the issue of capital punishment, we can turn to the broader question of "just punishment." In keeping with the contention that our natural law–based common agreement ethic is applicable to issues *beyond* just war, this particular question extends the discussion opened with capital punishment. Since punishment is dispensed through a legal system supported, inescapably, by moral ideals and common agreements that the law seeks to institutionalize and codify for purposes of social regulation, a further analysis, brief though it shall be, will indicate the implications of this ethic for social policy. The capital punishment discussion has implications for social policy, to be sure, for if the guidelines (i.e., criteria) for just execution are examined carefully and in light of actual experience, the execution practice will inevitably fail to meet the tests of moral justification. The rational conclusion of this failure is that executions should, as a moral matter, stop. Just punishment will also have significant implications for social policy, but before suggesting what those might be, let us sketch what a theory of "just punishment" would look like using our just war–related ethical model.

THE PROBLEM OF RACIAL DISPARITIES

Crime is an arousing yet difficult issue in American society. Elections are won due to the stances political figures take on crime. Candidates viewed as "soft on crime" do not typically fare well in their quest for public office, and the example of Michael Dukakis opposing the death penalty in a debate with then vice president George H. W. Bush in the 1988 election makes the point. "Law and order" is a continual electoral theme in American politics, but policies governing punishment for criminal offenses have produced a justice system marked by racial and class disparities. In his influential book *Malign Neglect: Race, Crime and Punishment in America*,[19] Michael Tonry has chronicled how the "war on drugs" pursued by the Reagan and Bush administrations led to disproportionately high incarceration rates and inequalities in sentencing for poor people and blacks compared with middle-class whites. The war on drugs led to legislative, judicial, and even policing efforts that imposed a disproportionately harsh burden on minority groups, especially inner-city black males, who were most likely to be visible to police and arrested. Sentencing for the possession and sale of crack cocaine, for instance, used and sold mainly by blacks in the inner city, was much more severe than for powder cocaine used by whites in more suburban settings, despite the same pharmacological composition and effect of the drug.[20] The war on drugs led to a rewriting of sentencing laws. Possession of three grams of crack cocaine in Minnesota, for example, could bring a maximum twenty-year sentence compared with five years for powder and sentencing recommendations of forty-eight months for crack compared with probation for powder; in federal sentencing guidelines, one gram of crack is treated as the equivalent of one hundred grams of powder.[21] Mandatory sentences were introduced, and penalties became harsher. The war on drugs led to sentencing policies that were race and class biased, and this bias is the origin of the swelling of the American prison system population that today bestows on the United States the dubious honor of the highest per capita imprisonment rate in the world. Note that I shall be relying on Tonry's study in what follows because his analysis and call for reform appeals implicitly to the ethic of "just punishment" to be laid out in the following paragraphs, Tonry being one more example of a thinker making an implicit appeal to the common agreement ethic I have been advocating, in this instance an ethic relevant to "just punishment."

Tonry's study examined the policies pursued in the 1980s that led to the racial disparities in sentencing, and he notes, "A virtuous government would take account of the likely racial effects of contemplated policies. . . . Current patterns of racial injustice in the justice system (and the welfare system) will continue until governments reject them because they are wrong."[22] Contrary to conventional wisdom and electioneering slogans, imposing harsher penalties has little effect on crime rates, it does not treat offenders with drug problems, and the criminal justice system continues to lock up more black offenders than white. Blacks account for about 13 percent of the population, but they represent half of all incarcerated Americans. Human Rights Watch reported in 2008:

> Statistics released . . . by the Bureau of Justice Statistics, a branch of the US Department of Justice, show that as of June 30, 2007, approximately 2.3 million persons were incarcerated in US prisons and jails, an all-time high. This represents an incarceration rate of 762 per 100,000 US residents, the highest such rate in the world. By contrast, the United Kingdom's incarceration rate is 152 per 100,000 residents; the rate in Canada is 108; and in France it is 91. . . . The new statistics also show large racial disparities, with black males incarcerated at a per capita rate six times that of white males. Nearly 11 percent of all black men ages 30 to 34 were behind bars as of June 30, 2007.[23]

Tonry lays the blame for this situation on politics and policies rather than on the criminal justice system itself, but the criminal justice system, in following the policies set by elected officials and governmental leaders, becomes the instrument of the policy and thus cannot be exempted from examination and even moral critique. And while he does not exempt individual offenders from responsibility, Tonry insists that the fact of disadvantage be taken into account in any effort to create a just response to an offense against law and society.

In contemplating the moral issues involved in sentencing and punishment, we need to find some common agreements underwriting the problem of punishment itself. There are, of course, many theories of punishment. They range from retributive "just deserts" ideas, where inflicting pain on an offender for the pain the offender caused establishes the mechanism of justice, to consequentialist theories that focus on rehabilitation as the way to achieve and advance the greatest societal benefit. Restitution and restorative notions of justice are also relevant to the justice system question.

A common agreement or moral presumption must underwrite any theory of "just punishment" as it addresses the moral meaning of sentencing procedures. Such a presumption would rest on an appeal to the goods of life, which, as we have argued previously, people will pursue however they are situated in life, since it is their nature to do so. Law provides a means for establishing order in society so that people can pursue the goods of life, and political and governmental systems devise laws in order to regulate human interactions and relationships and thus maintain the orderly societal conditions necessary for human flourishing. Laws may be inherently coercive, but ideally they seek to institutionalize a moral reality, namely, that people are bound together in a social framework of mutual respect and obligation.

When the law is broken and an offense committed, relationships are broken, the bonds of societal unity are strained or even severed, and the conditions for flourishing are adversely affected, even undermined. The conditions of societal peace and harmony that make human flourishing possible must be restored to equilibrium when injury, harm, or offense unjustly deprive persons of their well-being and negatively affect the ability of persons to enjoy goods of life. Those who harm others can deprive their victims of the ability to enjoy such goods as bodily integrity, or meaningful interaction with one's environment, or the freedom to work or play, or the capability to experience pleasure or aesthetic delight—or, in extreme offense, even the good of life itself. Our justice systems are, from a moral point of view, designed to effect the process of putting right the upset moral equilibrium created by offense, which identifies a societal response aimed at rectification. And to engage the process of rectification is to aim at restoring persons to their position as persons of integrity deserving of respect and just treatment from others. Rectifying justice would also require that victims of offense receive fair compensation for losses incurred by injury or offense. Our justice systems represent the whole of society acting to address a relational fracture created by some wrongdoing or the infliction of some harm, the intention being to repair that fracture of injustice and restore the equilibrium and balance of justice. Justice in this moral sense refers to rectification or the process of putting upset things right.

On this understanding, just punishment could be said to rest on a guiding moral presumption or common agreement that can be expressed as follows: *To pursue the goods of life in a way that leads to human flourishing, hu-*

man beings are obligated to respect one another and order society in ways that promote peaceful, responsible, and harmonious relationships with others. This articulation of a common agreement is meant to satisfy the moral point of view, with its concern for universalizability, benevolence, impartial justice, and normative principles. It is not offered to endorse any particular political philosophy, theory of government, or ideology.

Of course, human beings sometimes do not respect one another but act in ways that harm or injure others. When this happens, some effort to rectify the relational imbalance created by the offense—the harmful or injurious act—is necessary, for wrongful and injurious acts disrupt social harmony and undermine human flourishing. Acts that violate respect for persons, or undermine social harmony, or create conditions of disorder that upset the peace do not call in the first instance for punishment of the offender. What justice requires is rectifying action that restores the balance and harmonious relationships between offender and offended upset by a wrongful and injurious act of injustice. It is perhaps worth noting that the idea of rectifying justice was Aristotle's original notion of retribution. By retribution, he meant a rectifying justice, a justice that put things right and restored relational harmony.

In light of the moral presumption above, let us note that the vast majority of offenses people commit against one another in everyday life may be rectified by apology, by some act of contrition subsequent to an apology, or by some effort at restitution for losses suffered. But as the severity of offense increases, rectifying the imbalance created by the offense becomes more difficult, and punishment becomes an option when the imbalance is so severe that society itself, and not just an individual victim, is harmed and thus demands rectifying action due to the injury it claims to receive. A punishment that is aimed at rectification would address the fact that offenders misuse their freedom—such misuse of freedom can be viewed as posing a continuing threat to societal harmony. A rectifying punishment would insist that offenders take responsibility for their offenses and submit to rectifying action, which in the case of serious criminal offenses would be this: that punishment must be directed at the moral center of the personality where decision making went astray in a misuse of freedom, requiring, then, that freedom be restricted or even taken away, at least until such time as it is determined that the offender may resume life in society respectful of persons and committed to using freedom responsibly.

Restricting freedom—and imprisonment is only one means by which this can be accomplished—can serve the ends of a rectifying justice by protecting society while also restoring the offender to a harmonious relationship with the whole society. Whether incarceration is the best means to accomplish rectification and restoration is, of course, open to question, and individual cases should be examined. Often a victim never receives compensation when an offender goes off to prison, and revisionist theories of justice, such as restorative justice, are making a more complicated move, requiring that an offender directly address the injustice dealt a victim. Making restitution directly to the offended offers a more productive means for rebalancing the upset scales of justice and thus addressing the harm experienced by an aggrieved society when a criminal offense occurs.

It may well be that people queried about the idea of fair punishment will respond with a retributivist response that a punishment should impose like harm for like harm, as in "an eye for an eye." But if the moral presumption underwriting punishment is, in fact, a true common agreement having to do with restoring relational harmony, reasonable people of goodwill should, upon reflection, acknowledge that the purpose of punishment is not to inflict pain, especially on the body, which is not the moral center of the human person, but to meet a justice demand that those who have misused freedom ought to have their freedom abridged. The misuse of freedom poses a continued threat to the well-being of the moral community and the flourishing of individual members. Confinement or incarceration for serious offenders is in order and can serve the just end of rectifying an imbalance in relationship created by an offender's wrongful and injurious act. But lesser crimes may be better dealt with by posing another kind of restriction on freedom, such as requiring that an offender make restitution to the victim. "Eye for an eye" thinking is widespread, and we should surely take account of it since our effort here is to conform thought with experience—and there is no doubt that the American incarceration rate reflects a widespread retributivist attitude toward crime. But eye-for-an-eye thinking is also divorced from the *experience* of persons who want protection from crime and who, if victimized, want a just response to the harm that has been visited upon them.

Eye-for-an-eye thinking may be invoked as shorthand for a rectifying justice response, but few hold to such a notion *literally*, since it is in the demand for rectification, not retribution, that people *seek* justice. In 2004, an Iranian woman was blinded by acid thrown at her by a marriage suitor she had rejected. She appealed to Sharia law, and the courts granted that her attacker could be similarly blinded by acid as punishment—the ultimate literal case of eye-for-an-eye justice. Reasonable people of goodwill the world over reacted in horror.[24] Such harsh retribution is at odds with the rectifying justice that seeks the ends of harmonious relationships and a society restored to peace. Would not a just response to the Iranian woman's tragic situation have been to abridge the offender's freedom and insist that he contribute to his victim's upkeep and comfort and medical expenses for the rest of his (or her) life? Such a punishment would have constituted a serious long-term restriction on the offender's freedom while requiring, in the interests of a rectifying justice, that he make restitution to the individual he had harmed, whose injuries were permanently disabling and debilitating, whose need for care is lifelong, and who would benefit by the support and assistance the offender could offer as the one responsible for causing devastating suffering. Rectifying justice is about the effort to restore balance and harmony; it is not motivated by revenge, and it does not amount to eye-for-an-eye retribution.

THE CRITERIA OF JUST PUNISHMENT

If we allow that punishment has a legitimate role in regulating society for certain identifiably serious offenses, how do we ensure that punishment and the legal system's procedures in sentencing are just? How do we allow sentencing when our moral presumption is geared toward harmony and social relationships? We are led by that presumption to do something other than righteously demand punishment when an unjust injury occurs. The justice demand ought to be aimed at a rectification that restores relationship to the end of human flourishing, not only for society and the victim of an offense, but for the offender as well. Drawing in part from Michael Tonry's reflections on the American criminal justice system, I suggest the following criteria as the justice concerns that should govern just punishment and just sentencing. Some of these criteria will be similar to those invoked in the death penalty discussion, but here the focus is not on the weightier question of justified killing, but on a restoration of societal harmony in the wake of offense:

1. Punishment and sentencing of offenders must be legitimately authorized.
2. There must be just cause for inflicting a punishment, which is to say, the offense itself must be sufficiently grave that society itself is aggrieved and the community well-being is adversely affected.
3. The motivation for punishment must be justice, not vengeance.
4. Punishments must be distributed and administered fairly, without accidental features such as race, religion, class, or sex affecting administration of the punishment.
5. Punishment and sentencing must express cherished values and be a part of a sanction that seeks to restore peace and harmony and even restitution for aggrieved parties.
6. Punishments ought not to be cruel and dehumanizing but should observe the law of parsimony (i.e., the least harsh sentence) and aim at restoring offenders to their rightful place in the moral community.

7. Punishment ought to be sought as a last resort, with every effort made to restore the relationship of offender and offended by means of restitution for an offended person's pain, loss, and suffering.
8. Punishment ought to restore a value equilibrium distorted and upset by the wrongdoing.
9. Punishment policies must observe a principle of proportionality in a social justice sense, for if not all persons have the same opportunity to participate in society, economic and social disadvantage must be seen as "affect[ing] the benefits of autonomy that produce obligation." The sentencing system should therefore demonstrate willingness to mitigate sentences by taking into account both social injustices and the personal circumstances of individual offenders.[25]

Let me briefly comment on each of these criteria of just punishment.

1. The first criterion, dealing with legitimate authority, is meant to locate authority for the dispensing of justice within an accountable and reviewable justice system. This criterion dispenses with any justification for private revenge or for vigilantism, both of which tear at the fabric of social peace and harmony.

2. The just cause criterion requires first of all that the facts of an offense be laid out, rightly attributed to an offender, and then made available to public scrutiny. Punishment should follow those offenses only where it is clear that offenders have adversely affected the well-being of society and continue to pose some threat by their misuse of freedom. If the offense does not rise to that level, some other means of addressing the injustice of the offense ought to be found, such as a restorative justice agreement where individuals make restitution for the loss or suffering they have caused a victim. Punishment ought to be reserved for certain serious offenses where the damage or harm done by an offense can be shown to adversely affect societal well-being. Punishment ought not to be an assumed response to every offense but a considered and measured response justified by the details of the offense, which could certainly include such things as an offender's contrition, willingness to make restitution, and the like. Again, prison is one option, but there are others, including public service and a restitution action conformed to the details of the loss experienced by a victim.

One can only wonder at what a just punishment would look like for white-collar executives involved in matters such as the Enron debacle: the harm visited on society and on thousands of people, many of them public servants, and their pension plans certainly was sufficiently severe to warrant punishment. One major offender died before going to trial, but certainly justice would have been served if all wealth were taken from the responsible executives and their families or anyone close who benefited from their misdeeds; if that wealth were then liquefied and directed into the very accounts where the losses were suffered; and if, as punishment, the individual offenders were required to do community service as recompense for the pain and suffering they caused. Social harmony and just punishment would require that these individuals be taken away from the levers of power and out of the lifestyle that led to their acts of irresponsible wrongdoing, turned by a societal demand for rectifying justice in another direction, and then forced into a lifestyle where they could do no such harm again. Societal protection and a restoring of social harmony—these ends embodied in the moral presumption could be effected by such a "punishment" response. What seems abundantly clear is that putting Enron corporate criminals in prison and allowing them (and their families) to resume their lives in comfort after ruining thousands of people's lives hardly seems a "punishment-fits-the-crime" solution. Just cause requires that an offense rise to the level where the harms inflicted affect the peace and harmony of society so that punishment is justified; what form that punishment ought to take is open for review and consideration, but clearly a "just punishment" theory would want to consider a punishment fitting to the offense and aimed in the direction of restoring an individual to relationship with those injured by the offense.

3. The motivation for punishment should not be simple retaliation or vengeance, although it is conceivable that for especially heinous offenses a strong sense of "just deserts" for evil deeds could be deemed in order on a theory of just vengeance, if you will, one based on the idea that vengeance should be seen as an exception and not the rule. But in the same way that just punishment turns away in the first instance—literally the first criterion—from private or vigilante justice, which is more than likely vengeance driven, the motivation for punishment ought to be concern for the rectifying of wrongs and the restoration of harmony and peace. Although vengeance has been the subject of a resurgence of defense in recent years, especially in an interesting if not necessarily compelling argument by Peter French,[26] vengeance can derail the objectives of justice, make bad situations worse, and prevent even the possibility of reconciliation and forgiveness. When justice is the motivation for punishment, attention turns to the need to reestablish right relationship between perpetrator and victim and perpetrator and society, which allows room to consider the context for offenses, mitigating circumstances, and the role of social disadvantage. Vengeance can so isolate the issue of responsibility on perpetrators, removing them from situation and context and attributing to them complete responsibility, that assessing contributing factors beyond the individual can gain no hearing. It was not justice but a desire for vengeance that motivated Inspector Javert to hound Jean Valjean without mercy in Victor Hugo's *Les Misérables*, and the fact that the

original crime was breaking and entering and a theft of bread was simply not relevant to Valjean's pursuer, relevant though it be to any moral analysis of Valjean's criminal situation. Punishment can have a constructive role to play in the justice process, but it must be conformed to justice as rectification rather than handed over to the destructiveness of vengeance.

4. The nondiscrimination and fairness issue points to such policy decisions as those involved in the "war on drugs." That war was an "unjust war" in large part because it targeted black and minority neighborhoods. "Black Americans are less likely to have used drugs than whites are, for all major drugs except heroin," writes Tonry, "but the arrest percentages by race bear no relation to drug use percentages," so overwhelmingly do black proportions and percentages outstrip those of whites, with the biggest rise after 1980.[27] Between 1980 and 1990, drug arrests and imprisonment of blacks for drug offenses in Pennsylvania rose 1,613 percent, resulting in a 58 percent nonwhite prison population.[28] Punishments that reflect discriminatory policies cannot be said to be just, and one response to the increase in the prison population due to changes in drug laws was the demand for mandatory minimum sentences, which simply increased the discriminatory effect since minorities were subject to "easy" arrest in urban areas compared with whites, whose drug dealing took place in harder-to-detect suburban settings. The point of this information is that punishments to be just need to be above suspicion on the question of discrimination, and the transformation of the criminal justice system in the wake of the "war on drugs" has left convincing evidence of racial disparities and thus an unfair distribution of punishments.

5. Punishment and sentencing must express cherished values and be a part of a sanction that seeks to restore peace, harmony, and even restitution for aggrieved parties. This criterion opens up the possibility of responding to offenses in ways that seek to put things right for victims, and given the nature of some of the offenses that land people in jails and prisons, it should affect how certain types of crimes are framed for societal response. That is, rather than thinking about drug use as simply a crime that must be punished, harm-reduction strategies could be imposed, treating the negative effects of drug use as a public health problem, as is done in the Netherlands, where, with small amounts of marijuana actually sold legally in cafes, authorities claim that their approach has reduced crime, lessening the likelihood of thefts to secure money to buy drugs while also weakening the illicit drug delivery system. A justice system committed to restoring persons to society, fostering greater social harmony, and preserving cherished values will not ignore drug use, but will so reframe the meaning of drug use in society that different kinds of justice responses can take place, including harm-reduction approaches and increased treatment rather than imprisonment. These are justice responses

that "punish" offenders in the sense of depriving them of freedom and constricting choices, but not incapacitating them for citizenship, which is what the prison experience does to many who end up incarcerated.

6. Punishments ought not to be cruel and dehumanizing but should observe the law of parsimony[29] that aims at restoring offenders to their rightful place in the moral community. Michael Tonry's advocacy of "the least harsh sentence" by an invocation of the law of parsimony aims at this end, proscribing punishments for crimes that entailed no "unnecessary suffering" while "imposing the least severe punishment that meets legitimate social purposes" in every instance.[30] No punishment should ever be harsher than deserved—mandatory sentences and "three-strikes" laws that can put shoplifters in prison for life are examples of sentences that focus on crimes and not on persons, and they have led to egregious injustices being meted out. Punishments need to take into account an individual offender's circumstances, including the role that social and economic disadvantage can play in certain kinds of offenses, and the criminal justice response ought to be to fit a punishment to a crime, to prevent unduly harsh sentences by allowing mitigating circumstances to play their role, and to think of alternative sentences such as community service and restitution in tort offenses.

7. Punishment ought to be sought as a last resort, with every effort made to restore the relationship of offender and offended by means of restitution for an offended person's pain, loss, and suffering. Giving judges discretion to impose the least harsh sentence (parsimony) and a wide range of alternatives to imprisonment will go a long way toward making a criminal justice system more just in distribution of punishments and responses to crime. This last-resort feature is in play for all those offenses that are mitigated by first offense or otherwise handled by imposing a suspended sentence. It is not in play, however, in another sense, namely that many offenses are directed toward a prison sentence without a full exploration of an offender's circumstances, such as a breadwinner being taken away from the family, which is then reduced in circumstance and set on a course of greater hardship. Alternative sentencing and restorative justice practices can go a long way toward reforming a justice system that has placed too many offenders in prison with no benefit to the offender, the victim, or society.

8. Punishment ought to restore a value equilibrium distorted and upset by the wrongdoing. This criterion restates ideas already mentioned, but the importance of stating the justice aim of restoring the value equilibrium between offender and both victim and society is that this criterion identifies a measure for determining how successful a punishment has been. In other words, this criterion looks back on a punishment to consider the effects of the punishment, to see whether the value equilibrium has, in fact, been restored. Other

criteria dealing with the issue of social harmony, the ends of societal peace and restored relationships, guide punishment prospectively. This criterion takes a retrospective look at all that transpires around a punishment to see whether the ends sought by punishment were or are being achieved. If not, the punishment itself may be deemed a contributing injustice, and the other criteria should be looked at to discern where the injustices are likely to have arisen.

9. Punishment policies must observe a principle of proportionality. A punishment must in some way fit the crime—it must not be harsher than the crime merits, and it ought to take account of the fact, now well established, that resorting to ever harsher sentences, as is often advocated by candidates for public office, has little to no effect on crime rates. The offender, not the offense, must be the object of sentencing. Every offender has a story, and many of those in prison today are poor, members of a minority, and in a variety of ways socially disadvantaged. Sentencing must take that into account and respond accordingly. Judges need discretion, latitude, and authority to direct offenders to alternative sentences and treatment, and sentences that are directed by political policy—mandatory sentences—must be opposed as unjust if they assume that, say, the use of crack cocaine is racially neutral when we know it is not. As we noted in opening this discussion, certain policies have the effect of widening racial disparities, and when this occurs, punishments are not proportionate to the crime. That blacks should serve sentences on average 43 percent longer than whites for drug arrests is disproportionate and morally wrong. A justice system that truly seeks justice must attend to issues of proportionality and focus on individual offenders and their circumstances.

We have been examining the kinds of moral criteria that would guide reflection for those entrusted with devising a system of just punishment and just sentencing through a criminal justice system. In the background is a moral presumption that regulates the behavior of citizens in society as they seek to live in a condition of social harmony and peace. But when offenses occur, this common agreement, just war–related ethic will guide reflection on how, in a moral sense, a just system ought to be devised.

The objection could be raised that this presentation does not reflect our current system of criminal justice and therefore contradicts one of the purposes for opening this ethical study, namely, that the thinking of many on the issue of just punishment has not produced a system that reflects those moral concerns, so that what we are dealing with is a situation where thought and experience simply do not meet. It could be argued that the presentation just made places thought out ahead of our experience with criminal justice, for what we have been doing is floating ideas that do not seem to reflect the mainstream of thinking about what a criminal justice system should be. Two responses are necessary.

First, since the ethical criteria protect the moral presumption and seek always to defend and restore it to a regulative position, one could say that any empirical and experiential failures to meet the justice criteria amount to a moral criticism. We are in the realm of ethics and not politics—the commonly agreed-upon presumption and criteria we advanced articulate a moral understanding reasonable people of goodwill can be expected to avow. A critical application of the criteria may lead to the conclusion that on the basis of an empirically informed critical examination, the criminal justice system is unjust and in need of correction. This would parallel what we saw in the case of just war, namely, that a use of force that fails to satisfy the criteria of just war is an unjust use of force. In both cases the common agreement ethical criteria present a tool for critical analysis on the question at hand, the use of force or just punishment. This critical function is and should always be integral to the way the ethic functions, for the criteria articulate a standard of the good, right, and fitting—and a standard of justice. The failure to meet the standard yields the conclusion that what one is doing is not the good, right, and fitting thing to do; and the actions that fail the test or do not meet all the conditions yield the moral conclusion that those actions are not morally justified. What are the practical implications of this? It could mean what Scottish philosopher Anthony Duff says, "Punishment is not justifiable within our present legal system; it will not be justifiable unless and until we have brought about deep and far-reaching social, political, legal, and moral changes in ourselves and our society."[31] That is not to say that, practically speaking, we shut down our criminal justice system but to say, rather, that the system we have devised to deal with offenders is not a just system. It is in need of correction. The moral chore, then, is to advocate and undertake the work of making the system conform to the standards of justice articulated by the ethic of just punishment.

But this then leads to another, second issue. If in fact there seems to be a gap between the system of justice dispensation we have created and our best ethical thinking, have we not failed to articulate ideas of justice that people actually use and that are then most at issue in any formulation of a common agreement? The question is empirical—do people avow the common agreement underwriting our justice system and just punishment as we have suggested, or has this been an exercise in pie-in-the sky, warm and fuzzy thinking that is, in fact, divorced from the more common demand for eye-for-an-eye retribution?

This is a fair question, and my response to it is that the argument I have been making is a moral argument, a plea for a way of doing ethics, not a platform for running for office. Public discourse over our criminal justice system is notoriously shallow, and one of the major practical justifications for the death penalty is that by supporting it, candidates for office meet the public test of being "tough on crime." With that test for public office met, candidates are exempted from further conversation and public dialogue about just punishment and a just criminal justice system. I would bridge the apparent gap between thought and experience posed by the question we have asked and urge first a reconsideration of the fundamental grounding of our ethic in the moral point of view. This theory of just punishment may not win a political debate about crime, but it does express the moral point of view. Recall that the moral point of view asks that moral perspectives be submitted to a test of universalizability. As a practical matter, if reasonable people of goodwill were asked to universalize one of two options, either harsh retribution or the kind of just punishment theory I have laid out here, understanding that what they chose would apply not only to miscreants, wrongdoers, and criminals, but *equally to themselves and their loved ones* if they happened to fall into one of those categories themselves, they would without doubt recoil in horror at having to enter the justice system they support from the outside but have never experienced personally.

Few citizens have investigated that system far enough to understand what it can do in terms of creating and perpetuating destructiveness in the societal fabric. Ethics requires an act of imagination around the principle of universalizability, and it is beyond conceiving how supporters of harsh retribution could maintain that perspective and submit to it willingly when a moral perspective was offering a reasonable alternative that focused not on exacting pain and retaliation, but on seeking to put things right, restore persons to a position of well-being, and bring about societal harmony. I do not deny that in common experience there is high support for retribution, but neither can I imagine that that perspective could be universalized, as if a parent—any parent—would willingly say, "Yes, I understand my son has been found guilty of a drug offense, so I believe he should be sent to a chain gang or to thirty years in prison for that offense"—things that have actually been done—if a theory of just punishment is offering treatment, alternative sentencing, and attention to a rectifying punishment that fits the crime.

In the heat of public debate over controversial issues, we sometimes confuse political expediency with moral deliberation, and we can forget that a moral perspective asks us to universalize actions, so that what is wrong to do to one person is wrong to do to any person. This theory of just punishment is conformed to the moral point of view, and I believe it actually does meet the test we have set for this ethic—that it reconcile thought and experience. If reasonable people of goodwill seek social harmony and peace, they will seek to create a justice system that restores harmony and peace when it is upset and broken by criminal activity. From a moral point of view, they ought to demand a justice system that conforms to a moral vision where thought is reconciled with experience.

Chapter Eight

The Ethics of Abortion
The Question of Innocence

The just war criteria have traditionally been divided between those that justify resorting to force (*jus ad bellum*) and those that govern conduct during war (*jus in bello*). These are often distinguished as the criteria policy makers have to consider versus those that confront the military on the battlefield. The distinction is useful but not critical since all criteria of just war must be satisfied if a war or, more precisely, a use of force is to be considered morally permissible.

We have been referencing just war thinking to gain access to the ethic behind and then beyond just war, but the criteria of just war present valuable tools that can help sort out a number of difficult moral issues. The noncombatant immunity provision of the *jus in bello* criteria is a case in point. This *jus in bello* criterion states that noncombatants are to be exempted from any application of force, and it imposes on those engaged in combat operations a requirement to exercise due diligence to protect noncombatant civilians in any use of force. This is a deontological respect-for-persons principle embedded in the just war criteria. This criterion focuses on civilians not materially involved in the conflict where force is being used, and it imposes on combatants the duty to shield noncombatants from injury and violation. Morally speaking, these noncombatants are nonparticipants who have a right not to be harmed; combatants have a duty to respect that right; and holding the status of noncombatant suffices to afford protection. Another way to understand this provision is to say that it establishes an easily graspable notion of *moral innocence*.

A war in which innocent civilians are intentionally targeted for harm cannot satisfy the noncombatant immunity provision, and those seeking to inflict such harm are, under just war, acting immorally. Combatants cannot reasonably justify harming noncombatants on a claim of self-defense or self-protection. The status of noncombatants as "innocent" derives from the fact that they intend no

173

harm and pose no threat of harm to the parties in conflict, and they do not need to be defended against. Therefore, they are to be exempted from the conflict and never made a target of military action, coercion, or acts of aggression. To make noncombatants military targets, to strike directly at innocent civilians with lethal force, even if done for the purpose of terrorizing them so that the enemy might more swiftly seek a cessation of hostilities, constitutes an immoral act under just war; and those who violate this provision may be charged with war crimes, even murder. The moral point of view and natural law ethics insist that innocent civilians be immune from aggression and harm. Not only must pains be taken to assure that they are excluded from hostilities, but active steps must be taken to afford them actual protection.

"Innocence" is a critical concept in moral thinking, and it makes a dramatic appearance in deliberating the ethics of war, but not only on this issue. The question of innocence is central to the abortion debate, and for many, it is the critical concept in deciding that abortion is morally wrong. "The developing form of human life that is killed in abortion is innocent; therefore, abortion is wrong," we often hear it said. In this chapter, I wish to use the concept of *moral innocence*, a notion central to just war thinking in its criterion of noncombatant immunity, to elucidate the central problem of the abortion debate—the question of fetal status. I shall then turn in the concluding chapter back to war and to an interpretation of noncombatant immunity in the context of our common agreement ethic that war is an unwelcome state of affairs, an evil in human existence, and accordingly that war and the use of force ordinarily ought not to be used to settle conflicts.

ABORTION: THE CRITICAL
PROBLEM AND THE PROJECT

The *moral* question at the heart of the abortion debate is a simple one: can the killing that takes place when an abortion is performed be justified? Complicating the question is the fact that the moral status of the fetus is in dispute: is it or is it not to be regarded as a person? Let us stipulate that no consensus exists on the question of fetal status. Let us also stipulate that ascribing personhood to a developing form of human life is a moral, not a scientific question. Personhood, after all, is a moral category with attendant rights, foremost among them being a right to life. The moral community has a duty to protect persons and shield them from harm; persons have a right not to be harmed. The divisiveness over the question of fetal status in the so-called abortion debate has prevented a strong morally moderate position on abortion from making headway in both public and professional discussions of the issue. This is curious in light of the fact that a morally moderate position on abortion is simple enough to formulate: some abortions are permissible and others are not. The primary ethical quandary in abortion focuses on the question: How are we to tell the difference?[1]

In the spirit of opening up the possibility of a morally moderate position on abortion, I shall examine an issue that prevents the moderate position from gaining a hearing, and that is the underanalyzed if not overlooked notion central to the abortion debate—fetal innocence. The unarticulated assumptions attached to the idea of the innocent fetus have contributed immeasurably to abortion becoming an intractable moral dispute where moderate views are shunned by both abortion rights defenders and their opponents.

My purpose is to examine fetal innocence and a suppressed metaphysical claim attaching to it that renders abortion by definition an unjustified killing, hence the interpretation of abortion as "murder," even "genocide." Were the fetus a person—and that itself is a profoundly arguable claim—we should inquire into issues of moral meaning with the ethical chore being to examine the situation and determine whether there were sufficient warrants to justify an abortion. Again, the *moral* question in abortion should be this: which abortions are justifiable and which are not? But that is not what we do; and that is not how the issue is framed. Many hold that abortions are *by definition* illicit and beyond justification; and those who hold such a view offer as their justification the explanation that the fetus is innocent and thus protected from *even the possibility* of abortion. My argument here is that appeal to fetal innocence as a justification for opposing abortion—any and all abortions—can be shown to interject a nonmoral "sectarian" religious viewpoint that functions to elevate the fetus above and beyond the moral category of person. I propose to examine our ordinary moral sense of innocence so that this sectarian religious viewpoint might emerge more clearly, and I shall use as an ethics resource a feature of just war thinking, the noncombatant immunity provision of the *jus in bello* criteria, which, I argue, allows the contrasting religious-sectarian view to stand out in strong relief against our ethic of common agreement.

Exposing the differences between moral and religious views of innocence allows us to see that the abortion debate is something other than disagreement based on common moral assumptions; furthermore, the sectarian view of innocence I shall present here poses challenges for the religious point of view itself. I contend that once the *nonmoral* religious meaning of innocence is exposed, many who oppose abortion on religious grounds may find themselves surprised and even offended by what the nonmoral viewpoint on "innocence" actually commits them to theologically.

MORAL INNOCENCE

Opponents of abortion often rest their opposition in the idea that the developing form of human life—the conceptus/zygote/embryo/fetus—is innocent and therefore deserving of protection. This argument itself holds that *person* is a moral category and that persons command respect in virtue of being persons; furthermore, "respect for persons" necessitates an acknowledgment of a person's right to life while imposing a corresponding duty on others not to deprive a person of that right. The disputed logical move is what follows from these two premises, namely, that ascribing personhood—and thus a right to life—to the fetus logically imposes a duty not to kill it. Since abortion is a killing—by this logic the killing of a person—abortion represents a moral evil and should not be permitted. The logic is not at issue. The point of contention is whether the fetus ought to be treated as a person.

In the ordinary course of moral thinking and analysis, we might be able to grant for the sake of argument that a fetus is a person or should be treated as if it were one, and that concession (which I now do grant for the sake of argument) would not in and of itself lead to a wholesale objection to abortion. Why? Because moral reflection usually proceeds from a recognition that the world is imperfect and that values can come into conflict; that uncertainty and problems present themselves in such a way that perplexities arise in the moral life; that we have to face those perplexities and in the context of freedom and finitude make difficult decisions that can result in ending life. Furthermore, a natural law ethic would hold that goods of life can come into conflict with one another, and sometimes even the good of life can be justifiably overridden in the effort to pursue and protect other goods—life itself is not an absolute good.

Nonetheless, the killing of persons is presumptively a terrible moral offense, and this is not in dispute. Sometimes, however, we are able to justify certain killings of persons, not that we desire another person's death but because events may conspire to create situations where a decision to kill reflects a judgment that a use of force, which may regrettably be a use of lethal force, is the least wrong, bad, or evil thing that could be done in a difficult and perplexing situation. Would a rational person of goodwill want to avoid being in such a situation? Of course. But we know that in police actions, there are times when a threat to the lives of persons, including threats to police officers themselves, may require a use of lethal force. Using lethal force in such situations is not desired and should not be intended, but it may come about due to circumstances in which some individual poses a threat to others, and such an individual—a member of the moral community, a person—is killed to protect others. Life is not an absolute value in the realm of moral thinking, and practical reason recognizes that persons have a duty to defend themselves and to protect others facing the threat of lethal harm.

In our ordinary moral discourse, we make reference to "innocent" persons. We acknowledge in the moral life the threat to innocent lives posed by a terrorist or armed bank robber who may be panicking, and what we mean by "innocence" in such situations is that persons so threatened, all of whom possess a right to life, have been positioned by unwanted life circumstances to be in harm's way. These persons are agents and capable of action; their right to life is protected by their nature as rational beings and by their inclusion in the moral community; and it would be morally wrong to intentionally kill one of these nonthreatening "innocent" persons. The duty to protect them may lead others, say, the police, to use deadly force to prevent them from being harmed.

This duty to protect innocent persons because they are persons and possessed of a right to life has been enshrined in just war thinking. For underwriting the tradition of just war thinking and even its use as a tool for military justification is a moral framework—a structure for moral thinking—that is enormously practical and helpful for thinking through our experiences of moral conflict and ethical dilemmas. To reiterate what we have mentioned several times in these pages: the just war ethic presumes reasonably that force ordinarily ought not to be used to settle conflicts and then imposes various tests of justice that must be satisfied if that presumption or common agreement is to be lifted and a use of force justifiably undertaken for limited and specific purposes. The tests of justice—the *jus ad bellum* criteria so familiar to us—deal with such matters as competent authority, just cause, announcement of intention, last resort, and so on. The classic theory also sets forth *jus in bello* requirements that govern the actual use of force once a use of force has been justified and is under way. These two constraints consist of a proportionality requirement that the use of force must be proportionate to the end of peace—this deals with weapons or actions that are disproportionate and ought not to be used—and a "noncombatant immunity" provision. This last criterion of just war thinking directs combatants in a conflict to protect noncombatant persons. Noncombatants are not to be directly attacked, and, as we already mentioned, every reasonable effort must be made to protect them from harm. Noncombatant immunity makes reference to what we typically call "innocent persons."

The just war tradition provides a moral framing of the idea of "innocence." Noncombatants are immune from the use of force, and it is presumptively wrong to directly use force, especially lethal force, against them. They are innocent. They are bystanders in the bank that is being robbed; they are in the line of fire when warring parties unleash urban mop-up operations; they are in office buildings and subways when terrorists strike; they are children walking in fields where land mines have been buried. Directly intending to harm and kill noncombatants, those not party to a conflict where lethal force is being used, is, according to the just war ethic, morally wrong. Targeting civilians for harm to achieve some end is wrong; using terrorist tactics, which by definition are directed at civilian noncombatants, is wrong; and every effort must be made, just war wants to say, to prevent harming these "innocent persons."

Just war thinking, however, is not absolutist, and the noncombatant immunity provision is not absolutist, as if there could never be an allowable (albeit rare) exception. If we invoked the double-effect doctrine, we could say that the killing of noncombatant innocent persons may be deemed allowable if it would prevent an even greater evil, if every conceivable effort is made to prevent such killing, and if the death of an innocent occurs as the result of a regrettable and foreseen—but always unintended—consequence of a morally legitimized use of force. Sometimes in the terrible messiness of life, using force to aim at a good effect, such as self-defense or protection of noncombatants, and avoid evil can nonetheless yield a bad consequence, including the unwanted and unintended killing of noncombatants. As discussed in chapter 1, the doctrine of "double effect" has been devised in the natural law tradition to accommodate the moral reality that an unintended bad effect, a secondary "lesser evil" consequence, may be allowed for serious "proportionality" reasons. And that lesser evil may actually include the loss of human life when "innocent" persons are put in harm's way and then actually harmed, even killed, in pursuit of a good end, such as self-defense. The "innocents" who might perish are recognized in the just war tradition as moral agents, as fully endowed members of the moral community who bear a right to life and a right not to be harmed. What this means is that the just war tradition does not absolutize the claim of innocent, noncombatant persons to a right to life but holds open the possibility through "double effect'" that the justification for the loss of "innocent life"—regrettable as it is—may be accommodated as a matter of the utmost moral seriousness.[2]

I want to suggest that the *just war tradition provides us with a reasonable moral framing for the idea of the "innocent person,"* the moral meaning of "innocent" clearly invoking the idea that persons not party to a conflict must be exempted from harm. "Innocence," then, shields persons from direct or intentional harm even when targeting them for harm might, in some deliberations, hasten a good end such as the cessation of hostilities or the restoration of peace. The just war ethic, however, condemns the evil act of directly killing innocent civilians—terrorizing them—in order to bring about a quicker end to the war, good end though that be.

The intention to respect and thus not harm innocent noncombatants is a moral requirement—a duty—under just war, but the world is messy and human beings, however good their moral theories, are not capable of pure actions. The use of force always leads to coercive actions of one kind or another, and coercive force—even that of nonviolent resistance—puts people in harm's way. We noted earlier that Martin Luther King Jr. used to worry enormously about starting nonviolent boycotts because they yielded economic consequences that could not easily be contained. King and Gandhi were attentive to this concern that the just war tradition calls its noncombatant immunity provision, and both sought to confine the harms generated by their activity, directing it at the resisters themselves, and not toward others, not even their adversaries. Despite their clear intentions not to harm others, both proceeded with their direct-justice action programs aware that not all the attendant harms could be contained as they wanted.

In summary: In the moral life, the sense of natural justice based on reason commends to us that persons not involved in a conflict should be immune from harm. The just war tradition articulates this moral insight by means of the "noncombatant immunity" provision in the *jus in bello* criteria. Recognizing the status of individuals as innocent—as innocent bystander or innocent civilian—imposes restraints and protections, but the problem is that those protections are not absolute. The moral reality is that if every reasonable effort has been made to realize the intention of not harming them and combatants actively seek to protect them, even the deaths of innocents may be deemed justifiable. Innocence is attached to agency, and parties using force are morally constrained by a duty to respect the life and even the well-being of noncombatant, innocent persons, but "innocence" is never so absolutized that an exception cannot be made. A just war ethic allows that an unintended harm can, in certain circumstances, be accepted as a regrettable "lesser evil" when aiming directly at achieving some greater good while also seeking to prevent some greater evil. Even proponents of nonviolence face the prospect that nonviolent tactics may, as both Gandhi and King understood, place innocent persons in harm's way.

ABORTION AND THE INNOCENT FETUS

Thus far I have explored the moral meaning of "innocent person" by considering how a common agreement ethic expressed through the just war tradition approaches this topic. That tradition, so closely associated with moral reflection on the question of using force, advances the criterion of "noncombatant immunity" as a moral construction of "innocent person." In that just war tradition, persons not party to a conflict are afforded a presumptive protection of their right to life, even their right not to be harmed, although the protection is not absolute. This discussion has set the groundwork for the next move in the argument. We turn now to the abortion issue and consider the matter of fetal innocence.

Two questions arise. The first concerns the innocent person identified by the just war "noncombatant" immunity provision and how it might transfer to the "innocent fetus." The second question concerns the conflict of values that arises when a woman as moral agent experiences an unwanted pregnancy. On the assumption that only a pregnancy that could be described as "unwanted" is a legitimate candidate for abortion consideration, the conflict that arises is that between the good of fetal life on the one hand and, on the other, practical reason, which is the good at issue when a woman exercises autonomy to make decisions about her reproductive health. The central question to ask, then, is this: When such a conflict of values arises, what protections can be claimed for the fetus in virtue of its status as innocent?

If we call on the resource of the "noncombatant immunity" provision of the just war tradition to inform us of the moral meaning of "innocent person," it is reasonable to argue that a fetus is not in any obvious way party to a conflict, certainly not by an exercise of intentionality on the part of the fetus. The fetus, then, is an "innocent" *in the moral meaning of that term, and, as innocent, it thus deserves protection from harm.* The moral status of the fetus is, as a matter of sociological fact, in dispute. But the moral point of view would insist that even if the fetus were to be regarded as an actual person and thus endowed with full membership in the moral community, including the moral duty to respect its right to life, its status as a person does not bestow an *absolute immunity* from harm. Such absolute immunity attaches neither to the fetus nor to any member of the moral community.

To regard the fetus as a person is to ascribe to the fetus protections that attach to any other person, and an innocent civilian in time of war deserves to be protected from harm, much as a fetus-as-person would deserve to be protected from abortion. But those protections are not absolute. The natural law, just war model does not deal in absolutes, and fetuses, even considered as a particular class of persons, cannot be exempted from inclusion in the moral arena where we confront complexity, perplexity, and the messiness of life. The fetus cannot be abstracted from the world of moral conflict and dilemmas as if inflicting harm or even killing an embryo or fetus is ruled out as a formal impossibility. On the contrary, it is a descriptive fact that the embryo or fetus *can* become enmeshed in conflicts over values and goods. A pregnant woman *can* experience a pregnancy she did not welcome or for some other reason may not want to continue, and when this occurs she *can* face a conflict.

As a rational moral agent, a woman in this situation must exercise practical reason to determine whether the fetus's claim to immunity from harm can be overridden, and justifiably so.

In the abortion debate, people who defend abortion rights would argue that the fetus is not a person, due perhaps to developmental immaturity or its situation of dependency. Mary Anne Warren's classic argument is that the fetus does not possess the attributes of personhood recognized by members of the moral community—self-awareness, ability to use language, and whatever criteria for personhood one would present; therefore, the fetus does not enjoy the protections afforded persons and can be aborted, killed, without that killing amounting to a moral offense.[3] Pro-life persons recognize fetal personhood, but even those who are not absolutists would reasonably acknowledge certain cases in which abortion could be justified. Those situations have typically been incest, rape, and "to save the life of the mother." Since rape and incest have been losing support as justifications from many pro-life supporters, my focus will be on "save the pregnant woman's life."[4]

Pregnancy is a medical condition that can threaten a woman's life.[5] When such a threat to life occurs, we can say that a conflict arises involving two innocents, the pregnant woman and the embryo/fetus, both of whom possess a right to life and a right not to be harmed. When such a medical situation arises, medical authorities may determine that abortion is the medical option necessary to save the woman's life. The fetus is still innocent in the sense that it poses no threat to the woman's life due to any intention it has formed to harm her, yet, from a moral point of view, the embryo or fetus does in actuality pose a material threat and from that threat a woman may die. The medical condition where the woman's life is in danger then allows us to describe the embryo or fetus as a material aggressor threatening harm notwithstanding its status as innocent and despite any intention to do harm. From the moral point of view, then, just as any person has a natural right to protect his or her life from harm, a woman whose life is endangered because of the medical condition of pregnancy has a right—some would actually claim a *duty*—to protect herself and preserve her life from this threat, even if it costs the life of an innocent fetus.

Whatever "innocent" may mean for those who ascribe innocence to the fetus-as-person, reasonable persons of goodwill in the context of moral life and relationships allow that in certain cases—certainly if the pregnant woman's life were in danger—*fetal innocence should not overrule the good of a woman acting to save her life*. Even those who hold that the fetus is a person could by an exercise of practical reason be expected to say that a fetus could be aborted, and justifiably so, for the good of preserving and defending the pregnant woman's life.

So taking as the critical proposition for moral analysis "abortion to save the life of the mother," we see *agreement* between those who hold that the fetus is a person and is therefore deserving of immunity-from-harm protections and pro-choice advocates who deny fetal personhood. The common moral agreement is this: If a complication in the medical condition of pregnancy endangers a woman's life, any claim of a fetus to a right to life grounded in its status as an innocent person can be overruled for rational and justifiable reasons. In arriving at this conclusion we see the good of practical reason functioning.

From a moral point of view, what has been argued thus far is not really controversial. We have been saying that if a medical condition threatened a pregnant woman's life and the only way to save her life was through abortion—a killing of the fetus—that killing, regrettable as it might be, would be deemed morally allowable. On this point, both pro-life and pro-choice proponents would agree, remembering that we are holding pro-life proponents to the moral point of view, which is nonabsolutist and thus open to possible abortion exceptions. For reasonable people of goodwill, even for people in general opposed to abortion, saving a woman's life amounts to so grave a situation that abortion in such a case is an easily justified exception. It is beyond this point that things get interesting.

What about those who hold that abortion is *never* allowable—*absolutely impermissible*—and invoke fetal innocence as the reason for this claim? My case is that in the moral life, this move cannot really be made reasonably and coherently, for conflicts in value, even conflicts involving the value of life, are possible, and life cannot reasonably be thought of as an absolute value that will always and in every situation trump other values. The fact is that life as a biological reality can be a value that comes into conflict with other values, else we would be morally obligated, for example, never to terminate life support so long as we can keep biological processes—one definition of life—going regardless of the patient's condition or expressed instructions otherwise. Moral reasoning values life, even in a preeminent way in a hierarchy of values since all other values depend upon it, but it does not absolutize the value of life, nor does it deny the possibility that ending life could be morally justified. Reason and morality would assert that fetal life ought to be valued, but not in an absolute sense that it would trump the life of a woman whose pregnancy was threatening her life; and this would hold even for those committed to the view that the fetus is a person and possesses a right to life.

I would make this case even by appealing to the natural law tradition of the Roman Catholic Church, which preserved and developed the just war tradition. For it was in that tradition that the noncombatant immunity provision and the doctrine of double effect were developed, which in a sense detached the idea of persons being innocent from any absolutist notion of innocence. The doctrine of double effect, recall, allows for the overruling of noncombatant immunity in situations of serious value conflict, such as in self-defense. One of the ironies of the current abortion debate is that the teaching of the Roman Catholic hierarchy has, in fact, absolutized the value of the fetus, *absolutized its immunity*, yet moral teaching in the Roman Catholic Church has always tried to avoid absolutism. That moral tradition has, if I may as an outsider describe this feature of the Roman Catholic tradition, allowed for loopholes in the interests of justice and in recognition of the impossibility of acting purely or being godlike in our moral knowledge or moral action. Just war thinking itself is a model of such hesitation in the face of absolute certainty, for it provokes an ethical model of moral moderation: it structures moral reflection so that the guidelines of the theory allow one to say that some uses of force are justifiable and others are not. This is moral moderation that eschews a strict pacifism yet also imposes constraint on the use of force, even when one's cause seems just. Applying this mode of thinking to abortion, a similar moral claim could be inferred: some abortions are permissible, others not.

The hierarchy of the Roman Catholic tradition has addressed the idea of fetal innocence in different ways,[6] and just as change has been under way in movement toward absolutizing the value of the fetus in, say, the Republican platforms of 2004 and 2008, where "rape, incest and to save a mother's life" were for the first time dropped from the anti-abortion plank, the Roman Catholic position has similarly changed. Consider how American jurist and moral philosopher John Noonan rehearses the history of the Catholic moral tradition in its nonabsolutism, pointing out how it once addressed the idea of a justified abortion in the sole situation of a mother's life being in danger:

> In Catholic moral theology, as it developed, life even of the innocent was not taken as absolute. Judgments on acts affecting life issued from a process or weighing. Even with the fetus weighed as human [as "person" in the moral sense I have been using], one interest could be weighed as equal or superior: that of the mother in her own life. The casuists between 1450 and 1895 were willing to weigh this interest as superior. Since 1895, that interest was given decisive weight only in the two special cases of the cancerous uterus and the ectopic pregnancy. In both of these cases the fetus itself had little chance of survival even if the abortion were not performed.[7]

This understanding of the moral tradition asserted a strict protection for the fetus but not an absolute protection. Contrast this with a statement from Pope John Paul II:

> The moral gravity of procured abortion is apparent in all its truth if we recognize that we are dealing with murder and, in particular, when we consider the specific

elements involved. The one eliminated is a human being at the very beginning of life. No one more absolutely *innocent* could be imagined. In no way could this human being ever be considered an aggressor, much less an unjust aggressor!

Then, quoting from "Instruction on the Respect for Human Life," John Paul continues:

> The human being is to be respected and treated as a person from the moment of conception; and therefore from that same moment his rights as a person must be recognized, among which in the first place is the inviolable right of every innocent human being to life.[8]

The papal statement regards abortion as murder. It justifies that characterization of the abortion as "killing" by appealing to the idea that the human being is *innocent*—with the pope providing the emphasis—but more than that, "absolutely innocent."

Recognizing the fetus as absolutely innocent has the effect of removing the fetus from a moral framework where even an innocent fetus regarded as a person could conceivably be killed in the face of a conflict where some other value might trump that of the fetus-as-person's right to life. Noonan identifies one situation—only one—in which abortion could be justifiably performed because the pregnant mother's right to life supersedes that of the fetus: "that of the mother in her own life." Yet the papal statement turns away from this morally compelling "loophole" to dictate the idea that in the moral teaching of the Roman Catholic hierarchy, no woman has any right to directly intend the killing of the fetus. Be clear: even to save her own life, such a direct killing cannot be sanctioned.[9] Noonan is calling on the Roman Catholic hierarchy to reassert the mother's right to save her life if her very life is threatened by medical complications in pregnancy, but what must be made clear is that he does so *against* the papal statement. In John Paul's statement, abortion is murder—unjustified killing—and is always so. The life of the fetus *always* trumps that of the woman. And that is the moral teaching of the Roman Catholic Church's hierarchy. A pregnant woman does not have the moral right to receive abortion not only in cases of rape and incest, but *not even to save her own life*. And the critical move that allows for the elevation of the fetus to a status where its life is to be valued above its mother is, in the pope's word "*innocence*." The fetus, he insists, is "absolutely innocent."

Pope John Paul II italicizes "*innocent*"—I would italicize "*absolutely*." And that is because the pope is using "absolutely" not as a linguistic intensifier but as a descriptor of fetal metaphysical status. Absolute innocence renders fetal life immune from harm and unassailable by value conflicts. As such, killing a fetus can never be justified, which is to say *there are never any reasons that could justify an abortion*, not even a "lesser evil" reason that might permit an abortion as a last resort to save a woman's life. In the pope's view, the fetal right to life cannot be trumped for putatively justified reasons because no reason could ever mount a challenge to the fetal right to life. No justification for overruling the fetal right to life could ever be adduced. The good of fetal life cannot be put into conflict—that good overrules and suppresses any value conflict. Nothing can ever be either theoretically or practically of higher value, even in a rare exception, than the fetus. The question this prompts is this: in the moral life, do we know of anything of comparable value to this absolutely innocent fetus? What could it be? What does this extraordinary heightened valuation of fetal life mean in moral terms?

ABSOLUTE INNOCENCE:
THE METAPHYSICAL TRUMP

I have been contemplating these questions for some time, and the insight I offer came to me when I was a visitor in Japan. When I visited the ancient capital of Nara, Japan, a couple of years ago, I was struck by the free-roaming deer and was informed by my guide that deer are sacred in Nara. He then proceeded to tell me that in recent memory, a driver had accidentally hit a deer and killed it. The accident was particularly nasty, for the driver himself was killed. Despite the tragic loss of a human life, the state intervened to sue the survivors of the now deceased driver. With the law reflecting a Shinto valuing of sacred being, in this case the spirit-filled *kami* of the sacred deer, the family of the dead driver confronted both religion and law: killing a sacred deer is a terrible offense, a religious violation that carries with it a stiff, legally imposed penalty. Taken to court in metaphysical absentia, the deceased driver was tried for killing a sacred deer, found guilty, and sanctioned for his violation. His survivors were required to pay the fine. This situation was created because of the high valuation placed on the deer. And let us be clear about how this valuation was accomplished: the deer was recognized as spirit filled, and the protections accorded it were due to its status as divine.

Any injury that befalls a sacred deer due to human action constitutes in Japan—at least in Nara—a religious offense apart from any secular legal violation. The dead deer was enshrined with a religiously conceived, numinous sense of innocence so profound that even if it had caused the death of a person, any injury to the deer—however that injury might have actually occurred—always trumped any excuse, exception, or plea for mitigation: the one who caused the injury was guilty of a great offense because of the value of the being injured, and in this I think the sacred deer of Nara are akin to the fetus as John Paul II understands them in their status as absolutely innocent. There, too, is no excuse, exception, or plea for mitigation—there can be no "just abortion" just as there can be no justification for killing a sacred deer, even if the deer's death is accidental and caused the death of a person. In both cases, moral reflection leads to a recognition that *the issue here is not really moral*: the sacred object—the deer in Nara, the fetus for the pope—is being valued outside the categories of moral meaning. In both cases, moral meaning folds in the face of what moral reflection itself recognizes as *religious* valuation, and such valuation is what determines that a fetus is absolutely innocent and removed from any possible value conflicts. Such extramoral and religiously conceived valuation is what determines that a deer is worth more than a human being, so that its death requires a ritualistic atonement as a family, grieving the loss of a family member, is forced by law to pay a debt beyond rational moral proprieties.

Let me now connect more explicitly the sacred deer of Nara with the fetus elevated above morality by the pope. By describing the fetus as "absolutely innocent," the pope absolutized the fetus. He elevated its status beyond and outside of moral categorizes; and in this he was engaged in an act of valuation not at all unlike the Shinto-inspired legal proceeding that required the family of a dead deer killer to make restitution for a violation of the sacred. In both cases, at issue is an offense against an object of such extraordinary nonrational value that we are entitled to describe the object as sacralized. The object—the deer, the fetus—is regarded in both characterizations as sacred or holy and, as the pope said, "inviolable." It has been divinized. I use the Japanese Shinto example because this elevated divinizing valuation is easier to see in another culture than in one's own. Were we able to step outside our Western framework and see what is happening with the ascribing of absolute innocence to the fetus, we would, I suggest, draw a similar conclusion about the papal understanding, which is delivering to us what amounts to a divine fetus.

Lest this conclusion seem outrageous or implausible, let me ask a question about absolute innocence as part of the Christian, and especially the Roman Catholic, faith tradition: Where do we find absolute innocence? Who is to be regarded as absolutely innocent?

To answer this question, let us recall that in the moral framework, innocence attaches to persons who are actor-agents yet who are not themselves engaged as party to a conflict. By misfortune of place or perhaps of circumstance, they are subjected to harm when morally speaking, they ought to be immune from any infliction of harm by those engaged in the conflict. Violating this innocence, even if in some situations we can establish warrants for justifying it, is a serious moral matter, and justifying it is not easy to do. We often think of the moral offense involved when persons fitting the bill as morally innocent are subjected to harm, such situations as wrongfully convicting "innocent" persons and sending them to prison, or even worse, subjecting them to the death penalty; we think of the persons eating at McDonald's when an intruder opens fire and threatens their lives with a hail of gunfire. These situations describe the morally innocent persons suffering harm unjustly. The innocence, however, is not portrayed as absolute. If a S.W.A.T. team member killed the McDonald's gunman and accidentally killed an innocent bystander in the confusion of the situation, that death, however regrettable, would be deemed a tragic but allowable death under double effect, since the intention of the S.W.A.T. team shooters was to put an end to the threat and protect the innocent. Moral innocence is by definition not absolute; the innocence does not make reference to metaphysical status, but describes, rather, moral standing vis-à-vis a potential threat or harm. In the moral realm of self-other relations, innocence characterizes persons in their uninvolved and unwilled participation in a conflict that unwittingly draws them in and subjects them to harm, often tragically. Moral innocence does not obtain if persons willingly invite or participate in a conflict; it attaches, rather, to the exempt—those whom we describe as unwitting recipient, victim, noncombatant.

The Nara deer and the absolutely innocent fetus, however, are different. The innocence here is metaphysical, religious, and sectarian rather than moral and recognizable as universal. Attributing absolute innocence to the fetus actually elevates the fetus to a position above the moral category of person, and in that situation *the fetus is absolutely exempt from abortion, as are all other beings in its class or sharing its status*—I mean all fetuses. No fetus because of this status could be justifiably killed for any compelling moral reason—there is no possibility that the fetus could be intentionally killed on the idea that doing so would contribute to a greater good and thus constitute a "lesser evil."

Were we to take the moral stand that fetuses are persons with a right to life and therefore deserving of protection we would find ourselves at odds with this metaphysical notion of absolute innocence. For the moral idea of fetus-as-innocent-person would invite reflection on the idea that innocence in the relevant moral sense consists in the fetus lacking the capacity for willed action—a fetus cannot form intentions or act purposefully from motives. And the position that the fetus is morally innocent would not be lost even in the situation where a woman is facing pregnancy complications and chooses abortion. As a moral issue, what could be said even by one who holds the fetus to be a person and morally innocent is the same as what might be said of an innocent noncombatant killed in a just war: the fetus that dies, like the noncombatant, has not relinquished its status as innocent. It did not intentionally pose a harm. It became an unwitting subject of harm through an unfortunate accident of life circumstance. The value of innocence and the protections it affords persons is trumped by some other value, some greater good, such as saving the pregnant woman's life in the case of a "just abortion" or some greater good end in a use of force where despite efforts to prevent noncombatant casualties, innocent civilians nonetheless perish.

But the divine fetus is not the morally immune fetus whose immunity may be overruled in the complexity of the moral life. The divine fetus holds a metaphysical standing that overrules the pregnant woman's *in every case*, and *no abortion is permitted*—the fetus is protected, and absolutely so. And the two cases Noonan cites where medical action to save a woman's life allows for the embryo to die—ectopic pregnancy and the cancerous uterus—should not obscure the point as if these were abortion exceptions. Abortion, in the papal directive, is a direct and intentional killing of the fetus, and it is never permitted—it is always equivalent to murder. It is always unjustified, and what is killed in abortion is always "absolutely innocent." When an embryo dies in the medical correction of an ectopic pregnancy or a cancerous uterus, the action is simply not describable as "abortion." The medical interaction to save the woman's life is not a directly intended killing but an invocation of double effect. The Roman Catholic teaching about double effect is applied in the situation where the developing form of human life could not possibly survive and the pregnant woman would also inevitably die. But the teaching is clear. Directly killing a fetus to save a woman's life is not permitted. Where absolute innocence exists, the fetus trumps the mother—absolutely.

On this point, one cannot reasonably argue for a condition of mother-fetus "equal status" as Noonan does—that the mother is of equal or superior value to the fetus. If there is a threatening medical condition that would permit one of the two contestants for life—the fetus and the mother—always to trump the other due to its status as "innocent," then innocence becomes the defining characteristic that allows a superior status to be held. An either/or is involved. Either the mother is always justified in defending her life from the threat posed by a fetus, whether or not she opts to act for self-defense, or the fetus is absolutely protected from a direct killing—an abortion killing. Noonan, as a moral thinker advancing a moral point of view, is clear where he stands on this issue—the woman trumps the fetus when the woman's life is in danger. But the pope is also clear. Holding that the fetus always trumps the value of the woman and overrules any exercise of practical reason that might lead her to choose abortion, even for the reason of saving her own life, Pope John Paul II absolutizes the value of the fetus.

The elevation of the status of the fetus because of its absolute innocence is a remarkable development to consider. It is a position on "innocence" fraught with serious moral and religious implications. For how are we to understand such innocence? Innocence with such command as to overrule basic fixtures of moral thinking such as prudential self-regard—have we ever seen such a notion of innocence before? The answer to this last question is yes, but with a twist. For the answer is that such notions of innocence, foreign as they are to moral thinking, are quite familiar in religion. For Christians, absolute innocence attaches to God the Father, Jesus Christ, and the Holy Spirit, and for many Christians—Catholic Christians—Mary, Mother of God. These are all absolutely innocent beings. Extending this divine attribution of innocence to the fetus—to all fetuses—raises interesting theological questions about sin and original sin. For St. Augustine's idea that sin and original sin rest in concupiscence is being sidelined as the fetus is recognized *in utero* as a sinless being—metaphysical innocence when absolutized must identify a state of sinlessness.

Christian theology universally holds Jesus of Nazareth as the Christ to have been a man "born without sin," which is to say that Jesus was innocent—not in the moral sense of being akin to a noncombatant, but metaphysically innocent—absolutely innocent. To assure Jesus of such metaphysical innocence, the Roman Catholic hierarchy pronounced *ex cathedra* a doctrine regarding Mary's own "immaculate conception," the purpose of that being to guarantee that Jesus was free of the condition of original sin not only *in utero* but also *post utero*; the pope's statement seems to recognize all fetuses *in utero* as innocent in the metaphysical sense. (Where they differ from Jesus metaphysically on this view, I suppose, is that human fetuses are "born into" original sin, whereas Jesus Christ was not born into sin due to Mary's "immaculate conception.") Christian doctrine suggests that Jesus escaped the taint of original sin *post utero*; and original sin, for which baptism is needed to be put sacramentally right with God, is picked up biologically in the birth process, in leaving the woman's body and the innocence of the womb, or perhaps going through the birth canal, where some remnant of concupiscence persists and taints the emerging newborn with original sin.

Whatever the specifics of theological understanding, it is clear that the fetus as absolutely innocent is pure and without taint. Given the fact that a conceptus, zygote, embryo, or fetus is without volition and not an agent, that it cannot act and thus cannot sin, its status is that of metaphysical purity. The metaphysical claim that the fetus is absolutely innocent would inevitably lead to the conclusion that it too is, *in utero*, sinless, and, like the sinless Christ, godlike. In Christian doctrine, Jesus as Christ is metaphysically innocent, untainted by sin, and in that, Christ apparently shared in a *universal* fetal innocence. *In utero* Jesus would have been, in the pope's words, "absolutely innocent." The latter development of the Church doctrine of the immaculate

conception had the purpose of preserving Jesus's status of absolute innocence, which now means sinlessness during birth and even after birth so that
original sin was not transmitted to him going through the birth canal, where it
would seem innocence for the rest of us is lost. This theological excursion is
meant simply to suggest that a weighty theological implication hangs on the
idea of "absolute innocence." By his pronouncement, the pope is attributing
to the fetus—not only the absolutely innocent fetus that was Christ, but *every
fetus in every pregnancy*—absolute innocence, which is now discernible as
an attribute of divinity.

So let us be clear about the logic of what is being laid out here. The "absolutely innocent" teaching from John Paul II is stating that the fetus is of such
high value that it trumps the value of the pregnant woman when the medical
condition of her pregnancy is such that the pregnancy is posing a threat to
her health and even her life. The rational reasons for this trumping would be
either that the mother is not a person and the fetus is, or that the pregnant
woman is a person, but the fetus is something higher. The most logical candidate for what this "something higher" than a person might be is God. And
that is what I think the invocation of the idea of "absolute innocence" in the
abortion debate means—that the fetus is God. That is the valuation of fetal
life at issue in the abortion debate—it is not talked about, and it is suppressed
with good reason. To claim that the "innocent fetus" stands outside of moral
thinking and outside of ethical categories and then to regard the metaphysical
status of the fetus as godlike, even equal to God, would, in theistic theologies,
render the fetus an idol, an act of valuation that in theological categories is
itself sinful. Absolute innocence leads where absolutism always leads—to its
own contradiction. Absolute innocence leads to what monotheistic religion
identifies as the grave sin of making false gods—idolatry.[10]

For those who hold to a view of absolute innocence and the metaphysics
that gives rise to such standing, the fetus is divine—it is godlike, it is God.
That is, I believe, a conclusion that necessarily follows from the idea that
the fetus is absolutely innocent and its interests *always* trump that of the
pregnant woman. The dim awareness that the mother ought to hold this very
same trumping power over the fetus is what is responsible, I think, for the
pro-choice conclusion that the fetus is not really a person and should not be so
regarded. And this conclusion rests on the *morally* sound notion that a pregnant woman is morally entitled to defend her life, a view that was affirmed
for many centuries in the Roman Catholic moral tradition. The moral point of
view would insist, and any theory of "just abortion" would establish under a
criterion of *just cause*, that a pregnant woman can act prudentially to protect
herself, and the right of self-defense holds even when the fetus is regarded as
a person. The pope, however, denies that the fetus could ever be an aggres-

sor due to its status as absolutely innocent, but a "just abortion" view, once constructed on the order of a just war model, would allow that even when the fetus is an unintentional innocent aggressor, it can pose a material threat to the pregnant woman's life. The pregnant woman as a rational agent possesses the right—even a duty—to protect herself from such a threat; and reasonable people of goodwill would recognize this right and duty. The pope will not brook any consideration of such a situation. The fetus cannot be even a material aggressor, *ever*: it is innocent; it is divine. It is akin to the deer in Nara. A religious, sectarian valuation has removed it from the rational constraints of the moral life and reframed the meaning of its status outside the rational framework of moderate moral thinking and evaluation.

CONCLUSION

Articulating the religious-sectarian dynamic that conceptualizes the fetus in terms of "absolute innocence" enables us to see why the abortion debate is so intractable. That the fetus's status as "absolutely innocent"—a religious understanding—has infiltrated the moral category of "personhood" is clear from the words of Pope John Paul II himself, since in the above statement he insists that the fetus be recognized as a person with a right to life (moral language) but then also insists that the fetal person further be acknowledged as "absolutely innocent," language foreign to moral discourse and practical reasoning. This way of injecting sectarian religious conceptions into a moral discussion pits moral apples against religious oranges. A profound claim attends the attribution of absolute innocence to the fetus-as-person: the fetus is presented as protected from abortion in every conceivable circumstance because it is metaphysically inviolate—that is the meaning of absolute innocence. The "innocence" descriptor suggests that the fetus transcends the moral category of personhood in a metaphysical belief system where the fetus is, in the sacred space of the prebirth womb, innocent because it is not tainted by sin, even original sin. If it were subject to characterization as "sinful," how could it be described as "absolutely innocent"? That a fetus is innocent because it is sinless transcends moral categories, and no moral justification can allow the fetus to be killed for only the morally good purpose of saving the pregnant woman's life; for the woman does not enjoy the status of absolute innocence: no "person" does. The value of the woman's life is simply incommensurate with the religiously framed metaphysic of fetal being.

The abortion debate becomes divisively intractable at the point where moral argumentation collapses into sectarian religious conceptions, which then supersede moral issues and justice concerns. Granting that a pregnant woman is a person who is of equal value to every other person in the moral community and then granting the fetus power to trump a fully endowed member of the moral community in every situation for the sectarian reason that its metaphysical status is superior to the woman's moral status as person renders the woman less than a person. Either that or it elevates the fetus to a supramoral status. In the latter case, the fetus becomes divine—at least that is how the moral point of view would interpret this shift to some kind of transcendent or supramoral valuation. Killing the fetus is abhorrent not for the moral reason that it is a killing and killing is always subject to moral inquiry and critique and is presumptively wrong, but because destroying fetal life is absolutely wrong as an assault on the holy—it is akin to killing God. And if that is what is at stake, it is no wonder that religious enthusiasm has turned fanatical and that some religiously inspired persons have actually killed physicians who perform abortions. Such physicians are not medical practitioners, but God killers, and those who hold this view will inevitably interpret what they did as absolutely justified. They will understand that there was nothing wrong in killing an abortion provider—one such killer in the United States expected, up to the moment of his execution, to be reprieved by a pro-life governor.[11]

The divine fetus poses a terrible threat to the well-being of the moral community. It allows a metaphysic related to sectarian views about "sinlessness" to enter—in a subversive and unarticulated way—into deliberations concerning when and under what circumstances abortions may be justified as morally allowable killings. If we construe abortion as a *moral* issue, however, practical reason will insist on subjecting the killing involved in abortion to critical analysis. Relying on practical reason, people of goodwill will evaluate the conditions and circumstances that make abortion a live option in particular circumstances; and from the moral point of view this can happen even if we grant the fetus "person" status, which, again, many people for good reason do not do. The "just war" criterion of "noncombatant immunity" allows us to move from "noncombatants" to "innocent persons" and then imposes a requirement to protect those innocents from direct and intentional harm. The moral point of view, however, would resist absolutizing the innocence of these noncombatant innocents. The noncombatant immunity provision of the just war ethic insists that in some always regrettable and unwanted circumstances the death of innocents might be allowable, although the criterion presumes that ordinarily they would not be justified and therefore can be regarded as morally impermissible.

Clearly a moral presumption on the abortion question would entail the common agreement that pregnancy is an ingredient in promoting the good of life and ordinarily, abortion ought not to be performed. But lacking a "just abortion" ethic akin to that of "just war," the debate about abortion constitutes something other than a moral debate over justification and permissibility.[12] When moral debate is overruled by a sectarian declaration that the fetus is absolutely innocent, thus inviolate and never to be directly harmed, a nonmoral religious belief becomes the sole and unassailable determinant of action. Against such a position the moral point of view, if not exactly rendered irrelevant, at least is positioned so that it can exert little, if any, rational influence.

My view is that ascribing absolute innocence to the fetus is a religious valuation representing a sectarian point of view. People are, of course, free to hold such a belief—religious people believe lots of things, and they can believe that a fetus *in utero* is divine if they wish. But such a belief ought to be identified as a sectarian belief, and accordingly, such a belief ought not to be directing or even influencing social policy about an issue such as abortion. In a moral debate, many reasons can be cited to justify abortion, that of *saving the life of the pregnant woman being by any moral account the least controversial reason imaginable.* In fact, when a woman's life is at stake in a pregnancy complication where abortion is a medical necessity, abortion is more a duty than a right. Invoking a sectarian notion of fetal innocence under the protection of religious freedom is, of course, as appropriate as allowing any other religious belief to be held as long as that belief does not pose harms to people. But imposing such a belief on persons in a pluralistic society privileges a sectarian view and threatens to abridge religious freedom; and to be protected under the rubric of religious freedom are the many different views about fetal status and the permissibility of abortion to be found in different religious communities.[13]

If ethical debate over abortion can identify then quarantine sectarian claims about fetal life as absolutely innocent, our public discourse over abortion could assert the kind of regard for fetal life that fits into a moderate "just abortion" moral framework where some abortions, like some uses of force, are permissible and others not. Such a "common agreement" ethic would be grounded in a universal moral presumption that life is good and that pregnancy is a means to promote the value of life so that pregnancy ought to be regarded, morally, as a presumptive good. The ethic would then proceed to identify the moral chore on the abortion question not as protecting the inviolability of the fetus but as demanding that we ask the hard moral question about which pregnancies could and which could not be justifiably terminated in the context of those pregnancies deemed "unwanted." Moral reflection would attend to the difficult issue about justified abortion and proceed in the same way just war thinking addresses the justifiability of a use of force out of the presumption that some uses of force are justifiable and others, not.

The abortion debate is intractable because a sectarian viewpoint, represented by the idea of "absolute innocence," has skewed the terms of the debate and made rational conversation difficult and in some contexts impossible. Those who want to affirm an absolutely innocent fetus should be free to do so. The moral community, however, should resist this absolutizing tendency borne of sectarian metaphysical commitments and reframe the abortion debate, centering it on the imperfections of existence and the conflicts that arise over goods and values. Even the preeminent value of life ought not to be so valued in a moral discussion that it is transformed into an "absolute good" that trumps every other value. Such absolutizing of value evades the messiness and the complexity of the moral life while creating for rationality moral chaos.

Chapter Nine

The Ethics of War
The Question of Innocence

Our study of the common agreement ethic has taken us behind—and beyond—just war. The opening of the moral innocence question in the previous chapter brought us back into consultation with an actual criterion of just war thinking—the noncombatant immunity provision. We showed how this criterion transferred to the abortion question and affected moral reflection, for we were able to distinguish moral from metaphysical notions of innocence, which helped to clarify what abortion means as both a moral and a religious issue.

Questions about the moral meaning of innocence are no less important when the issue before us is war itself. As we began this study with an analysis of the limitations and possibilities of just war thinking and then clarified the "common agreement" ethic both behind and beyond just war, we find ourselves now able to look again at war and consider the ethical constraints on war in light of our ethical analysis. So we come full circle—back to the question of war and uses of force. What impact does the criterion of "noncombatant immunity" have on our thinking about the ethics of war? What is the meaning of moral innocence in time of war, and what obligations do those who engage in war owe to the "innocent"? With these questions we shall conclude this study, our effort in these final pages being to show how the common agreement ethic affects our thinking about the possibility of just war.

NONCOMBATANT IMMUNITY: INTRODUCTION

The greatest injustice in war—any war—is the victimization of noncombatant civilians. Civilians are by definition not armed or equipped for self-defense; they are acknowledged by common moral agreements and the protections of international law to be exempt from involvement in the violence of war; yet by any empirical analysis, they constitute the group most subjected to violence, suffering, and death as the victims of war. Although nonthreatening and immunized from harm, noncombatant civilians are nonetheless victims of unjust involvement in war; in addition, they bear an inequitable and disproportionate amount of suffering compared with combatants. Warfare deaths are always deserving of moral analysis, and in what follows we shall consider both the fact of civilian death inequities as well as moral responses to the injustice this represents, paying attention to war makers who target civilians for military purposes and terrorists who do so for political goals. Our "common agreement" ethic will enable us to argue that moral thinking must reprioritize noncombatant immunity in our thinking about the ethics of war. The question will be asked, "What would change in the world of war making and geopolitics if the moral community (not to be equated with the international community) were to insist that noncombatant immunity be the primary consideration in any conflict threatening violence and collective killing?"

CIVILIAN DEATHS: THE ISSUE OF INEQUALITY

Of the estimated fifty-five million casualties suffered in World War II, more than thirty million of them were civilians. Four countries—China, Russia, Poland, and Germany—accounted for 85 percent of those noncombatant deaths and injuries.[1] Iraq Body Count, which has been documenting verified civilian deaths in the Iraq War since 2003, places the number of civilian war dead in that country at around 114,000 as of the end of 2011.[2] Exact numbers verifying civilian deaths in the Iraq War are not available, but estimates as of the end of active United States involvement in December 2011 put the number at 1.4 million dead.[3] The British journal *Lancet* had estimated "excess deaths" in Iraq from 2003 to June 2006 at more than 650,000, a figure that would include death from lawlessness, degraded infrastructure, and poor health care;[4] and the Opinion Research Business poll, which had interviewed Iraqis in August 2007 about deaths in their families, put the estimates of civilian deaths at more than one million since the start of the war.[5] All of these figures are estimates based on various statistical research methods, and none is beyond dispute or without controversy.

What cannot be disputed, however, is the fact that civilians die in war and sometimes in horrendous numbers. War is never so constrained that war makers avoid making casualties of civilians. If the numbers from World War II are any guide, civilians can expect to make up more than half—a good majority—of the number of war casualties. And any in-depth analysis of a war zone would show what the *Lancet* estimators did: excess deaths—the deaths that noncombatant civilians suffer, not only from the consequences of actual combat, but from deaths caused by the destruction unleashed by war. Excess deaths cannot be confined to a moment of engaged combat but identify those deaths that occur from the consequences of war—in hunger, disease, poverty, homelessness, and social and economic dislocation. And it is worth noting that war technologies have been employed to develop weapons that are designed to produce just such "lingering effects"—the antipersonnel, chemical, biological, or nuclear weapons that generate suffering and death beyond the moment of engaged conflict. The destructive lingering effect of war and of such weapons is, and is intended to be, borne primarily by civilians. More than 70,000 died in Hiroshima from the direct atomic blast, but more than 200,000 died up to five years after the bombing, victims of radiation poisoning.[6]

A second indisputable matter is that these deaths of civilians are unjust. Civilians are possessed of a status that exempts them in war from direct and intentional harm. Accordingly, the warring parties are constrained—morally constrained—from inflicting direct harm on noncombatants. Although death is itself no evil but a natural end that comes to all, and although war, while always unfortunate and always to be avoided if possible, may yet be justified in certain restrictive circumstances, "civilian deaths" in war are undoubtedly a great evil. Failure to prevent civilian warfare deaths can deprive even an apparently justified war of its claim to justification. We can invoke a variety of moral theories to derive these judgments; we may even appeal to the more intuitive standard of "common decency." Even in the face of the contemporary geopolitical situation, where terrorism is a tool of conflict, where war itself is a murky guerrilla business, and where the combatant/noncombatant distinction is blurred as agents of warfare violence hide among a population of noncombatants—even then, the moral idea holds that in war, any war, civilian deaths are wrong and civilians hold a presumptive moral right not to be harmed in war.

THE JUST WAR TRADITION AND NONCOMBATANTS

Both ethics and law recognize war as an unfortunate state of affairs much to be avoided, and both have thus placed limits on war. The international community has recognized the transgression of those limits in the legal concept of a war crime, which is not always directed toward civilian victims but, then again, often is. In ethical reflection, the deontological principle of respect for persons can be invoked to condemn the torture and wanton destruction of noncombatant civilians even as, à la Nuremberg, this moral attention to disrespect of persons is also adjudged to defy the international legal frame of rule-bound warfare practices. Acts deemed "terrorism" may or may not fit the contextual definitions of a war crime—and what constitutes a war crime may certainly be influenced by the dynamic of victory and loss and the power of winners over losers. But not disputable is that destruction of civilians provokes profound moral questions whenever it arises. The Allied policy of targeting civilian populations in Germany during World War II found Churchill himself justifying what he would explicitly characterize as "terror" bombing;[7] and contemporary terrorist activity such as that organized by al Qaeda provides a non-nation-state-based, postmodern ideological program of disruption that targets civilians for casualty production in pursuit of religiopolitical ends. Targeting civilians defines the terrorist act, and it identifies what is morally objectionable about terrorism. The terrorist act is immoral because it cannot be universalized—no reasonable person would say what is allowable to do in the act of terror is thus allowable to do to me and to those I love; it cannot be grounded in any normative principle expressing benevolence or serving the interests of justice.[8] The victim of terrorism, having given no cause to warrant an application of deadly force, is the anonymous and undeserving victim of injustice.

An ethics tool relevant to civilian protection is found in the just war tradition, which extends as far back as Cicero and which is operative in international law today. The criteria of just war, as we have noted several times in these pages, present a set of inexplicit, broadly, even vaguely worded guidelines that are intended to frame issues related to the use of force, which are then open to debate in terms of the specifics of a conflict. The applicability of the criteria is indeterminate regarding the specifics of any particular conflict where the use of force is contemplated, but the more significant limitation of just war thinking is that lacking any normative principle to underwrite the criteria, just war cannot be said to be an ethic.

It could be, however, and that has been our argument throughout this book. We have argued in this book, particularly in our opening chapters, that the articulation of a common normative agreement or moral presumption to the effect that "force ordinarily ought not to be used to settle conflicts" would satisfy the demand of moral philosophy that a defensible, benevolent, just, and universalizable moral foundation be laid so that an action guide acceptable to the whole moral community can thereby be established on the question of the use of force. With this common moral agreement in place, the criteria of just war thinking are transformed to serve as an actual ethic to guide the process of making an exception to the rule *that force ordinarily ought not to be used to settle conflicts*. A nonabsolute presumption of nonviolence grounds the ethic of a just war on this understanding.

If just war is transformed into an ethic, lifting the presumption against using force in conflict situations is hard rather than easy to do, for the presumption is against the use of force, and this has implications for noncombatant immunity. The noncombatant immunity provision now has the force of a moral norm that ought to be observed in the context of a universalizable moral requirement. In other words, the idea that noncombatants are to be protected is transformed from a justice-related but vague guide into a universal prescription that lays a moral requirement not only on the parties to a conflict but in a larger sense on the whole moral community. That is what an ethic accomplishes, and this is what a *just war ethic* would demand. The responsibility for protecting the civilian noncombatant from the harm of conflict and violence does not simply fall on the warring parties, though of course they have that obligation as well. War is chaos, collective killing, and moral violation; and as history, common sense, and our experience of war tell us and as we have already acknowledged, warring parties do not succeed in preventing civilian harm—sometimes, as in the case of Allied bombing during World War II, Hitler's "final solution," Pol Pot, or Mai Lai—pick your atrocity—civilians are actually *targeted* for abuse, degradation, destruction.

War creates the context for collective killing involving persons whose status exempts them from violation and injustice. The moral issue, then, is where to locate responsibility for protecting civilians when the parties to conflict do not meet their obligations to respect civilian immunity. Transforming just war from a set of morally relevant concerns that provide cover or justification for uses of force, usually understood to be violent force,[9] into an actual ethic that is universally binding on reasonable persons of goodwill who live in moral community, has the profound consequence of turning responsibility for civilian protection over to the moral community itself. This is one way to establish moral justification for humanitarian intervention. Organizational and political issues may be difficult—that is a given—but the point is that this kind of just war ethical thinking makes clear the moral duty to protect noncombatant civilians. It is as if the moral community were saying, "Be in conflict—conflict is natural; but the limit on your conflict is the use of violent and destructive force as it involves, and especially as it is directed toward, noncombatant civilians." The moral community, comprising reasonable persons of goodwill, must insist on the protection of noncombatant innocents, and it must direct to warring parties a directive to stop any intentional killing of civilians. Persons who hold the status of noncombatant civilians must be exempted from harm in conformity to just war principles. Furthermore, the noncombatant immunity provision of just war requires that a "stop-the-killing" directive be issued to parties in conflict as a moral imperative. All reasonable people recognize this imperative as such, although it is not, unfortunately, in the logic of war, actually observed in practice. This gap between moral knowledge and wrong-ful action—between thought and experience—is the moral issue that presses on the moral community and demands response.

PRACTICAL CONSIDERATIONS

As we transform just war thinking into a just war ethic, the project that pre-occupied us in chapter 1, we can ask a provocative question concerning the practical significance of allowing noncombatant immunity to gain deeper traction in our ethical thinking and consider the practical ramifications of such a change. What would happen if the protection of noncombatant civilians became the rallying just war ethical priority for the entire moral community?

Let me suggest three responses to this question, briefly:

1. A new emphasis on the protection of noncombatants reminds persons of goodwill and conscience that war is itself an inadequate conflict-resolution strategy. That recognition could affect the organization of international responses to the usually local or regional conflicts in which noncombatant civilians are threatened with direct harm from warfare violence. When the noncombatant immunity provision is transformed into a universal moral pre-scription, the entire moral community faces the obligation to protect civilians. The moral community must respond to incidents of targeted civilian violence, especially genocide, by demanding that such killing stop. If there is a global ethic—global, as Peter Singer says, "in the sense of drawing on aspects of ethics common to all or virtually all human societies"[10]—one of the obvious principles or ethical standards that seems a likely candidate for universal con-sent is the moral, common-decency recognition through practical reason that the killing of civilians is wrong and that whatever the issue of the conflict, the moral imperative is first of all to stop the killing and protect civilians. Civilian killing, being of universal moral concern, must lead to an application of pres-sure on the institutions of government and other international organizations so that they organize a response to war and civil strife. Employing nonviolent force, because it interrupts the spiral of violence and creates the conditions necessary for a more just conflict aftermath, ought always to be the mode of protection; and it should not be relinquished without overwhelming evidence of its failure.

And applying such force faces problems. Of course, the integrity of na-tional boundaries and sovereignty must be respected, but the protection of civilians in places such as Darfur or Iraq, the Congo or Rwanda are moral ne-cessities. And there are other considerations as well: the question of political resolve even to enter a killing zone; concerns about mistaken, self-deceptive or ideologically driven interventions, which may or may not be truly humanitarian; the problem of cultural imperialism; and the issue of organizing multilaterally through an organization such as the UN to stop civilian deaths. All of these require some kind of consistency of response, else a politics of inequality is simply perpetuated, with some civilians in some quarters being more important to save than others. The United Nations is the organization best positioned to organize a response to the tragedy of civilian killing, but the UN's own structure and decision-making processes pose significant obstacles for decisive action when the aim is civilian protection. Elevated attention to noncombatant immunity will call for changes in the structure and functioning of the UN, perhaps along the lines of the European Union, which sets minimum ethical standards for admission.[11] This is a complicated geopolitical issue beyond the scope of the present inquiry, but the suggestion here is that organizing so that a "responsibility to protect" overrules the idea of a "right to intervene" refocuses the work of the UN and authorizes a multilateral response to the reality of war and the inevitable consequence of unjust warfare deaths. United Nations reform is one practical consequence that follows from elevating noncombatant immunity to a position where the moral community and the international community act meaningfully as one to stop slaughter and protect civilian populations.

2. An ethic supporting noncombatant immunity will acknowledge that warfare not only unjustly targets civilians for destruction but can by means of destructiveness make of noncombatants another kind of victim, what I would call a "perpetrator victim." P. W. Singer has chronicled how children—in Afghanistan, Iraq, and Pakistan—have been denied noncombatant status only to be then coercively pressed into service as soldiers.[12] And war can turn neighbor on neighbor, one civilian against another: the Hutu perpetrators of genocide in Rwanda were not mercenaries but neighbors. A recent study of the Murambi massacre in Rwanda points out that the forty thousand civilian Tutsis who died in the compound where they had all been assembled were slaughtered by their noncombatant neighbors: "My father was a victim of the war, and my brother killed my stepmother because she was a Tutsi and I did not prevent him from killing her"—said one Hutu killer.[13] War can transform noncombatants into victim perpetrators of unjust violence, and a focus on the centrality of noncombatant protection must include attention to the reality that conflict not controlled and restrained may extend the destruction of war by creating perpetrator victims.

Terrorists actually count on this happening. In the logic of terrorism, the successful terrorist is one who provokes an excess response from the authorities. That excess of violence and destructiveness inevitably includes a victimizing of noncombatant civilians, who will become politicized by their experiences, made militant by resentment over personal losses suffered, and then become motivated to help extend the violence even further. Protecting noncombatant civilians must also attend to the noncombatant who may be changed by the conflict as social pressures or even outrage at the injustice of civilian casualties perpetuate, expand, and deepen the conflict. This wrong is addressed by acting consistently with an elevated attention to protecting noncombatants.

3. And finally, the effort to position noncombatant immunity to a privileged place of moral attention must reassert the primacy of the common moral agreement that force must not be used to settle conflicts. Attending to the practical difficulties and the wrongness of violating noncombatant immunity reminds us that the common agreement that force ordinarily ought not to be used to settle conflicts is still the morally grounded position to take on war, and this is the explicit grounding of the just war *ethic*. If civilians are drawn into conflict, if they are victimized and made to suffer the inequities of war, including unjust and inequitable death, a moral response is called for. That moral response ought to be articulated not in the language of moralizers but in a language familiar to persons of goodwill and conscience, who are then charged with the responsibility of bringing a sense of natural justice and decency, which is perhaps easier to find in private life, into public life and discourse, where it is so often relinquished—and then into the realities of political conflict. Respect for the noncombatant and recognition of the obligation to protect the noncombatant offers a moral agreement around which to rethink the politics of conflict and transform the processes by which human beings unjustly visit death on one another in war.

Notes

INTRODUCTION

1. J. J. C. Smart, "Utilitarianism," in *Vice and Virtue in Everyday Life: Introductory Readings in Ethics*, 2nd ed., ed. Christina Sommers and Fred Sommers (San Diego: Harcourt Brace Jovanovich, 1989), 100.

2. See Thomas Mappes and David DeGrazia, eds., introduction to *Biomedical Ethics*, 6th ed. (New York: McGraw-Hill, 2006), 5.

3. Immanuel Kant, *Groundwork of the Metaphysic of Morals*, trans. H. J. Paton (New York: Harper & Row, Harper Torchbooks, 1964), 88.

4. Kant, *Groundwork of the Metaphysic of Morals*, 96.

5. Gregory Pence, *The Elements of Bioethics* (New York: McGraw-Hill, 2006).

6. Kant himself would not have endorsed such a "one solution" notion, at least according to Allen W. Wood in his book *Kantian Ethics* (Cambridge: Cambridge University Press, 2008), but my point here is about absolutism, to which some Kantians gravitate.

7. James Rachels, "Kant and the Categorical Imperative," in *Vice and Virtue in Everyday Life: Introductory Readings in Ethics*, 2nd ed., ed. Christina Sommers and Fred Sommers (San Diego: Harcourt Brace Jovanovich, 1989), 135.

8. See Rachels, p. 144: "Rules, even within a Kantian framework, need not be regarded as absolute. All that is required by Kant's basic idea is that when we violate a rule, we do so for a reason that we would be willing for anyone to accept, were they in our position." This appeal to a nonabsolute universalizability will play a role in my discussion of the just war–related ethic, the subject matter of this book.

9. Jeremy Bentham, *The Principles of Morals and Legislation* (1781), at http://www.constitution.org/jb/pml.txt, accessed October 11, 2011. See chapter I (II) "The Principle of Utility" and chapter IV (V, VI), "Value of a Lot of Pleasure or Pain, How to Be Measured."

10. John Stuart Mill, "Utilitarianism (1861)," in *The Collected Works of John Stuart Mill, Volume 10—Essays on Ethics, Religion, and Society*, ed. John M. Robson, Introduction by F. E. L. Priestley (Toronto: University of Toronto Press; London: Routledge and Kegan Paul, 1985), 212. Accessed from http://oll.libertyfund.org/title/241 on October 15, 2010.

11. I do not discuss here rule utilitarianism, which asserts that the rightness of an act is based on the maximizing of utility associated with rules that in general establish a utilitarian determination of contemplated actions, so, since lying would usually not meet the maximizing of utility requirement, rather than testing every possible lie, one simply follows a rule against lying. But the foundation of rule utilitarianism is still a determination of maximum utility, so the focus on act utilitarianism seems more appropriate for these comments.

12. "200 Lies per Day Just to Cope with Reality," *ShortNews.com: The News Community*, January 16, 2001, accessed August 4, 2009, http://www.shortnews.com/start.cfm?id=2738.

13. James Geary, "Deceitful Minds: The Awful Truth about Lying," *Time*, March 13, 2000, accessed July 6, 2010, http://www.time.com/time/europe/magazine/2000/313/deceit.html.

14. David Nyberg says in his book *The Varnished Truth*: "Truth telling is morally overrated. . . . Being against all deception is as wrong-minded as loathing all bacteria—including the ones responsible for wine and cheese. A lifetime of relationships is inconceivable without deception." Quoted in Geary, "Deceitful Minds."

15. Sometimes human subjects do consent to being deceived, as when human subjects in medical research agree to receive a drug not knowing whether it is the experimental drug. The case could be made that a Kantian notion of "informed consent" protects all human subjects, but this is not always practical in certain protocols. I'm thinking here of psychological protocols where outright deceptions occur in order to achieve the data results of an experiment. Institutional review boards can allow such deception but do so only because they will then require a debriefing that explains the real object of research. This could be said to amount to an ex post facto statement of informed consent. The debriefing thus lessens the risk of harm to the subject. My point, however, is that a Kantian could object to such a deception since it treats the subject disrespectfully, that is, as if the person were not worthy of being told the truth. The truth, however, would interfere with the advance of knowledge, and we are back to a conflict between the duty to pursue knowledge and the duty to tell the truth (or not lie).

16. I owe this insight to Thomas P. Kasulis. It is worth noting that there are differences among utilitarian philosophers. Bentham, for instance, held that social punishment would increase disutility, while J. S. Mill argued that right action was the result of common agreements about happiness ("the greatest happiness principle"), which were tied to "a higher mode of existence" such that he would argue the quality of actions lead to happiness—thus his famous remark that a dissatisfied human being would always be happier than a satisfied pig, and Socrates happier than a satisfied fool, cited in endnote 10.

17. Mill was reputed to have an IQ over 200. See, for instance, http://listverse.com/2007/10/06/top-10-geniuses.

18. Michael Brannigan, *Ethics across Cultures: An Introductory Text with Readings* (Boston: McGraw-Hill, 2005), 15–16.

19. The practical extermination of political opponents is all too familiar an example, but one worth noting as often justified on utilitarian grounds. Utilitarian justifications can often be found in the writings of historians wanting to "explain" morally reprehensible acts. One example: the first-century BCE Roman soldier-politician Crassus planned to slaughter his remaining ninety-nine slaves because two escaped slaves were believed to have murdered his cousin, which was later shown not to be the case. The idea was that in a time of Spartacus's slave revolt, a harsh response to such slave insubordination was necessary to prevent even further slavery insurrection, and Crassus's biographer, F. E. Adcock, invokes a utilitarian ethic to evaluate Crassus's contemplation of mass murder: "Times were desperate, and desperate measures were needed . . . [and] it would not be fair to criticize Crassus's behavior as unnaturally vicious." Quoted in Steven Saylor, *Arms of Nemesis* (New York: Ivy Books, 1992), 319. In another direction altogether, consider the subject of taboo sexual relations across the species boundary as discussed by noted utilitarian philosopher Peter Singer. See Peter Singer's utilitarian discussion of sex with animals in "Heavy Petting," *Nerve* (2001), at http://www.utilitarian.net/singer/by/2001---- .htm (accessed October 14, 2011).

20. The goods of life, which are examined at length by natural law theorist Germaine Grisez, will be discussed in the next chapter. We can say to the interested reader that these goods include matters such as life itself, physical integrity, the capacity to experience pleasure and aesthetic enjoyment, the freedom to work and play, the development of personal identity, friendships, and loving relationships, and practical reasonableness. Germain Grisez and Russell Shaw, *Beyond the New Morality: The Responsibilities of Freedom*, 2nd ed. (Notre Dame, IN: University of Notre Dame Press, 1974), 61–62.

CHAPTER 1:
JUST WAR AS AN ETHIC

1. Andre Fiala, *The Just War Myth: The Moral Illusions of War* (Lanham, MD: Rowman & Littlefield, 2008), 3.

2. Fiala, *The Just War Myth*, 3.

3. See a discussion relevant to this issue in Joseph Capizzi and Helmut David Baer, "Just War Theory and the Problem of International Politics: On the Central Role of Just Intention," *Journal of The Society of Christian Ethics* 26, no. 1 (Spring/ Summer 2006): 163–75; and Helmut David Baer and Joseph E. Capizzi, "Just War Theories Reconsidered: Problems with Prima Facie Duties and the Need for a Political Ethic," *Journal of Religious Ethics* 33, no. 1 (March 2005): 119–37. The latter article provides important insights about the differences between a prima facie ethic and a political ethic and discusses just war insights from ethicists Lisa Sowle Cahill and James F. Childress. I discuss how the common agreement ethic differs from a prima facie ethic below (chapter 4).

4. John Finnis, *Natural Law and Natural Rights* (Oxford: Clarendon Press, 1980), 16.

5. Grisez and Shaw, *Beyond the New Morality*, 61–62.

6. Joseph Boyle, "Just War Thinking in Catholic Natural Law," in *The Ethics of War and Peace: Religious and Secular Perspectives,* ed. Terry Nardin (Princeton: Princeton University Press, 1996), 43.

7. St. Augustine, in "Letter 189 Letter to Boniface," writes, "Peace should be the object of your desire; war should be waged only as a necessity, and waged only that God may by it deliver men from the necessity and preserve them in peace. For peace is not sought in order to [stir up] the kindling of war, but war is waged in order that peace may be obtained. Therefore, even in waging war, cherish the spirit of a peacemaker, that, by conquering those whom you attack, you may lead them back to the advantages of peace; for our Lord says: Blessed are the peacemakers; for they shall be called the children of God." *New Advent,* http://www.newadvent.org/fathers/1102189.htm, accessed August 22, 2010. Thomas Aquinas quotes this passage in *Summa Theologica* part II-II, question 41, "Of War." The other translation is found in Peter S. Temes, *The Just War: An American Reflection on the Morality of War in Our Time* (Chicago: Ivan R. Dee, 2003), 9.

8. John Finnis, "The Ethics of War and Peace in the Catholic Natural Law Tradition," in *The Ethics of War and Peace: Religious and Secular Perspectives*, ed. Terry Nardin (Princeton: Princeton University Press, 1996), 17.

9. Finnis, "The Ethics of War and Peace," 33.

10. John Finnis points out that this is the case with Aquinas in *S. T.* II-II (qq. 24–43, prolog. to q. 43) (vices opposed to *caritas*), and in Suarez's tract "De caritae" in *De triplice virtue theologica*, section 13 on "De bello." See Finnis for complete references (qq., 24–43, prolog. to q. 43); and in Suarez's tract "De caritae" in *De triplice virtue theological*, section 13 on "De bello," see Finnis, "The Ethics of War and Peace," 35, for complete references.

11. St. Augustine, *City of God*, trans. Henry Bettenson, intro. John O'Meara (New York: Penguin Classics, 1984), section 19.7, 861–62.

12. Marcus Tullius Cicero, *De Officiis/On Duties*, trans. Harry G. Edinger (New York: Bobbs-Merrill, 1974), I (34), 19.

13. Cicero, *De Officiis/On Duties*, 217.

14. Bernard T. Adeney, *Just War, Political Realism, and Faith* (Lanham, MD: Scarecrow Press, 1988), 24.

15. William R. Stevenson, *Christian Love and Just War* (Macon, GA: Mercer University Press, 1988), 37.

16. Augustine, *Contra Faustum*, XXII, 74. Quoted in Thomas Aquinas, *Summa Theologica*, q. 40, 1, 1265–73, http://www.newadvent.org/summa/3040.htm.

17. Augustine, *Contra Faustum*, 41.

18. John Langan, "The Elements of St Augustine's Just War Theory," *Journal of Religious Ethics* 12 (Spring 1984): 43–44.

19. See John Mark Mattox, *St. Augustine and the Theory of Just War* (New York: Continuum, 2009). Mattox argues that despite the lack of a systematic theory of just war in his several disparate writings on the topic of war, Augustine still presents arguments and positions that display a remarkable "unity . . . apparent in his just-war thought" (5).

20. See Alexander of Hales, "Virtuous Dispositions in Warfare," in *The Ethics of War: Classic and Contemporary Readings*, ed. Gregory M. Reichenberg, Henrik Syse, and Endre Begby (Oxford: Blackwell Publishing, 2006), 156–59.

21. Finnis, "The Ethics of War and Peace,"18.

22. Thomas Aquinas, *Summa Theologica*, II-II, q. 40, "On War," trans. Fathers of the English Dominican Province (Chicago: Encyclopedia Britannica, 1952), p. 578.

23. Thomas Aquinas, *Summa Theologica*, II-II, q. 64, article 7, "Whether it is permissible to kill a man in self-defense?" in *The Ethics of War: Classic and Contemporary Readings,* ed. Gregory M. Reichenberg, Henrik Syse, and Endre Begby (Oxford: Blackwell Publishing, 2006), 190–91.

24. United Nations, *Charter of the United Nations*, http://www.un.org/en/docu ments/charter. Chapter VII, Article 51 reads:

> Nothing in the present Charter shall impair the inherent right of individual or collective self-defense if an armed attack occurs against a Member of the United Nations, until the Security Council has taken measures necessary to maintain international peace and security. Measures taken by Members in the exercise of this right of self-defence shall be immediately reported to the Security Council and shall not in any way affect the authority and responsibility of the Security Council under the present Charter to take at any time such action as it deems necessary in order to maintain or restore international peace and security.

St. Augustine, incidentally, did not include a right to self-defense under his early formulation of just war since Christians were not to kill over their own lives or property.

25. Thomas Aquinas, *Summa Theologica,* II-II, q. 64, article 7, 7, in *The Ethics of War.*

26. See Hugo Grotius, "The Theory of Just War Systematized (On the Law of War and Peace)," reprinted in *The Ethics of War*, 385–437. See also the helpful discussion of Grotius in David L. Clough and Brian Stiltner, *Faith and Force: A Christian Debate about War* (Washington, DC: Georgetown University Press, 2007), 57.

27. Richard P. McBrien, *Catholicism: Study Edition* (Minneapolis: Winston Press, 1981), 1036.

28. See the outstanding "Secular Just War Theory" chapter in Kenneth L. Vaux, *Ethics and the Gulf War: Religion, Rhetoric, and Righteousness* (Eugene, OR: Wipf & Stock, 2003), 120–45.

29. Daniel C. Maguire, *Ethics: A Complete Method for Moral Choice* (Minneapolis: Fortress Press, 2010), 9.

30. Maguire, *Ethics*, 9, also discussed on 85.

31. McBrien, *Catholicism: Study Edition*, 1036.

32. Thus does Michael Walzer write in "A Dissenting View," *New Republic* 85 (September 23, 1981): 13–14: "The bombing of Hiroshima was an act of terrorism; its purpose was political, not military. The goal was to kill enough civilians to shake the Japanese government and force it to surrender. And this is the goal of every terrorist campaign."

33. For an in-depth discussion, see Hans Blix, *Disarming Iraq* (New York: Pantheon, 2004).

34. This is controversial terrain, since Derrida's aporetic or deconstructionist ethic is often criticized as expressing a wildly nihilistic relativism that would counter the premises of ethical thinking. Some scholars have argued that despite Derrida's suspicion of the logocentrism giving rise to ethics, in the attention he gives to violence, justice, personhood, responsibility, and decision making in the instant, his work

does finally constitute an ethic. See the argument, for example, of Marko Zlomislic, *Jacques Derrida's Aporetic Ethics* (Lanham, MD: Lexington Books, 2007).

35. Joseph Runzo, "Religion and Ethics in a Global World," in *Ethics in the World Religions*, ed. Joseph Runzo and Nancy M. Martin (Oxford: One World, 2001), 23. The reference to the moral point of view is meant to distinguish the idea of an ethic as proposed here from a kind of ethic that might arise contrary to the moral point of view, the idea being that action guides and rule-governed behavior—an ethical system of sorts—could be claimed for the worst kinds of actions and systems of behavior. So a social order that practices genocide against a minority could claim to have an ethic in the sense that they avow a rule-governed system of behavior aimed at certain ideas of goodness—the problem is that such an ethic is not conformed to the moral point of view, as the subsequent discussion above will make clear.

36. The shortest and most devastating critique of moral relativism as incoherent is found in John Hospers, "The Problem with Relativism," in *Vice and Virtue in Everyday Life: Introductory Readings in Ethics*, 2nd ed., ed. Christina Sommers and Fred Sommers (San Diego: Harcourt Brace Jovanovich, 1989), 157–62. The ultimate argument against ethical relativism is existential, for such an ethic cannot be lived: it is the ultimate example of an ethic where thought is divorced from experience. As a teacher I note that I have offered to abide by a relativistic ethic with students trying to persuade me of its reality, but when I offer to accede by giving them a grade of F for reasons related to my own idea of pedagogy, none has urged me to follow through and live out with them the ethic they think is right. Usually I receive comments that such an action would not be right, that it would be unjust or unfair, and by that appeal the point is made.

37. See Lloyd Steffen, *Holy War, Just War: Exploring the Moral Meaning of Religious Violence*, Lanham, MD: Rowman & Littlefield, 2007) for an extended discussion of this claim.

38. Abraham Lincoln, "Speech at Worchester, Massachusetts, September 12, 1848," in *Collected Works of Abraham Lincoln, Volume 2*, ed. Roy Basler (New Brunswick, NJ: Rutgers University Press, 1953), 3–4.

39. This excludes moral relativism, ethical egoism, and moral absolutism.

40. Joseph Runzo, "Religion and Ethics in a Global World," in *Ethics in the World Religions*, ed. Joseph Runzo and Nancy M. Martin (Oxford: One World, 2001), 23.

41. See Keith Ward's discussion of benevolence in "Religion and the Possibility of a Global Ethic," in Runzo and Martin, *Ethics in the World Religions*, ed. Joseph Runzo and Nancy M. Martin (Oxford: One World, 2001), 41–43.

42. For an accessible discussion of justice as both social and individual, see Maguire, *Ethics*, 51–75.

43. This is one of the critical points made in John Rawls's influential work, *A Theory of Justice* (Cambridge: Harvard University Press, 1971, 1999), which upholds the idea of justice as fairness. Rawls endorses the "impartial justice" ethical ideal in all he does to articulate an "original position" and its "veil of ignorance" construct that establishes theoretically that no persons are to be privileged on the basis of incidental features such as gender, class, race, or religion but only in the grounds of their basic humanity.

44. Runzo, "Religion and Ethics in a Global World," 23.

45. There are, of course, critics of the Golden Rule, as in J. S. Mill's point that on the Golden Rule, an individual facing prison might actually wish that those who would imprison him also be set free if they were in that individual's position—so the formality of the rule is satisfied, but justice is not done. I would not look so deep—the Golden Rule (and its Silver and Platinum versions) has timeless features that commend it to us as an action guide aimed at goodness, so as I would not wish to be a slave I should never act to enslave another. This moral focus is not to be confused with relative cultural preferences, for clearly it would be a mistake to invoke the Golden Rule to insist that everyone use forks rather than chopsticks.

46. The idea of "ethical egoism"—that one should act in ways that benefit oneself and no others—is, like ethical relativism, taken to be incoherent as an ethic. Whereas ethical relativism fails to acknowledge any notion of universalizability and normative principles that transcend the limitations of cultural or group (or even individualistic) particularities, ethical egoism fails to meet the requirements of actually being an ethic due to its failure to attend to other-regardingness and benevolence.

47. Runzo, "Religion and Ethics in a Global World," 23.

48. I have been working with this idea of a moral presumption since the 1980s. The original paper delivered in 1989 is available now as "Reflections on Abortion: The Conflict of Moral Presumptions," in *The Living Theological Heritage of The United Church of Christ: United And Uniting (Living Theological Heritage of the United Church of Christ, Volume 7)*, ed. Frederick R. Trost and Barbara Brown Zikmund (Cleveland: Pilgrim Press, 2005), 471–76. Ideas from this initial discussion were developed in Lloyd Steffen, *Life/Choice: The Theory of Just Abortion*, rev. ed. (1994; repr., Eugene, OR: Wipf & Stock, 1999). This book explores how just war thinking translates into an ethic applicable to the abortion issue, thus addressing issues other than war. A more complete discussion of "moral presumptions" can be found in that text. Discussions of a "moral presumption against violence" in just war theory have been prominent in religious ethics for quite some time, the earliest perhaps being Ralph Potter, *War and Moral Discourse* (Richmond, VA: John Knox Press, 1973), 61. See also J. Philip Wogaman, *Christian Moral Judgment* (Louisville, KY: Westminster John Knox Press, 1989), 63–64; James B. Childress, "Just War Criteria," and J. Bryan Hehir, "The Just War Ethic and Catholic Theology," both in *War or Peace? The Search for New Answers*, ed. Thomas A. Shannon (Maryknoll, NY: Orbis, 1980), 42 (Childress) and 18 (Hehir); David Hollenbach, *Nuclear Ethics: A Christian Moral Argument* (Notre Dame, IN: University of Notre Dame Press, 1990), 372. The presumption against violence was also central to the United States Conference of Bishops document *The Challenge of Peace: God's Promise and Our Response—A Pastoral Letter on War and Peace—May 3, 1983* (Washington, DC, 1983), http://www.zero-nukes.org/pdf_files/Challenge_of_ Peace.pdf: "Catholic teaching begins in every case with a presumption against war and for peaceful settlement of disputes. In exceptional cases, determined by the moral principles of the just-war tradition, some uses of force are permitted" (2); and the United Methodist Council of Bishops, *In Defense of Creation: The Nuclear Crisis and a Just Peace* (Washington, DC, 1986).

49. I say "of a sort" because the "principles" or propositions at issue here are not absolute, and some ethical perspectives, particularly some versions of deontological or Kantian ethics, would consider a principle by definition to be an exceptionless rule.

50. "Lying" also carries a negative moral valence, and one could legitimately ask why "lying" is not akin to "murder" as an issue in moral language. We undoubtedly face certain ambiguities in our moral language. "Murder" as a morally unjustifiable homicide does not seem to me to parallel lying, which identifies a linguistically explicit statement designed to mislead belief, thus making it a particular form of "deception." "Homicide" is a rather neutral term, with "killing" a term embodying a presumptive wrongness, and both terms can be qualified as justified or unjustified. "Murder" embodies a moral conclusion; deceptions need not be as a class so close to that valence, as when an actor deceives an audience with a fine performance. Lying to save a life, as in the Nazi pursuer case, puts a duty not to lie in conflict with a duty to save a life, so that lying yields before the more serious duty; and the phenomenon of the "white lie" points to a deception that does not harm and is aimed at some social good. So lying can permit some qualification. I do not deny the negative moral valence of "lying," but I think some terms, such as "murder" and "terrorist," function in the language to embody a *moral conclusion* that is at the end of deliberation; and such terms function with an inflexibility that is meant to exclude, by definition, any justified instance. This issue about moral language is discussed at greater length in chapter 4.

51. Michael Walzer, *Just and Unjust Wars* (New York: Basic, 1977), 261. Churchill is here cited as having used the term "terror bombing."

52. For a more in-depth discussion of what constitutes a moral presumption and how it embodies a vision of goodness, see Steffen, *Life/Choice*, 30–34.

53. This is a controversial claim from a natural law perspective. While natural law thinkers could accept some notion of obligation and duty (one can find duty in Plato), the idea of maximizing pleasure or happiness as advocated by Bentham and Mill, respectively, provokes the natural law critique that no physical or biological state or circumstance commends a duty or obligation, and I accept this. But what if the principle of utility were not pleasure, or happiness, or even love, as Joseph Fletcher argued in *Situation Ethics*—what if it were simply goodness? The idea of maximizing goodness is a short step away from the idea of promoting goodness, and natural law is concerned to promote goodness, to extend goodness and the result of good action to as many people as possible, which is, in a sense, "utilitarian" as well as an expression of benevolence. Utilitarianism has flaws to be sure, but I am here offering the view that attending to consequences based on a principle of promoting goodness ("the greatest good for the greatest number") is something natural law must contend with since I am convinced that reasonable people employing practical reason as their natural endowment actually use this kind of thinking in their experience of the moral life, and if we are conforming thought to experience, this inclusion—this nod to utilitarianism—is necessary as a truth about moral experience.

54. The theoretical pacifism to which I refer is that of the absolutist pacifist who would, as in an ethic of nonresistance to evil, deny the good of practical reasonableness and, like Tolstoy, drawing on the Matthean Gospel "resist not evil" stance,

refuse to oppose injustice and evil. That is one form of pacifism—an absolutist form to be sure. Just war thinking, which eschews on principle any type of absolutism—it is always open to considering exceptions—opposes this kind of absolutist pacifism.

CHAPTER 2:
NONVIOLENT RESISTANCE AS A USE OF FORCE

1. Martin Luther King Jr., *A Testament of Hope: The Essential Writings of Martin Luther King, Jr.*, ed. James M. Washington (New York: HarperSanFrancisco, 1986), 109. Hereafter cited as *TofH*.

2. Quoted in Hanes Walton Jr., "King's Philosophy of Nonviolence," in *Martin Luther King Jr.*, ed. Thomas Siebold (San Diego: Greenhaven Press, 2000), 87.

3. M. K. Gandhi, *Non-Violent Resistance (Satyagraha)* (New York: Schocken Books, 1951), 32. Hereafter cited as *Satyagraha*.

4. M. K. Gandhi, *Satyagraha*, 251.

5. And both knew that in an empirical sense it could work, Gandhi having achieved his political goals of independence and King being convinced by Gandhi's example. For a discussion of historical examples where nonviolent resistance achieved substantive political and social change, see Richard B. Gregg, *The Power of Nonviolence*, 2nd ed. (New York: Schocken Books, 1966). Gregg's first edition was dated 1935, and he had been a member of Gandhi's ashram; but by the time of the second edition, he was able to invoke not only examples involving nineteenth-century Hungary and pre-apartheid South Africa but more recent successes in India, Denmark, Norway, and the King-led boycott in Montgomery.

6. For a discussion of Tolstoy's nonresistance pacifism as the expression of absolutized, and therefore demonic, religion, see Lloyd Steffen, *Holy War, Just War*, 143–70.

7. Gandhi, *Satyagraha*, 161.

8. Martin Luther King Jr., "Pilgrimage to Nonviolence," in *TofH*, 39.

9. Martin Luther King Jr., " Pilgrimage to Nonviolence," in *The Papers of Martin Luther King, Jr., Vol. IV*, ed. Clayborne Carson (Berkeley: University of California Press, 2000), 479. King's interactions with Niebuhr are significant and need more scholarly attention. Niebuhr writes in *Moral Man and Immoral Society* (New York: Scribners, 1932) that whites will admit blacks to equal station in the United States only if "forced" to do so, but that any attempt by blacks to secure equality by means of violence will fail, and that the "techniques of non-violence" will be important in that struggle: "Non-violence is a particularly strategic instrument for an oppressed group which is hopelessly in the minority and has no possibility of developing sufficient power to set against its oppressors. The emancipation of the Negro race in America probably waits upon the adequate development of this kind of social and political strategy." (See 252–54.) King distances himself from Niebuhr, but his indebtedness to Niebuhr is clear, and King will acknowledge it several times, including references in King's famous *Playboy* interview and even in "Letter from Birmingham City Jail."

King makes reference to Niebuhr and cites his perspectives from *Moral Man and Immoral Society* as handy reference points, and neither of these two works is derived from research but out of those sources that are King's own resources. My thanks to Thomas G. Poole for discussing the Niebuhr-King connection in some detail with me.

10. Gandhi and King will both claim that the spiritual power of nonviolence is spiritually based and noncoercive. But this is arguable given the kinds of activities nonviolent resistance sponsors. Boycotts and refusal to pay taxes are exertions of power designed to have an effect on social arrangements, and Gandhi and King both associate nonviolence with noncooperation. While nonviolent resistance may not constitute physical coercion, Reinhold Niebuhr observes that it "results in consequences not totally dissimilar from violence . . . non-violence does coerce and destroy." See Reinhold Niebuhr, *Moral Man and Immoral Society* (New York: Scribner, 1932), 241.

11. As just war requires discussion and debate—it settles no particular conflict itself but provides a structure for analysis and debate applicable to any conflict—I would make bold to say that as a framework for moral engagement, just war is a friend of engaged, informed democratic citizenship.

12. Martin Luther King Jr., "Letter from Birmingham City Jail," *TofH*, 290. See note 30 for Erik Erikson's observation on Gandhi's commitment to what could be called data collection, analysis, and assessment.

13. Tolstoy was an absolutist, and I have analyzed his perspectives on nonresistance to evil in *Holy War, Just War: Exploring the Moral Meaning of Religious Violence*. Gandhi is not an absolutist: "No man can claim that he is absolutely in the right," he writes (*Satyagraha*, 17); and he holds open a justified use of physical force: "I do believe that where there is only a choice between cowardice and violence I would advise violence" is in Gandhi's short essay, "Doctrine of the Sword [August 11, 1920]," in *The Penguin Gandhi Reader*, ed. Rudrangshu Mukherjee (New York: Penguin, 1996), 99. King will say, "I am committed to nonviolence absolutely" ("Showdown for Nonviolence," in *TofH*, 69); and in his later writings makes of nonviolence a "philosophy of life" (ibid.). But King also talks about nonviolent resistance as a method (if not technique) and never positions it to the absolutist position Tolstoy did, where pacifism became, in a sense, absolute, God. Gandhi admired Tolstoy (as did King) and actually corresponded with him and received aid from him, but even Gandhi found Tolstoy's assertion of pacifism as absolute—as God—difficult, since the implication was that it denigrated other religious forms, which upset Gandhi. For more on this, see Martin Green, *Gandhi: Voice of a New Age Revolution* (New York: Continuum, 1993), 194–96.

14. Gandhi and King both observe this prohibition on the use of force—even nonviolent force, as the discussion of last resort in the next section will demonstrate.

15. Writes King in "Letter from Birmingham City Jail," "We can never forget that everything Hitler did in Germany was legal—and everything the Hungarian freedom fighters did in Hungary was illegal. It was illegal to aid and comfort a Jew in Hitler's Germany." *TofH*, 294–95.

16. James Turner Johnson, *The Holy War Idea in Western and Islamic Traditions* (University Park: Penn State Press, 1997, 2001), 50–51. Johnson writes that this appeal to papal authority was modified so that the official rationale was directed toward

the just war ideas of defense against attack, punishment of attackers, and retaking things wrongfully taken by attackers (51), thus turning the crusade into a unifying war of liberation.

17. Bruce Lincoln, "Appendix: 'Instructions to Hijackers,'" in *Holy Terrors: Thinking about Religion after September 11* (Chicago: University of Chicago Press, 2003), 93–98.

18. This is what I did in my book *Holy War, Just War*. I would note that holy war can cross over into "just war." In *The Holy War Idea in Western and Islamic Traditions*, 45, James Turner Johnson identifies two just war criteria that apply to holy war, the one relevant to this discussion being the appeal to transcendent authority, "either given directly from God or mediated through the religious institutions in some way."

19. Gandhi, *Satyagraha*, 95, 271.

20. Gandhi, "Fifteen Instructions to Volunteers [17 April 1918]," in *The Penguin Gandhi Reader*, 131.

21. King, "Walk for Freedom," in *TofH*, 83.

22. Quoted in Hanes Walton Jr., "King's Social and Political Ideology," 88.

23. Although discussing Gandhi and King here, I would note the explicit appeal to just cause when the Dalai Lama offered in his acceptance speech for the Nobel Peace Prize the words, "Our cause is just," thus justifying the continued use of nonviolent resistance to the Chinese occupation of Tibet. If the criteria of just war thinking are related to common agreements and rationality as I am arguing here, then in the course of reflection on the question of force and resistance to injustice, rational people should be expected to appeal to these criteria in the normal and ordinary course of their rational deliberations. This is what I believe actually happens.

24. Gandhi, *Satyagraha*, all quotes in paragraph from 381.

25. King, "Non-Violence: The Only Road to Freedom," *TofH*, 57.

26. King, "Non-Violence: The Only Road to Freedom," *TofH*, 57.

27. King, "Playboy Interview," *TofH*, 344.

28. Gandhi, *Satyagraha*, 87.

29. King, *TofH*, 484–85.

30. Gandhi on truth as the end: "Without Ahimsa (nonviolence) it is not possible to seek and find the truth. Ahimsa and Truth are so intertwined that it is practically impossible to disentangle and separate them . . . ahimsa is the means and Truth is the end. Means to be means must always be within our reach, and so ahimsa becomes our supreme duty and Truth becomes God for us. If we take care of the means, we are bound to reach the end sooner or later" (Gandhi, "Excerpt from a Letter to Narandas Gandhi [28–31 July 1930]," in *The Penguin Gandhi Reader*, 112. With noninjury and nonviolence intertwined with truth itself, the end sought is by definition a noninjurious and peaceful community. King likewise says: "We will not obey unjust laws or submit to unjust practices . . . our aim is to persuade. We adopt the means of nonviolence because our end is a community at peace with itself. . . . We are ready to suffer when necessary and even risk our lives to become witnesses to the truth as we see it." *TofH*, 484–85. Both, then, point to the end of truth and the means as integral of achieving the goal of peace.

31. King, *TofH*, 291.

32. Gandhi, *Satyagraha*, 4, 23.

33. Erik Erikson, *Gandhi's Truth: On the Origins of Militant Nonviolence* (New York: Norton, 1969), 414.

34. King, "Nonviolence and Racial Justice," *TofH*, 8, 9. King would be even more explicit about victory and the nature of the victory, *TofH*, 257: "Be assured that we'll wear you down by our capacity to suffer, and one day we will win our freedom. We will not only win freedom for ourselves; we will so appeal to your heart and conscience that we will win you in the process, and our victory will be a double victory."

35. Gandhi, *Satyagraha*, 353.

36. Gandhi looked to history to argue that the "force of truth or love," not that of "force of arms," yields success: "The greatest and most unimpeachable evidence of the success of this force is to be found in the fact that, in spite of the wars of the world, it (the force of love or truth) still lives on," in *The Penguin Gandhi Reader*, 47. He was also prepared to recognize success if only one person performed the program of *satyagraha* correctly and in the true spirit: "In Satyagraha success is possible even if there is only one Satyagrahi of the proper stamp" (Gandhi, *Satyagraha*, 30). The reader is referred to Richard B. Gregg, *The Power of Nonviolence*, for historical examples of nonviolent resistance effecting positive political and social change.

37. See note 8 and the relevant text previously quoted, where King says pacifism is not sinless but "a lesser evil in the circumstances."

38. King, "Nonviolence and Racial Justice," in *TofH*, 7.

39. Gandhi, *Satyagraha*, 36.

40. McBrien, *Catholicism: Study Edition*, 1039.

41. King, "The Case against Tokenism," *TofH*, 110.

42. Gandhi, *Satyagraha*, 6.

43. King, "The Rising Tide of Racial Consciousness," *TofH*, 149.

44. Gandhi, *Satyagraha*, 148. On Niebuhr, see note 10 above.

45. The doctrine or principle of double effect deems licit an unwanted and negative secondary effect of an action if it is not directly intended and it is the foreseen but unwanted result of pursuing a good end that outweighs the harm of the secondary effect. Double effect is discussed in chapter 1.

46. I would note that one can find in Gandhi, for instance, his lengthy deliberation process being exposed as he writes about how he has been pressured and even rebuked for delaying engagement: "Today I am doing what the nation has been yearning for during the past ten years. Have I not been rebuked for delaying civil disobedience? Have not the friends angrily said, 'You are stopping the progress of the nation toward its goal'. . . . But suddenly I saw the light. And so I am out for battle and am seeking help on bended knee." Cited in note 3.

47. King, "The Social Organization of Nonviolence," *TofH*, 33.

48. Gandhi, *The Penguin Gandhi Reader*, 101–2.

49. Let me push the issue about proportionality further, asking the same question raised in the text but in a different way. Gandhi and King both understood that their methods would be met with violence. They clearly thought that they were meeting violence with superior weapons and would ultimately win. But there is a time-frame issue that is relevant to thinking about proportionality here. Time frame is always

relevant to proportionality since a poisoned well continues to poison after the conflict is over, and thus it is deemed an immoral, disproportionate act of war under just war; nuclear, biological, and chemical weapons are likewise disproportionate in impacting the parties to a conflict long after the conflict has ceased to exist. So the question to be raised is whether their objective to shame their opponents and convert them from their ways of oppression required that the oppressor do things worthy of evoking a shame response. That shameful acts were committed is not in dispute, but using the criterion of proportionality, we might ask a moral question, namely, "Is the desire to persuade and convert an enemy so necessary a task of resisting injustice that one is morally authorized to put oneself in situations where one provokes behavior—violent, destructive behavior—of such a character that it would evince shame in its perpetrator?" In other words, does the idea of volunteering and agreeing through "informed consent" to subject myself to violence and even death in the struggle for justice represent a proportionate action if what I am doing is potentially consenting to my death or being subjected to violence? And can I do so with only the justification that I am sacrificing myself to convert an enemy and provoke a shame reaction that may not come for a very long time—and is likely not to be provoked in the person who kills me? Does proportionality impose a relevant time restriction such that my sacrifice at the moment may not prove to be proportional if its effect does not take place until some distant future moment after I have suffered harm? (This question explains why King so often invoked the idea that history is on the side of justice, since he obviously thought about justice in long spans of time, as his Christian tradition would have encouraged him to do.) Does "informed consent" to the prospect that I might be harmed or killed adequately cover this? Poisoning a well or deploying a nuclear weapon may in fact prove effective in ending a particular conflict, but just war does not countenance either of them because of a disproportionate effect over time, and the issue is whether nonviolent resistance might be subject to a time restriction analogous to those kinds of actions.

50. See note 10.

51. Consider, for example, John Langan's presentation of just war in Augustine in "Elements of St. Augustine's Just War Theory," 19–38.

52. That absolutism of any kind necessarily entails its own contradiction as a function of the meaning of "absolute" is discussed in Steffen, *Holy War, Just War*, 23–42.

CHAPTER 3:
THE HYBRID ETHIC AND ITS APPLICATION

1. I hesitate to use this term, "objectivity," but only because of the way it is associated with scientism. I would hold that "objectivity" in this natural law philosophical sense identifies the ways things are with people in their commonality, which is publicly observable in that they pursue recognizable "goods of life," and this then allows us to speak meaningfully about "human nature." If this is what is meant by objectivity, subjectivity in all likelihood, rather than being something like ungrounded

opinion, becomes a form of objectivity that is for some reason not publicly observable or even available. (I owe this distinction to Thomas P. Kasulis.) Proponents of the "ethics is subjective" view do not or cannot articulate how a "subjective" ethical view could be divorced from our common understanding about what would constitute good and right action. Were we to find someone who believed that no promise should be kept and then offered that as a universal (thus ethical) prescription, that individual would rightly be considered somehow outside the confines of the moral community, even "unreasonable." Such a claim is not subjective in the sense that it is private and inaccessible to others. Rather, that prescription not to keep promises could be judged wrong when set against the moral standards reasonable people of goodwill accept for themselves and for others and understand to be universally applicable. Science and faith in science has unfortunately co-opted our understanding of objective and subjective.

2. Another prominent exemplar of this way of doing ethics is Abraham Lincoln, who also practiced a "hybrid" ethic that was constituted by studied virtue cultivation, attention to duties and principles, and practical consideration of consequences consistent with utilitarian thinking. See Lloyd Steffen, "The Ethical Complexity of Abraham Lincoln: Is There Something for Religious Ethicists to Learn?" *Journal of the Society of Christian Ethics* 31, no. 2 (2011): 74–99.

3. Cicero, *On Duties*, ed. M. T. Griffin and E. M. Atkins (Cambridge: Cambridge University Press, 1991), 7.

4. Cicero, *On Duties,* 3, 4; although this particular translation is taken from Cicero, *On Moral Obligation*, Book I, Ch. 2, trans. John Higginbotham (Berkeley/Los Angeles: University of California Press, 1967), 40.

5. Cicero, *On Duties*, 3.

6. Cicero, *On Duties*, 3, 7, 9.

7. Montague Brown, *The Question for Moral Foundations: An Introduction to Ethics* (Washington, DC: Georgetown University Press, 1996), 106.

8. Cicero, *On Duties*, 3.

9. Cicero, *On Duties*, 6.

10. Cicero, *On Duties*, 65.

CHAPTER 4:
USING THE "COMMON AGREEMENT" ETHIC

1. Aristotle, *Nicomachean Ethics*, II, par. 6, trans. W. D. Ross, in *Complete Works of Aristotle Vol. I*, Revised Oxford Translation, ed. Jonathan Barnes (Princeton: Princeton University Press, Bollingen Series LXXI, 2, 1984), 1748.

2. This is not an argument for relativism, but rather the opposite. A moral relativist would deny that an evolution in moral consciousness could take place. There is only what they believed in Aristotle's day and what we believe in ours—that's it; there is no overarching moral standard in play for the relativist, for there are no universals (except that, ironically and incoherently, of relativism itself).

3. Dick Francis, *Forfeit* (New York: Pocket Books, 1975).

4. Aristotle, *Rhetoric*, I, par. 13, trans. J. Barnes, in *Complete Works of Aristotle*, *Vol. I*, Revised Oxford Translation, ed. Jonathan Barnes (Princeton: Princeton University Press, Bollingen Series LXXI, 2, 1984), 2187.

5. Peter Singer, *One World: The Ethics of Globalization* (New Haven: Yale University Press, 2002), 106–49.

6. Robert N. Van Nyk, "When Is Lying Morally Permissible? Casuistical Reflection on the Game Analogy, Self-Defense, Social Contract Ethics, and Ideals," *Journal of Value Inquiry* 24 (1990): 155.

7. Aquinas, *Summa Theologica* II-II, q. 110, article 4, reply objection 5, 1662.

8. See "Introduction."

9. Victor Frankl, *Man's Search for Meaning* (New York: Washington Square Press, 1984), 70, 79.

10. All I mean by "intention" here is a forward-looking reason for action, to be distinguished from backward-looking reasons for action, which we more typically identify with "motives."

11. Sissela Bok, *Lying: Moral Choice in Public and Private Life* (New York: Vintage, 1978, 1979), 97.

12. Bok, 98.

13. Bok, 103

14. Bok, 116.

15. Mark Twain (Samuel Clemens), "On the Decay of the Art of Lying," Kindle edition, 78–85.

16. Robert C. Solomon, *Ethics and Excellence: Cooperation and Integrity in Business* (New York: Oxford University Press, 1992), 104.

17. J. O. Urmson, "The Interpretation of the Moral Philosophy of J. S. Mill," in *Theories of Ethics*, ed. Philippa Foot (Oxford: Oxford University Press, 1967), 128–35; R. B. Brandt, *A Theory of the Good and the Right* (Oxford: Oxford University Press, 1979).

18. Daniel C. Maguire, *Ethics: A Complete Method for Moral Choice* (Minneapolis: Fortress, 2010), 115.

19. W. L. Reese, "Utilitarianism," in *Dictionary of Philosophy and Religion: Eastern and Western Thought* (New Jersey: Humanities Press, 1980), 601.

20. W. D. Ross, *The Right and the Good* (Oxford: Clarendon Press, 1930), 22.

21. Maguire, *Ethics*, 116.

22. Ross, *The Right and the Good*, 19.

23. Lloyd Steffen, *Life/Choice: The Theory of Just Abortion* (Eugene, OR: Wipf & Stock Publishers, 1999, 2004). This book argues that there is a moral presumption against abortion but that a conflict in the goods of life—that of preserving and promoting life on the one hand, and exercising practical reason, which includes the exercise of choice and respect for the autonomy of women as fully endowed members of the moral community able to make decisions about their reproductive health, on the other—provokes abortion as a live moral question. The criteria that guide decision making involve competent authority, just cause, last resort, medical success, the preservation of values/nonsubversion of the value of life; and a prior-to-promise criterion

to govern the timing question of when in pregnancy it is no longer morally justified to proceed with an abortion. These are discussed in detail in *Life/Choice*.

CHAPTER 5:
THE ETHICS OF PHYSICIAN-ASSISTED SUICIDE

1. Kevorkian's case rested on appeal to the Ninth Amendment, which grants rights held by the people and not explicitly enumerated in the Constitution, including for Kevorkian a right to die. See Jack Kevorkian, *Amendment IX: Our Cornucopia of Rights* (Penumbra Press, Bloomfield Hills, MI, 2005).

2. For the way other countries have dealt with the issue, see the discussion below.

3. Physician assistance in dying is the preferred tag for the moral issue under examination here, but I prefer the language of physician-assisted suicide since it does present a language that pushes the moral issue—the patient who pursues this option is seeking to self-kill—suicide; and physician assistance in dying can cover much broader ground, including aspects of palliative care and pain management, which are not so controversial.

4. In the United States, Oregon, in a law passed in 1997 and affirmed by the Supreme Court in January 2006, authorizes physician-assisted suicide only; Switzerland in a 1941 law permits physician- and nonphysician-assisted suicide only; Belgium in 2002 authorized euthanasia but does not define the method; and since April 2002 but permitted by the courts since 1984, the Netherlands authorized voluntary euthanasia and physician-assisted suicide.

5. The American Geriatrics Society has offered the following position in its "Ethics Position" statement of 2007, accessed January 2008, http://www.american-geriatrics.org/products/positionpapers/vae94.shtml: "For patients whose quality of life and expected lifespan has become so limited as to make earlier death preferable to prolongation of life, the professional standard of care should be that of aggressive palliation of suffering and enhancement of opportunities for a meaningful life, not that of intentional termination of life."

6. These concerns are stated in the American Geriatrics Society, "Ethics Position."

7. CNN, "Euthanasia Now Legal in Holland," CNN (April 1, 2002), accessed May 15, 2007, http://archives.cnn.com/2002/WORLD/europe/04/01/netherlands .euthanasia.

8. Religious Tolerance, "Physician Assisted Suicide (PAS) outside the U.S., Canada, Holland, and UK," accessed May 18, 2007, http://www.religioustolerance .org/euth_wld.htm.

9. Many professional medical organizations, including the American Medical Association and the American Geriatrics Society, have explicitly stated opposition to physician-assisted suicide.

10. Since I am arguing that this way of moral thinking is accessible, I share that these conditions are not drawn from a professional ethics resource but from undergraduate students in a bioethics course I taught. The setup was to describe, first, the

just war ethic—the criteria of just war attached to the moral presumption against using force. Then this model of moral reflection was presented to students for consideration of the issue of "physician-assisted suicide." The in-class chore was to specify conditions on the moral presumption that physicians should ordinarily not agree to participate in the direct killing of a patient or assist a patient's suicide; and several of these "criteria" were suggested by students in a class discussion.

11. State of Oregon, "Death with Dignity Act, Oregon Revised Statutes," Oregon .gov website, accessed May 2007, http://www.oregon.gov/DHS/ph/pas/ors.shtml.

12. State of Oregon, "Summary of Oregon's Death with Dignity Act—2010," accessed May 2011, http://public.health.oregon.gov/ProviderPartnerResources/Evaluation Research/DeathwithDignityAct/Documents/year13.pdf. The Oregon Death With Dignity Act can be located at this website, but it has been reprinted many other places, including Mappes and DeGrazia, eds., *Biomedical Ethics*, 420–25.

13. State of Oregon, "Oregon Resident Deaths by Age Group and County of Residence, 2010 Preliminary Data, " accessed December 2011, http://public.health.oregon .gov/BirthDeathCertificates/VitalStatistics/PreliminaryData/Documents/deathage.pdf.

14. State of Oregon, "Summary of Oregon's Death with Dignity Act."

CHAPTER 6:
THE ETHICS OF PATIENT NONTREATMENT

1. See Peter Singer, *Practical Ethics* (Cambridge: Cambridge University Press, 1979), 132: "Defects vary of course. Some are trivial, and have little effect on the happiness of the child or its parents; but other defects turn the normally joyful event of birth into a threat to the happiness of the parents, and any other children they may have." By this statement, I take it that a neonate may be defective even beyond "trivial" and thus should receive medical care, but some defects go to the issue of severity such that continued pain and distress raise the question, as Singer puts it, of whether the neonate's "life is worth living." This invokes the severity issue of the case I make here, though not necessarily the futility feature, as will be seen. Singer also moves beyond the "misery" factor to a broader view of utilitarian calculus, namely, the justifiability of killing a severely defective hemophiliac. The hemophiliac is bound to contribute to an aggregate disutility compared to another newborn whom the parents of the killed neonate could create to replace it, who would not produce such disutility. I am not a utilitarian and do not agree with this position. I raise the "misery" issue related to the assessment of the neonate's condition to indicate that even Singer seems to recognize the moral presumption issue here. Singer believes a severely disabled neonate can be aborted, but he goes further: an embryonic/fetal candidate for justified "abortion" is one who presents a defect that may not be actually discernible until inspected at birth, and by Singer's account, such a neonate could be justifiably killed, using a utilitarian calculus that takes into account the greatest aggregate happiness. Singer provokes serious issues, but I appeal to his argument in *Practical Ethics* to indicate that he does not oppose the moral presumption, the action guide regarding

patient nontreatment, important to my argument, and even seems to support it, as it would be reasonable to do. Admittedly he does not dwell on this feature because his interest is in the hard cases and he seeks to determine what utilitarianism will allow and should be done—and what is good to do—in cases of extreme defect.

2. I acknowledge that other questions press for attention, such as "Is there a moral difference between withdrawing and withholding care?" (which I think there is), and "How is 'allowing to die,' by the decision to act in a way that foresees death, not also intending death, so that letting die might be distinguished from 'killing' and thus with active euthanasia?" These questions, important though they be, lead us away from the specific issue of this inquiry, so let us turn back to possible conditions that would guide justified nontreatment of neonatal patients.

3. Richard C. Sparks, *To Treat or Not to Treat* (New York: Paulist Press, 1988), 317.

4. *Black's Medical Dictionary*, 41st ed., s.v. "anencephaly."

5. Sparks, *To Treat or Not to Treat*, 311.

6. Robert J. Echenberg, "Permanently Locked-In Syndrome in the Neurologically Impaired Neonate: Report of a Case of Werdnig-Hoffman Disease," *Journal of Clinical Ethics* 48, no. 3 (Fall 1992): 206–8. This case study is followed by three critical responses.

7. "Perinatal" refers to the period immediately before and after birth, which may be as early as the twentieth week of pregnancy and as late as four weeks after birth.

8. The 1982 Infant Doe case in the United States involving an Indiana newborn who was born with Down syndrome and correctable spina bifida is such a case. Infant Doe's spina bifida was correctable by surgery, but the parents did not approve the surgery option and asked that the infant be allowed to die because they did not want the burden of a seriously retarded infant. The parents asked the attending physician to withhold food and water from the infant. This parental decision was upheld by an Indiana court. It is generally agreed that the parents would have requested the necessary surgery if the baby had not been "retarded" due to Down syndrome, so it was not the uncorrected spina bifida that killed Infant Doe, even though spina bifida can sometimes be considered so serious a defect that it alone could provoke consideration of justified nontreatment. (See Echenberg, "Permanently Locked-In Syndrome"). In the Infant Doe case, the death resulted from a decision not to treat made by parents distressed by having to contend with the mental retardation accompanying the Down syndrome.

9. Dispatching a neonate with this condition using, say, a morphine injection to suppress breathing and hasten death does not seem to me to be outside the pale of justification as action addressing the best interests of the patient. Such action could be described perhaps as pain management rather than a killing, but it cannot be known for certain whether pain is even at issue since there is no self to experience or integrate sensation into pain, and controversy would arise over criterion number 6—diminishing respect for the good of life itself, a utilitarian-related criterion. But nontreatment itself does not seem morally controversial.

10. Echenberg, "Permanently Locked-In Syndrome," 208.

11. Echenberg, "Permanently Locked-In Syndrome," 208.

12. Echenberg, "Permanently Locked-In Syndrome," 207.

13. Robert D. Truog, "Locked-In Syndrome and Ethics Committee Deliberation," *Journal of Clinical Ethics* 48, no. 3 (Fall 1992): 209–10.

14. Robert F. Weir, "Abating Treatment in the NICU," *Journal of Clinical Ethics* 3, no. 3 (Fall 1992): 209–11.

15. T. F. Dagi, "Compassion, Consensus, and Conflict: Should Caregivers' Needs Influence the Ethical Dialectic?" *Journal of Clinical Ethics* 3, no. 3 (Fall 1992): 214–18.

16. For all that appears to be disagreement about the "ethics" of this case around attention to the grief reactions of staff, this case—the presentation and the respondents—actually provides a good example of how the "just nontreatment" ethic actually works. A common agreement to treat is acknowledged but then questioned due to the specific situation facing the medical team. Agreement is then reached that an exception should be made for a nontreatment course of action. That decision is derived from an evaluation of the patient's best interests in light of the medical situation. The other criteria are also observed, with the sticking point being the criterion that states that withdrawing treatment cannot be determined by the burdens imposed on others, including caregivers. The discussion about the role of nursing staff might make it appear that concern for the caregivers trumped concern for the patient and the patient's best interests, but that is actually not the case, at least as far as the nontreatment decision goes. As much as working for harmonious relations with medical staff on difficult cases is to be lauded, the just nontreatment ethic insists that the patient must be the central focus—and I believe that was accomplished so that the dispute then turns to how to implement the best-interest decision not to treat, which then led to a consideration of the role of caregivers. I do not see that the neonatal patient was in any way shortchanged ethically or that the patient's case failed to be vetted adequately through the ethical scheme I am supporting here.

CHAPTER 7:
THE ETHICS OF EXECUTION AND JUST PUNISHMENT

1. Death Penalty Information Center, "Fact Sheet," accessed September 9, 2010, http://www. deathpenalty info.org/documents/FactSheet.pdf. The numbers cited will of course change, but they are accurate as of this writing, and current figures may be consulted at the Death Penalty Information Center.

2. A preeminent good in virtue of the fact that the good of life is required for the pursuit or enjoyment of other goods, life is itself a good of life and it is a good in relation, and therefore potentially in conflict, with other goods of life.

3. For a complete discussion of these criteria, see Lloyd Steffen, *Executing Justice: The Moral Meaning of the Death Penalty* (Eugene, OR: Wipf & Stock, 2006).

4. Death Penalty Information Center, "Fact Sheet," accessed September 9, 2010, http://www.deathpenaltyinfo.org/documents/FactSheet.pdf; Federal Bureau of Investigation, accessed September 14, 2010, http://www.fbi.gov/ucr/cius2008/documents/expandhomicidemain.pdf.

5. Death Penalty Information Center, "Fact Sheet," accessed September 9, 2010, http://www.deathpenaltyinfo.org/documents/FactSheet.pdf; the number of 2008 murders is from "United States Crime Rates," accessed September 9, 2011, disastercenter.com/crime/uscrime.htm.

6. Death Penalty Information Center, "Fact Sheet," accessed November 2011, http://www.deathpenaltyinfo.org/documents/FactSheet.pdf; the number of 2010 murders is from "United States Crimes Rates," accessed November 2011, http://disaster center.com/crime/uscrime.htm.

7. The Antiterrorism and Effective Death Penalty Act of 1996, provisions of which were upheld in *Felker v. Turpin* (116S. Ct. 2333 [1996]), expanded the list of federal crimes that would be eligible for the death penalty to more than sixty, mainly involving drug-related issues. But even so, the connections of death penalty–eligible crimes can be traced to the act of aggravated murder.

8. It seems to me that the low number of executions relative to number of wrongful homicides begs a legal question as to whether execution is in fact "unusual" as distinct from cruel. The rareness with which it is imposed makes its application appear "freakish."

9. Immanuel Kant, *The Metaphysic of Morals*, trans. and ed. J. W. Semple (Edinburgh: Thomas Clark, 1836), 307. Kant writes that "no punishment ought to be inflicted out of hatred."

10. The case could be made that when the 1991 *Payne v. Tennessee* decision was made, allowing victim impact statements into the penalty phase of capital cases, the US Supreme Court actually turned from the historical understanding that punishments ought to be justice related and deal with wrongs rather than with harms. The difference is important. Evaluating a crime and just punishment has historically allowed a jury to assume that those who lose a loved one to a crime such as aggravated murder are harmed by that loss, so that the idea of dispensing justice was tied to the wrong committed and then addressing that wrong. By allowing harms to be presented to juries, the jury shifts attention to addressing harms, which is a natural incitement to vengeance. *Payne v. Tennessee* is a watershed in moving away from the idea that capital punishment, in order to be just, must focus on justice rather than vengeance. I preserve this criterion as stated because the weight of judicial history is on the side of justice rather than vengeance, and punishment incited by vengeance is at least inadequate, but more likely reprehensible from a moral point of view.

11. Refusing to make such a judgment about the criminal justice system as an unfair system, the court opted for a contrary position, that a defendant claiming discrimination had to show a specific act of discrimination in the defendant's particular case, but no broadside was allowed against the system.

12. This quotation is widely available. See for instance, That Religious Studies Website, "Capital Punishment," accessed September 3, 2010, http://www.that religiousstudieswebsite.com/Ethics/Applied_Ethics/Capital_Punishment/capital_ punishment.php.

13. For references to concerns with state paroling that would release a convicted murderer after seven years of imprisonment, see Richard C. Dieter, "Sentencing for Life: Americans Embrace Alternatives to the Death Penalty," posted February 09, 2003, accessed November 2010, http://www.deathpenaltyinfo.org/sentencing-life -americans-embrace-alternatives-death-penalty.

14. In *Blystone v. Pennsylvania* (1990), however, the US Supreme Court ruled that a Pennsylvania statute that imposed a mandatory death sentence where the jury finds no mitigating circumstances and one aggravating circumstance does not violate

the Eighth Amendment. This decision for the first time gave the legislature, rather than the jury, the ultimate decision over a death penalty decision and undermined the individualized hearing notion so important previously.

15. Violent offenders overall serve more time in prison than drug offenders. But consider that in 1994, when mandatory federal drug sentencing guidelines were in effect, Jack O'Malley, the Cook County state's attorney and president of the Illinois State Attorney's Association, wrote in the *Chicago Tribune* that the average Illinois murder sentence was thirty-three years but the average time actually served for murder was 10.3 years. Jack O'Malley, "Doing Real Time: Truth-in-Sentencing and Crime in Illinois," *Chicago Tribune*, April 28, 1994, at http://articles.chicagotribune.com/1994-04-28/news/9404280053_1_prison-sentences-previous-murder-illinois-house. A 2007 Huffington Post report discussing Manuel Noriega's seventeen-year imprisonment for drug trafficking noted this: "There are many Americans in prison that are serving sentences of more than 17 years for simple drug crimes. These are marginalized offenders who don't have the bargaining chips to establish deals." Anthony Papa, "Will Drug Lord Do Less Time Than Average American Nonviolent Drug Offender," Huffington Post, October 1, 2007, http://www.huffingtonpost.com/anthony-papa/will-drug-lord-do-less-ti_b_66612.html.

16. In fact, a portion of Steffen, *Executing Justice*, is dedicated to showing how using just execution demonstrates that execution is immoral. In my opinion, the "common agreement" ethics approach allows this conclusion to be drawn more conclusively than, say, utilitarian or deontological moral theories. My point here has been to argue for the "just execution" structure, which reflects an ethic—applying the ethic and applying the structure are different processes that yield potentially different conclusions. I show above how the legal system has applied it, but I argue in *Executing Justice* that an analysis of the *experiential* data involved in American execution is so flawed as to fail the test of the criteria for exemption from the common moral agreement standard. Thus is the conclusion drawn: capital punishment is impermissible because it lacks moral warrants. Put positively, it is immoral and should not be practiced.

17. See Steffen, *Executing Justice*, passim.

18. Pope John Paul II called capital punishment "cruel and unnecessary" in a papal mass homily in St. Louis, Missouri, January 27, 1999, saying, "Modern society has the means of protecting itself, without definitively denying criminals the chance to reform." Quoted in Catholics against Capital Punishment, "What the Vatican Has Said," accessed November 2010, http://www.cacp.org/vaticandocuments.html.

19. Michael Tonry, *Malign Neglect: Race, Crime and Punishment in America* (New York: Oxford University Press, 1995).

20. Tonry, *Malign Neglect*, 188.

21. Tonry, *Malign Neglect*, 188. The Obama administration early in the administration eliminated the disparity between crack and powder cocaine sentencing.

22. Tonry, *Malign Neglect*, 187.

23. Human Rights Watch, *US: Prison Numbers Hit New High: Blacks Hardest Hit by Incarceration Policy*, accessed September 20, 2010, http://www.hrw.org/en/news/2008/06/05/us-prison-numbers-hit-new-high.

24. A. Klinger, "Ameneh Bahrami's Revenge: An Eye for an Eye for Acid Victim," *Bild*, accessed September 21, 2010, http://www.bild.de/BILD/news/bild-english/

world-news/2009/03/26/acid-attack-revenge-eye-for-an-eye/iran-court-allows-victim-to-blind-culprit.html; http://www.bild.de/news/bild-english/news/iran-court-allows-victim-to-blind-culprit-7793964.bild.html.

25. Tonry, *Malign Neglect*, 159.

26. Peter French, *The Virtue of Vengeance* (Lawrence: University of Kansas Press, 2000).

27. Tonry, *Malign Neglect*, 108, 110.

28. Tonry, *Malign Neglect*, 115.

29. The law of parsimony, also known as Occam's razor, refers to the idea that the simplest of two competing theories is to be preferred—in this instance, the least harsh punishment.

30. Tonry, *Malign Neglect*, 151.

31. Anthony Duff, *Trials and Punishments* (Cambridge: Cambridge University Press, 1986); quoted in Tonry, *Malign Neglect*, 159.

CHAPTER 8:
THE ETHICS OF ABORTION

1. Asking "When does life begin?" in the hopes that science might settle matters not only exposes serious confusions about biology but then uses a scientific misunderstanding to extract a position of moral absolutism. See Maurizio Mori, "On the Concept of the Pre-embryo: The Basis for a New 'Copernican Revolution' in the Current View about Human Reproduction," in *The Future of Human Reproduction: Ethics, Choice, and Regulation*, ed. John Harris and Soren Holm (Oxford: Clarendon Press, 1998), 38–54.

2. For more on "double effect," see David L. Clough and Brian Stiltner, *Faith and Force: A Christian Debate about War* (Washington, DC: Georgetown University Press, 2007), 55–56.

3. Mary Anne Warren, "On the Moral and Legal Status of Abortion," *Monist* 57, no. 1 (1973): 43–61.

4. I am thinking of the platform of the Republican Party in the United States, which eliminated these exemptions from their pro-life plank in 2004 and 2008. This is mentioned in the text that follows.

5. There are those who deny that there is ever a medical reason for abortion. Irish oncologist Dr. John Crown, for example, has said he has never encountered a situation in which abortion was needed to save a mother's life, admitting that he has sometimes faced some "hard decisions re: chemotherapy in pregnancy." See Hilary White, "No Case Where Abortion Was 'Necessary to Save Mom,'" *LifeSiteNews.com: Life, Family, Culture*, Wednesday, February 22, 2012, http://www.lifesitenews.com/news/no-case-where-abortion-was-necessary-to-save-mom-eminent-irish-oncologist. But it has been accepted even in American law that abortion can be a procedure "necessary to save the life of the mother whose life is endangered by a physical disorder, physical illness, or physical injury, including a life-endangering physical condition caused by or arising from the pregnancy itself." This was the language used in a Nebraska Bill (23) cited in *Carhart v. Stenberg* 11 F. Supp. 2d 1099, http://voicesofamericanlaw

.org/media/documents/Carhart_trial_opinion.pdf. We can note, for example, that a woman suffering from primary pulmonary hypertension (PPH) faces a serious risk of death if she becomes pregnant, and pregnancy termination is a recommended medical procedure for those with this condition.

6. There is no one Roman Catholic teaching on abortion or any other moral issue unless one is using the hierarchical definition of the Church, which I do in the discussion about to commence. I acknowledge that other viewpoints are possible in the Church through the theological magisterium and through the *sensus fidelium* (the faithful laity who are neither hierarchs nor theologians). After all, the organization "Catholics for Choice" comprises Roman Catholics who object to the teaching of the hierarchy on matters such as contraception and abortion rights, but it is that hierarchical teaching to which I am referring in what follows.

7. John T. Noonan Jr., "An Almost Absolute Value in History," in *Vice and Virtue in Everyday Life*, 7th ed., ed. Christina Sommers and Fred Sommers (Belmont, CA: Wadsworth, 2006), 391.

8. John Paul II, "The Unspeakable Crime of Abortion," *Evangelium Vitae*, March 25, 1995, in *Biomedical Ethics*, 6th ed., ed. Thomas Mappes and David DeGrazia (New York: McGraw-Hill, 2006), 458.

9. In May 2010, a local bishop in Phoenix excommunicated a nun who approved an abortion to save the life of a pregnant woman. See Barbara Bradley Hagerty, "Nun Excommunicated for Allowing Abortion," National Public Radio, accessed November 2010, http://www.npr.org/templates/story/story.php?storyId=126985072.

10. I have argued that an absolute must, by encompassing everything, entail its own contradiction. See Steffen, *Holy War, Just War*.

11. On July 29, 1994, Paul Hill shot and killed Dr. John Bayard Britton and his bodyguard, retired Air Force Lt. Col. James Herman Barrett, outside the Ladies Center in Pensacola. Hill was executed in Florida in September 2003. A news report commented, "Hill showed no remorse and urged abortion foes to use whatever means to protect the unborn." Cited in FindArticles.com, accessed December 28, 2007, http://findarticles.com/p/articles/mi_qn4155/is_20030904/ai_n12510129.

12. Devising a theory of just abortion in parallel to the just war ethic, that is, a common agreement ethic that includes both an articulated common moral agreement (moral presumption) and accompanying justice-related criteria that would if satisfied allow a exception to that common agreement was the task I set for myself in *Life/Choice: The Theory of Just Abortion*.

13. For statements on the wide diversity of views on abortion among—and within—world religious traditions, see Lloyd Steffen, ed., *Abortion: A Reader* (Eugene, OR: Wipf & Stock, 2010).

CHAPTER 9:
THE ETHICS OF WAR

1. History Learning Site, "Civilian Casualties of World War Two," accessed March 10, 2010, http://www.historylearningsite.co.uk/civilian_casualties_of_world_war.htm.

2. "Iraqi Deaths from Violence 2003–2011: Analysis and Overview from Iraq Body Count (IBC)," Iraq Body Count, accessed January 2012, http://www.iraqbody count.org.

3. "Iraq Deaths," accessed December 2011, http://www.justforeignpolicy.org/iraq.

4. Gilbert Burnham, Riyadh Lafta, Shannon Doocy, and Les Roberts, "Mortality after the 2003 Invasion of Iraq: A Cross-Sectional Cluster Sample Survey," *Lancet* (October 11, 2006). See an online article by Les Roberts, professor of public health at Columbia, defending the *Lancet* findings: http://www.independent.co.uk/opinion/commentators/les-roberts-iraqs-death-toll-is-far-worse-than-our-leaders-admit-436291.html.

5. Opinion Research Business, "More Than 1,000,000 Iraqis Murdered," September 2007. Cited in discussion in http://en.wikipedia.org/wiki/ORB_survey_of_Iraq_War_casualties, where a report on the ORB report is available.

6. Department of Energy, "The Atomic Bombing of Hiroshima. August 6, 1945," accessed March 8, 2010, http://www.cfo.doe.gov/me70/manhattan/hiroshima.htm.

7. See Michael Walzer, *Just and Unjust Wars*, 255–61.

8. Of course, what constitutes an act of terrorism is worthy of consideration. Terrorist acts are committed by "civilized" nations, but war acts by civilized nations are rarely termed "terrorist"—even Churchill's bombing of German cities, which Churchill himself described as terrorist, are not remembered that way or compared with terrorist acts today, yet they certainly were directed at civilians. For an interesting analysis of the way "terrorist" is attached to those who are deemed in the eyes of civilized nations to be uncivilized, so that their war acts qualify as "terrorist," see Talal Asad, *On Suicide Bombing* (New York: Columbia University Press, 2007).

9. This is a reminder to the reader of the claim made in chapter 2 that the use of force can include nonviolent uses of force, with Gandhi and King being shown to be self-aware exemplars of nonviolence as a use of force.

10. Peter Singer, *One World: The Ethics of Globalization* (New Haven: Yale University Press, 2002), 142.

11. What does one do with, say, China, which might not meet the human rights standard? One suggestion that has been made is to limit China's representation while refiguring United Nations representation in accordance with world population, so that power is vested in a kind of world assembly. There are many ideas to consider, and my task is not to sort them out but to say that concern for civilian casualties in world conflicts presses the issue.

12. P. W. Singer, *Children at War* (New York: Pantheon, 2005).

13. Stephen Smith, "Massacre at Murambi: The Rank and File Killers of Genocide," in *Why We Kill: Understanding Violence across Cultures and Disciplines*, eds. Nancy Loucks, Sally Smith Holt, and Joanna R Alder (Middlesex, UK: Willan Publishing, Middlesex University Press, 2009), 194.

Bibliography

Adeney, Bernard T. *Just War, Political Realism, and Faith.* Lanham, MD: Scarecrow Press, 1988.

Alexander of Hales. "Virtuous Dispositions in Warfare." In *The Ethics of War: Classic and Contemporary Readings*, edited by Gregory M. Reichenberg, Henrik Syse, and Endre Begby. Oxford: Blackwell, 2006.

American Geriatrics Society (AGS). "Position Papers." Accessed January 2008. http://www.americangeriatrics.org/products/positionpapers/vae94.shtml.

Angell, M. "The Supreme Court and Physician-Assisted Suicide: The Ultimate Right." In *Taking Sides: Clashing Views on Bioethical Issues*, 12th ed., edited by Carol Levine. Dubuque, IA: McGraw-Hill, 2007: 88–97.

Anonymous, "200 Lies per Day Just to Cope with Reality," *Shortnews.Com: The News-Community.* Accessed August 4, 2009. http://www.shortnews.com/start.cfm?id=2738.

Aquinas, Thomas. *Summa Theologica, II.* Translated by Fathers of the English Dominican Province. Chicago: Encyclopedia Britannica, 1952.

Aristotle, *Nicomachean Ethics.* Translated by W. D. Ross. In *Complete Works of Aristotle, Vol. I.* Revised Oxford Translation, edited by Jonathan Barnes. Princeton: Princeton University Press, Bollingen Series LXXI, 2, 1984.

———. *Rhetoric.* In *Complete Works of Aristotle, Vol. I.* Revised Oxford Translation. Edited by Jonathan Barnes. Princeton: Princeton University Press, Bollingen Series LXXI, 2, 1984.

Asad, Talal. *On Suicide Bombing.* New York: Columbia University Press, 2007.

Augustine. *City of God.* Translated by Henry Bettenson. Introduction by John O'Meara. New York: Penguin Classics, 1984.

———. *Contra Faustum.* In Thomas Aquinas, *Summa Theologica*, Q. 40, 1, 1265–1273, at http://www.newadvent.org/summa/3040.htm.

Baer, Helmut David, and Joseph E. Capizzi, "Just War Theories Reconsidered: Problems with Prima Facie Duties and the Need for a Political Ethic." *Journal of Religious Ethics* 33, no. 1 (March 2005): 119–37.

———. "Just War Theory and the Problem of International Politics: On the Central Role of Just Intention," *Journal of the Society of Christian Ethics* 26, no. 1 (Spring/ Summer 2006): 163–75.

Bentham, Jeremy. *The Principles of Morals and Legislation* (1781). Accessed October 11, 2011. http://www. constitution.org/jb/pml.txt.

Blix, Hans. *Disarming Iraq.* New York: Pantheon Books, 2004.

Bok, Sissela. *Lying: Moral Choice in Public and Private Life.* New York: Vintage Books, 1978, 1979.

Boyle, Joseph. "Just War Thinking in Catholic Natural Law." In *The Ethics of War and Peace: Religious and Secular Perspectives,* edited by Terry Nardin. Princeton: Princeton University Press, 1996.

Brandt, R. B. *A Theory of the Good and the Right.* Oxford: Oxford University Press, 1979.

Brannigan, Michael. *Ethics across Cultures: An Introductory Text with Readings.* Boston: McGraw-Hill, 2005.

Brown, Montague. *The Question for Moral Foundations: An Introduction to Ethics.* Washington, DC: Georgetown University Press, 1996.

Burnham, Gilbert, Riyadh Lafta, Shannon Doocy, and Les Roberts. "Mortality after the 2003 Invasion of Iraq: A Cross-Sectional Cluster Sample Survey." *Lancet* 368, no. 9545 (October 21, 2006): 1421–28. doi: 10.1016/S0140-6736 (06) 69491-9.

Carhart v. Stenberg. 11 F. Supp. 2d 1099 (D. Neb. 1998). http://voicesofamerican-law.org/media/documents/Carhart_trial_opinion.pdf.

Catholics against Capital Punishment, "What the Vatican Has Said." Accessed November 2010. http://www.cacp.org/vaticandocuments.html.

Childress, James, B. "Just War Criteria." In *War or Peace? The Search for New Answers,* edited by Thomas A. Shannon. Maryknoll, NY: Orbis, 1980.

Cicero, Marcus Tullius. *On Duties.* Edited by M. T. Griffin and E. M. Atkins. Cambridge: Cambridge University Press, 1991.

———. *On Moral Obligation.* Translated by John Higginbotham. Berkeley/Los Angeles: University of California Press, 1967.

Clough, David L., and Brian Stiltner. *Faith and Force: A Christian Debate about War.* Washington, DC: Georgetown University Press, 2007.

CNN. "Euthanasia Now Legal In Holland." CNN.com, April 1, 2002. Accessed May 15, 2007. http://archives.cnn.com/2002/WORLD/europe/04/01/netherlands. euthanasia.

Dagi, T. F. "Compassion, Consensus, and Conflict: Should Caregivers' Needs Influence the Ethical Dialectic?" *Journal of Clinical Ethics* 3, no. 3 (Fall 1992): 214–18.

Death Penalty Information Center. "Fact Sheet." Accessed September 9, 2010. http://www.deathpenaltyinfo.org/documents/FactSheet.pdf.

Department of Energy. "The Atomic Bombing of Hiroshima. August 6, 1945." Accessed March 8, 2010. http://www.cfo.doe.gov/me70/manhattan/hiroshima.htm.

Dieter, Richard C. "Sentencing for Life: Americans Embrace Alternatives to the Death Penalty." Posted February 9, 2003, accessed November 2010. http://www.deathpenaltyinfo.org/sentencing-life-americans-embrace-alternatives-death-penalty.

Disastercenter.com. "United States Crimes Rates." Accessed September 9, 2010, and November 2011. disastercenter.com/crime/uscrime.htm.

Duff, Anthony. *Trials and Punishments*. Cambridge: Cambridge University Press, 1986.

Echenberg, Robert J. "Permanently Locked-In Syndrome in the Neurologically Impaired Neonate: Report of a Case of Werdnig-Hoffman Disease." *Journal of Clinical Ethics* 48, no. 3 (Fall 1992): 206–8.

Erikson, Erik. *Gandhi's Truth: On the Origins of Militant Nonviolence*. New York: Norton, 1969.

Federal Bureau of Investigation. Accessed September 14, 2010. http://www.fbi.gov/ucr/cius2008/documents/expandhomicidemain.pdf.

Fiala, Andrew. *The Just War Myth: The Moral Illusions of War*. Lanham, MD: Rowman & Littlefield, 2008.

Francis, Dick. *Forfeit*. New York: Pocket Books, 1975.

Frankl, Victor. *Man's Search for Meaning*. New York: Washington Square Press, 1984.

French, Peter. *The Virtue of Vengeance*. Lawrence: University of Kansas Press, 2000.

Gandhi, M. K. "Doctrine of the Sword [11 August 1920]." In *The Penguin Gandhi Reader*, edited by Rudrangshu Mukherjee. New York: Penguin, 1996.

———. *Non-Violent Resistance (Satyagraha)*. New York: Schocken Books, 1951.

Geary, James. "Deceitful Minds: The Awful Truth about Lying," *Time Europe* (March 13, 2000), 155, no 10. Accessed July 6, 2010. http://www.time.com/time/europe/magazine/2000/313/deceit.html.

Green, Martin. *Gandhi: Voice of a New Age Revolution*. New York: Continuum, 1993.

Gregg, Richard B. *The Power of Nonviolence*. 2nd ed. New York: Schocken Books, 1966.

Grisez, Germaine, and Russell Shaw. *Beyond the New Morality: The Responsibilities of Freedom*. 2nd ed. Notre Dame, IN: Notre Dame University Press, 1974.

Grotius, Hugo. "The Theory of Just War Systematized (On the Law of War and Peace)." In *The Ethics of War: Classic and Contemporary Readings*, edited by Gregory M. Reichenberg, Henrik Syse, and Endre Begby. Oxford: Blackwell, 2006.

Hagarty, Barbara Bradley. "Nun Excommunicated for Allowing Abortion." National Public Radio. Accessed November 2010. http://www.npr.org/templates/story/story.php?storyId=126985072.

Hehir, J. Bryan. "The Just War Ethic and Catholic Theology." In *War or Peace? The Search for New Answers*, edited by Thomas A. Shannon. Maryknoll, NY: Orbis, 1980.

History Learning Site. "Civilian Casualties of World War Two." Accessed March 10, 2010. http://www.historylearningsite.co.uk/civilian_casualties_of_world_war.htm.

Hollenbach, David. *Nuclear Ethics: A Christian Moral Argument*. Notre Dame, IN: University of Notre Dame Press, 1990.

Hospers, John. "The Problem with Relativism." In *Vice and Virtue in Everyday Life*, 2nd ed., edited by Christina Sommers and Fred Sommers. San Diego: Harcourt Brace Jovanovich, 1989.

Human Rights Watch. "US: Prison Numbers Hit New High: Blacks Hardest Hit by Incarceration Policy." Accessed September 20, 2010. http://www.hrw.org/en/news/2008/06/05/us-prison-numbers-hit-new-high.

Iraq Body Count. "Iraqi Deaths from Violence 2003–2011: Analysis and Overview from Iraq Body Count (IBC)." Accessed January 2, 2012. http://www.iraqbody count.org.

Johnson, James Turner. *The Holy War Idea in Western and Islamic Traditions*. University Park: Penn State University Press, 1997, 2001.

Just Foreign Policy. "Iraq Deaths." Accessed December, 2011. http://www.justforeign policy.org/iraq.

Kant, Immanuel. *Groundwork of the Metaphysic of Morals*. Translated by H. J. Paton. New York: Harper & Row, Harper Torchbooks 1953, 1964.

———. *The Metaphysic of Morals*. Edited and translated by J. W. Semple. Edinburgh: Thomas Clark, 1836.

Kevorkian, Jack. *Amendment IX: Our Cornucopia of Rights.* Bloomfield Hills, MI: Penumbra Press, 2005.

King, Martin Luther, Jr. "Pilgrimage to Nonviolence." In *The Papers of Martin Luther King, Jr., Vol. IV*, edited by Clayborne Carson. Berkeley: University of California Press, 2000.

———. *A Testament of Hope: The Essential Writings of Martin Luther King, Jr.*, edited by James M. Washington. New York: HarperSanFrancisco, 1986.

Klinger, A. "Ameneh Bahrami's Revenge: An Eye for an Eye for Acid Victim." *Bild.* Accessed September 21, 2010. http://www.bild.de/BILD/news/bild-english/world -news/2009/03/26/acid-attack-revenge-eye-for-an-eye/iran-court-allows-victim-to -blind-culprit.html; and http://www.bild.de/news/bild-english/news/iran-court -allows-victim-to-blind-culprit-7793964.bild.html.

Langan, John. "Elements of St. Augustine's Just War Theory." *Journal of Religious Ethics* 12 (Spring, 1984): 19–38.

Lincoln, Abraham. "Speech at Worchester, Massachusetts, September 12, 1848." In *Collected Works of Abraham Lincoln, Volume 2*, edited by Roy Basler. New Brunswick, NJ: Rutgers University Press, 1953.

Lincoln, Bruce. "Appendix: 'Instructions to Hijackers.'" In *Holy Terrorism: Thinking about Religion after September 11*. Chicago: University of Chicago Press, 2003, 93–98.

Maguire, Daniel C. *Ethics: A Complete Method for Moral Choice*. Minneapolis: Fortress, 2010.

Mappes, Thomas A., and David DeGraza, editors. *Biomedical Ethics*, 6th ed. New York: McGraw-Hill, 2006.

Mattox, John Mark. *St. Augustine and the Theory of Just War*. New York: Continuum, 2009.

McBrien, Richard P. *Catholicism: Study Edition*. Oak Grove, MN: Winston Press, 1981.

Mori, Maurizio. "On the Concept of the Pre-embryo: The Basis for a New 'Copernican Revolution' in the Current View about Human Reproduction." In *The Future of Human Reproduction: Ethics, Choice, and Regulation*, edited by John Harris and Soren Holm. Oxford: Clarendon Press, 1998.

Mukherjee, Rudrangshu, ed. *The Penguin Gandhi Reader*. New York: Penguin, 1996.

Nardin, Terry, ed. *The Ethics of War and Peace: Religious and Secular Perspectives*. Princeton: Princeton University Press, 1996.

Niebuhr, Reinhold. *Moral Man and Immoral Society*. New York: Scribner, 1932.

Noonan, John T., Jr. "An Almost Absolute Value in History." In *Vice and Virtue in Everyday Life: Introductory Readings in Ethics*, 7th ed., edited by Christina Sommers and Fred Sommers. Belmont, CA: Wadsworth, 2006.

O'Malley, Jack. "Doing Real Time: Truth-in-Sentencing and Crime in Illinois." *Chicago Tribune*, April 28, 1994. http://articles.chicagotribune.com/1994-04-28/news/9404280053_1_prison-sentences-previous-murder-illinois-house.

Opinion Research Business. "More than 1,000,000 Iraqis Murdered (September 2007)." Accessed March 3, 2010. http://en.wikipedia.org/wiki/ORB.

Papa, Anthony. "Will Drug Lord Do Less Time Than Average American Nonviolent Drug Offender." *Huffington Post*, October 1, 2007. http://www.huffingtonpost.com/anthony-papa/will-drug-lord-do-less-ti_b_66612.html.

Pence, Gregory. *The Elements of Bioethics*. New York: McGraw-Hill, 2006.

Pope John Paul II, "The Unspeakable Crime of Abortion," from *Evangelium Vitae* (March 25, 1995). In *Biomedical Ethics*, 6th ed., edited by Thomas Mappes and David DeGrazia. New York, McGraw-Hill, 2006.

Potter, Ralph B. *War and Moral Discourse*. Richmond VA: John Knox Press, 1973.

Rachels, James. "Kant and the Categorical Imperative." In *Vice and Virtue in Everyday Life: Introductory Readings in Ethics*, 2nd ed., edited by Christina Sommers and Fred Sommers. San Diego: Harcourt Brace Jovanovich, 1989.

Rawls, John. *A Theory of Justice*. Cambridge, MA: Harvard University Press, 1971, 1999.

Reese, W. L. "Utilitarianism." In *Dictionary of Philosophy and Religion: Eastern and Western Thought*, edited by W. L. Reese. Atlantic Highlands, NJ: Humanities Press, 1980.

Reichenberg, Gregory M., Henrik Syse, and Endre Begby, eds. *The Ethics of War: Classic and Contemporary Readings*. Oxford: Blackwell, 2006.

Religious Tolerance. "Physician Assisted Suicide (PAS) outside the U.S., Canada, Holland, and UK." Accessed May 18, 2007. http://www.religioustolerance.org/euth_wld.htm.

Roberts, Les. "Iraq's Death Toll Is Far Worse Than Our Leaders Admit: The US and Britain Have Triggered an Episode More Deadly Than the Rwandan Genocide." *Independent*, February 14, 2007. Accessed March 4, 2010. http://www.independent.co.uk/opinion/commentators/les-roberts-iraqs-death-toll-is-far-worse-than-our-leaders-admit-436291.html.

Ross, W. D. *The Right and the Good*. Oxford: Clarendon Press, 1930.

Runzo, Joseph. "Religion and Ethics in a Global World." In *Ethics in the World Religions*, edited by Joseph Runzo and Nancy M. Martin. Oxford: One World, 2001.

Saylor, Steven. *Arms of Nemesis*. New York: Ivy Books, 1992.

Singer, P. W. *Children at War*. New York: Pantheon, 2005.

Singer, Peter. "Heavy Petting." *Nerve* (2001). Accessed October 14, 2011. http://www.utilitarian.net/singer/by/2001----.htm.

————. *One World: The Ethics of Globalization*. New Haven: Yale University Press, 2002.

————. *Practical Ethics*. Cambridge: Cambridge University Press, 1979.

Smart, J. J. C. "Utilitarianism." In *Vice and Virtue in Everyday Life: Introductory Readings in Ethics*, 2nd ed., edited by Christina Sommers and Fred Sommers. San Diego: Harcourt Brace Jovanovich, 1989.

Smith, Stephen. "Massacre at Murambi: The Rank and File Killers of Genocide." In *Why We Kill: Understanding Violence across Cultures and Disciplines*, edited by Nancy Loucks, Sally Smith Holt, and Joanna R Alder. Middlesex, UK: Willan Publishing, Middlesex University Press, 2009.

Solomon, Robert C. *Ethics and Excellence: Cooperation and Integrity in Business*. New York: Oxford University Press, 1992.

Sparks, Richard C. *To Treat or Not to Treat*. New York: Paulist Press, 1988.

State of Oregon. "Death with Dignity Act, Oregon Revised Statutes." Accessed May 2007. http://www.oregon.gov/DHS/ph/pas/ors.shtml.

————. "Oregon Deaths by Age Group and County of Residence." http://www.dhs .state.or.us/dhs/ph/chs/data/ytd/deathage.pdf.

————. "Oregon Resident Deaths by Age Group and County of Residence, 2010 Preliminary Data." Accessed December 2011. http://public.health.oregon.gov/ BirthDeathCertificates/VitalStatistics/PreliminaryData/Documents/deathage.pdf.

————. "Summary of Oregon's Death with Dignity Act—2010." Accessed May, 2011. http://public.health.oregon.gov/ProviderPartnerResources/EvaluationResearch/ DeathwithDignityAct/Documents/year13.pdf.

Steffen, Lloyd. "The Ethical Complexity of Abraham Lincoln: Is There Something for Religious Ethicists to Learn?" *Journal of the Society of Christian Ethics* 31, no. 2 (Fall/Winter 2011): 74–99.

————. *Executing Justice: The Moral Meaning of the Death Penalty*. Eugene, OR: Wipf & Stock, 2006.

. *Life/Choice: The Theory of Just Abortion*. Eugene, OR: Wipf & Stock, 2004.

————. *Holy War, Just War: Exploring the Moral Meaning of Religious Violence*. Lanham, MD: Rowman & Littlefield, 2007.

————. "The Presumption of Peace: Where Just War and Nonviolent Resistance Meet (and Diverge)." In *Conflict and Conciliation: Faith and Politics in an Age of Global Dissonance*, edited by Jason W. Davareth. Dublin: Columba Press, 2007.

Steffen, Lloyd, ed. *Abortion: A Reader*. Eugene, OR: Wipf & Stock, 2010.

Stevenson, William R. *Christian Love and Just War*. Macon, GA: Mercer University Press, 1988.

Temes, Peter S. *The Just War: An American Reflection on the Morality of War in our Time*. Chicago: Ivan R. Dee, 2003.

That Religious Studies Website. "Capital Punishment." Accessed September 3, 2010. http://www.thatreligiousstudieswebsite.com/Ethics/Applied_Ethics/Capital_ Punishment/capital_punishment.php.

Tonry, Michael. *Malign Neglect: Race, Crime and Punishment in America*. New York, Oxford: Oxford University Press, 1995.

Truog, Robert D. "Locked-In Syndrome and Ethics Committee Deliberation." *Journal of Clinical Ethics* 48, no. 3 (Fall 1992): 209–10.

Twain, Mark (Samuel Clemens). "On the Decay of the Art of Lying." Kindle edition.

United Methodist Council of Bishops. *In Defense of Creation: The Nuclear Crisis and a Just Peace.* Washington, DC, 1986.

United Nations. *Universal Declaration of Human Rights.* Accessed October 2010. http://www.un.org/en.documents/udhr.

United States Conference of Bishops. *The Challenge of Peace: God's Promise and Our Response—A Pastoral Letter on War and Peace—May 3, 1983.* Washington, DC, 1983. http://www.zero-nukes.org/pdf_files/Challenge_of_Peace.pdf.

Urmson, J. O. "The Interpretation of the Moral Philosophy of J. S. Mill." In *Theories of Ethics,* edited by Philippa Foot. Oxford: Oxford University Press, 1967.

Van Nyk, Robert N. "When Is Lying Morally Permissible? Casuistical Reflection on the Game Analogy, Self-Defense, Social Contract Ethics, and Ideals." *Journal of Value Inquiry* 24, no. 2 (1990): 155–68.

Vaux, Kenneth L. *Ethics and the Gulf War: Religion, Rhetoric, and Righteousness.* Eugene, OR: Wipf & Stock, 2003.

Walton, Hanes, Jr. "King's Philosophy of Nonviolence." In *Martin Luther King Jr.,* edited by Thomas Siebold. San Diego: Greenhaven Press, 2000.

Walzer, Michael. "An Exchange on Hiroshima." *New Republic* 85 (September 23, 1981): 13–14.

———. *Just and Unjust Wars: A Moral Argument with Historical Illustrations.* New York: Basic, 1977.

Ward, Keith. "Religion and the Possibility of a Global Ethic." In *Ethics in the World Religions,* edited by Joseph Runzo and Nancy M. Martin. Oxford: One World, 2001.

Warren, Mary Anne. "On the Moral and Legal Status of Abortion." *Monist* 57, no. 1 (1973): 43–61.

Weir, Robert F. "Abating Treatment in the NICU." *Journal of Clinical Ethics* 3, no. 3 (Fall 1992): 209–11.

White, Hilary. "No Case Where Abortion Was 'Necessary to Save Mom.'" *LifeSiteNews.com: Life, Family, Culture,* Wednesday, February 22, 2012. http://www.lifesitenews.com/news/no-case-where-abortion-was-necessary-to-save-mom-eminent-irish-oncologist.

Wogaman, J. Philip. *Christian Moral Judgment.* Louisville, KY: Westminster John Knox Press, 1989.

Wood, Allen W. *Kantian Ethics.* Cambridge: Cambridge University Press, 2008.

Zlomislic, Marko. *Jacques Derrida's Aporetic Ethics.* Lanham, MD: Lexington Books, 2007.

Index

Lincoln, Abraham, 35, 216n2
Lockett v. Ohio, 154
love, 8–9,26, 28, 36, 54, 56, 59, 63, 66,
    71, 109, 198, 210n53, 214n36; law
    of love, 56
lying, 7–10, 12, 15, 33, 79, 99, 101–7,
    110, 118, 204n11, 210n50; white
    lies, 9, 103, 105, 210n50

Maguire, Daniel, 30–31, 108, 110
Marshall, Thurgood, 150
McBrien, Richard, 31
McCleskey v. Kemp, 152
Mill, John Stuart, 2, 6, 8, 11, 14, 33, 78,
    109, 204nn16–17, 209n45, 210n53
moderation (moral), 3, 39–40, 96, 100,
    113, 126, 147, 159, 174–75, 183,
    191, 193
moral community. *See* community
    (moral)
moral dilemmas 3, 6, 14, 23, 68, 84,
    100, 112 , 146, 175, 177, 180;
    performative, 41, 88–89, 92–93, 106;
    person (reasonable, goodwill), xi, 4–6,
    12, 14, 17, 25–27, 32–33, 38, 40–41,
    43–44, 46, 52, 67, 70, 73, 79, 81, 83,
    89, 90, 95, 97, 99–100, 103–5, 109,
    119, 121, 123, 130, 133–34, 137, 141–
    42, 154–55, 157, 164, 172, 177–182,
    191, 198–99, 205, 210n53; problem,
    xii, 3, 5, 5–15, 25, 73–74, 81, 94–95,
    100, 112, 118, 120, 130, 140–41, 174;
    violation, 12, 16–17, 23, 89, 118, 199
moral point of view, ix–x, 33, 35–39,
    43–45, 48, 51–52, 57, 59, 70, 74–75,
    82, 84–85, 89, 94, 96, 98, 101, 104,
    108–9, 111, 117, 124, 130, 134, 149,
    151, 162–63, 172, 174, 180–82, 88,
    190, 192–93, 208n35, 222n10
moral presumption. *See* presumption
    (moral)
murder, 41, 59, 86–90, 92, 102, 106,
    118, 125, 148–51, 153–54, 157–58,
    174–75, 183–84, 188, 205n19,
    210n50, 222n7, 223n15

natural law, 14, 16–17, 25–27, 30, 46,
    74–78, 80, 87, 93–94, 96–100, 107–
    9, 112, 117, 120–21, 146, 148, 155,
    158–59, 174, 176, 178, 180, 182,
    205n20, 210n53, 215n1
Netherlands, 122, 124, 168, 218n4,
newborns (disabled), 17, 83–84, 99,
    101, 104, 113, 118, 131, 133–41,
    146, 156, 219n1, 220n2, 220n8
Niebuhr, Reinhold, 54, 65, 70–71,
    211n9, 211n9, 212n10
noncombatant 17, 22, 30, 33, 41, 61, 65,
    69, 113, 174, 177–79, 187–89, 194
    97, 199, 100–102. *See also* innocent
    civilians
noncombatant immunity, xiii, 17, 22,
    30, 41, 43, 64–65, 70, 79, 113,
    173–75, 177–83, 192, 195–96, 199,
    200–202; absolute immunity, 180
nonresistance, 54, 56, 58, 67, 210n54,
    211n6. *See also* Tolstoy, Leo;
    pacifism
nonviolence, 26, 51–53, 56–57, 60–62,
    64–65, 67–69, 71, 198; as use of
    force, 52, 57–58, 62, 65–67, 71,
    75, 96, 99, 101, 178, 200, 212n14,
    214n36, 226n9
nonviolent resistance, xii–iv, 48–49,
    52–71, 75, 86, 117, 179, 211nn5 6,
    212n10, 210nn13–14, 214n36, 215n49
Noonan, John, 183–84, 188
normative principles. *See* ethics

Oregon. See Death with Dignity Act
organ transplantation, 6
other-regardingness, 36, 38, 40, 44, 47,
    74, 100, 111, 130, 134, 209n46

pacifism, 28, 48, 54, 56, 63, 67, 129,
    183, 212n13, 214n37; absolute, 54,
    56, 67, 210–11n54, 212n13 (see also
    Tolstoy, Leo); practical, xiii, 48;
    theoretical, xiii, 210n54
pain, 36, 65, 77–78, 92, 99, 103, 118,
    120, 122–23, 125, 127, 135, 137–38,

About the Author

Lloyd Steffen is professor of religion studies, university chaplain, and director of both the Dialogue Center and the Prison Project at Lehigh University in Bethlehem, Pennsylvania. A graduate of New College (Sarasota), an honors graduate of Andover Newton Theological School and Yale Divinity School, Steffen received his PhD in religious studies from Brown University. He is the author or editor of several books in philosophy of religion and ethics, including *Holy War, Just War: Exploring the Moral Meaning of Religious Violence*, published by Rowman & Littlefield (2007).